MORMON
ATHLETES
BOOK 2

MORMON ATHLETES
BOOK 2

William T. Black

Deseret Book Company
Salt Lake City, Utah

Library of Congress Cataloging in Publication Data

Black, William T., 1933-
  Mormon athletes II.

    1. Athletes—United States—Biography. 2. Sports—Religious
aspects—Mormon Church. I. Title.
GV697.A1B55 1982   796' .092' 2 [B]   82-14648
ISBN 0-87747-929-1

Perhaps it is the excess charge of the battery or, perhaps, the nature of the battery itself which lifts [the athlete] out of the sands of mediocrity. I choose to call this... quality, this distinguishing "plus," an inflammability of spirit. To me it is the ability of the imagination and the soul to catch afire and to burn with a hot, red glow. It is the susceptibility of the elements of personality to violent explosion under challenging conditions. With it, men ordinarily average and commonplace rise to heights. They express themselves in heroic deeds. They fatten on adversity. They welcome big challenges. They do their best and a little more in a crisis. They thrive on "tough-going."... Such is the real athlete. He possesses this extra quality. It is the ability to laugh in the teeth of a crisis and, instead of folding up or breaking under the strain, to lead his teammates out of the slimy mud and ooze of mediocrity to the sunkist heights. It is the ability to explode gloriously with power rather than to blow up in fragments of despair. You may name it what you will. I shall still choose to call it the Inflammability of the Spirit—the quality which enables that-which-makes-a-man to catch afire.

Ott Romney

CONTENTS

ACKNOWLEDGMENTS

xiii

INTRODUCTION

xv

DANNY WHITE

All-American Quarterback and Pro Football Player

1

DANNY VRANES

United States Olympian and All-American
Basketball Star

8

KIM TAYLOR

National Gymnastics Champion

14

DOUG PADILLA

NCAA Indoor Two-Mile Champion and American
Record Holder (Two-Mile and 5,000 Meter)

19

DEVIN DURRANT

The Best Prep Cager in the United States and Cougar
Basketball Star

27

TINA GUNN (ROBISON)

National Women's Collegiate Basketball Scoring
Champion and National Player of the Year

33

CURT BRINKMAN
Boston Marathon Wheelchair Champion
40

MERLIN OLSEN
All-American Football Player and Pro Superstar
45

JOHNNY MILLER
All-American and Golf Superstar
52

JEFF JUDKINS
Pro Basketball Player
59

JEAN SAUBERT
National Ski Champion and Olympic Silver Medalist
64

KEN SHELLEY
Outstanding Sportsman in the Winter Olympics 1972
69

HARMON KILLEBREW
Baseball Superstar
74

AB JENKINS
Champion Racer—Superman of Speed and Endurance
80

DANNY LOPEZ
Featherweight Boxing Champion of the World
85

VERN LAW
Pro Baseball Superstar and Cy Young Pitcher
90

ALF ENGEN
National Ski Champion: "Utah's Old Man of the Mountain"
99

LINN ROCKWOOD
National Public Parks Tennis Champion
106

KENNETH LUNDMARK
Swedish and NCAA High-Jump Champion
110

DALE MURPHY
Professional Baseball Player
115

LELEI FONOIMOANA
All-American and Olympic Swimmer
120

BOB RICHARDS
National Steeplechase Champion
125

MEL HUTCHINS
All-American Basketball Player and NBA All-Star
135

WADE BELL
National 880 Champion and Pan-American Games Champion
140

MIKE YOUNG
National and Pan-American Games Wrestling Champion and Wrestling Coach of the Year
144

ELDON FORTIE ("The Phantom")
All-American and Pro Football Player
148

NEIL ROBERTS
Phenomenal All-Around Athlete and Champion Coach
154

DOLORES LIER
Swiss National Skating Champion
162

REX BERRY
Pro Football Player
168

RICHARD GEORGE
National Javelin Champion and Olympian
172

DON FULLMER
American Middleweight Boxing Champion
178

BRAD HANSEN and the Wrestling Hansen Brothers
Brad Hansen
All-American and Record Performer
184
Mike Hansen
185
Laron Hansen
186
Mark Hansen
186
David Hansen
186
Ronnie Hansen
187

DICK MOTTA
NBA Coach of the Year and NBA Champion Coach
195

CECIL BAKER (1895-1980)
Track and Basketball Star and Super Coach
203

HOMER "PUG" WARNER (1896-1956)
All-Around Athlete and M-Men Basketball Originator
211

MICKEY OSWALD (1899-1977)
Outstanding All-Around Athlete and Super Coach
215

CLARENCE "ROBBIE" ROBISON
Track Star and Master Coach
223

GEORGE "DOC" NELSON (1890-1970)
Light Heavyweight Wrestling Champion of the World
and Fabled Wrestling Coach and Athletic Trainer
228

EUGENE "TIMPANOGOS" ROBERTS (1880-1953)
All-Around Athlete, Coach of Olympians, Master
Sports Innovator and Promoter
234

LaVELL EDWARDS
Outstanding Football Player and National Coach of
the Year
243

MIKE REID
All-American and PGA Golfer
251

LES GOATES (1894-1975)
Champion Sportswriter
256

MARV HESS
Outstanding All-Around Athlete and Hall of Fame
Coach
263

ANDERS ARRHENIUS
Swedish National Shot Put Champion and All-
American
268

BILLY CASPER
Golf Superstar
272

KEY TO ABBREVIATIONS
279

INDEX
281

ACKNOWLEDGMENTS

I want to thank my wife, Sandra, for her patience and support in this wonderful task; my daughter Stephanie for her help in transcribing my time-consuming and rapid dictations; my other eleven children (Lindsay, Robert, Lona, Jonathon, David A., Christian, Cynthia, David S., Timothy, Kristina, and Mark) for their love and support; Bonnie Roberts for typing the manuscript; all who have helped me gather the necessary information to do this work (*Deseret News* Information—Connie Christensen and staff; BYU Sports Information—Dave Schulthess; BYU Athletic Department; *Salt Lake Tribune* Sports Information; University of Utah Sports Information; USU Sports Information; BYU Alumni Center; BYU Archives; Utah Chapter of the Old Time Athletes Association; LDS Church Library and Public Affairs Division); *Salt Lake Tribune* sports editor John Mooney; *Deseret News* sports editors Hack Miller, Lee Benson, and Les Goates; *Provo Herald* sports editor Marion Dunn; the fine sportswriters on the many newspaper staffs for their excellent coverage of these athletes; Steven W. Heiner, Jr., for photographic assistance; and all the athletes and their families.

I thank Deseret Book Company for publishing this book, and especially I thank the great athletes and coaches and their families for their assistance.

INTRODUCTION

Researching the lives of the great Mormon athletes has been wonderful. All of the time and effort spent has been so rewarding to me that I can in no way convey the richness of blessings and experiences that have come into my life as a result of the research, studies, and interviews. In this book are the athletic accomplishments and philosophies of many Mormon athletes and also some of the great Mormon coaches who have influenced the lives of so many aspiring young men and women involved in athletics. Perhaps the most impressive aspect of my research has been the athletes' ideas, rather than strictly their deeds, for "as [a man] thinketh in his heart, so is he." (Proverbs 23:7.)

Danny Lopez, after he was beaten, before becoming featherweight champion of the world: "God helped me turn myself around. The Church helped me get back on my feet."

Eldon Fortie, entering the BYU Sports Hall of Fame with an incredible story as an all-American quarterback: "BYU provided me with a once-in-a-lifetime opportunity, and everything I have I owe to the school and the Church."

Clarence Robison, Olympian and former president of the NCAA Track and Field Coaches: "I've always felt that being a track coach gave me a great opportunity to build young men who are not only great athletes, but great citizens, great Christians. One of my goals is to build the whole man, not just his muscles."

Curt Brinkman, National and Boston Marathon wheelchair champion: "I just want to prove to others and to myself that there are things that one can do in a wheelchair that perhaps others cannot do."

Brad Hansen, all-American wrestler: "Never give up until the match is over. Learn to fight and give it all you have, every time, every practice and every match."

Ab Jenkins, internationally eminent auto racer, explaining his refusal to do an ad for a tobacco promoter: "The main reason is I think too much of the kids."

Dolores Lier, Swiss national ice-skating champion: "No

one should be fanatical enough to seek for success at any price, which is applicable both to the body and the spirit. I could never picture my own life without either the gospel or sports."

Ken Lundmark, Swedish and NCAA high jump champion: "My athletic career affected my ability to recognize the truths in Mormonism. In man's pursuit of excellence and perfection, the same basic principles operated in both athletics and Mormon doctrine."

Billy Casper, one of the all-time great golfers of the world: "I'm dedicating my life to helping my fellowman, and to sharing my talents and blessings with our fellowmen throughout the world."

Eugene Roberts, father of BYU athletics: "He wanted his boys to be 'fellow students,' participating not only in sports, but also in the whole social and academic life of the school. They should find ample compensation for athletic skills in the privilege they had of representing school and studentbody."

Richard George, world class javelin thrower: "The Church is the foundation of everything I do.... I would not have felt good competing in the Olympic games in the place of a mission, knowing that my first responsibility is to the Church."

Vern Law, UPI's National League Comeback Player of the Year and Cy Young Award (best pitcher in major-league baseball): "I often bow my head when I am pitching or even sitting on the bench and say a silent prayer. I simply ask for strength to do my best. I don't expect my prayers to be answered in a positive way immediately. I just want to be able to do my best. Prayer doesn't guarantee anything, but a person needs to be humbled once in a while."

Don Fullmer, American middleweight boxing champion: "If you want something bad enough, then there is a price to pay—and we have to be willing to pay that price."

Harmon Killebrew, American League Baseball Player of the Year: "Baseball has taught me a lot about life. I have felt the need to find a better purpose in life. This can be found in the gospel of Jesus Christ. I believe in God; it gives me a wonderful dimension in life."

Neil Roberts, praised by *Sports Illustrated* as "the greatest prep athlete in the U.S.": "I have always believed in pregame prayer. It has not mattered what religion, race, or standing the members of the team possessed—we have always participated in prayer—each member taking a turn."

Devin Durrant, "The best prep cager in the U.S.,"as he decided to interrupt his sports career for a mission: "Basketball is only ten years of a lifetime, and a lifetime is only a dot in the eternities.... It's nice, but... life will go on."

Linn Rockwood, national tennis champion: "I am going to go for every ball, every point of the match until somebody cracks—and it isn't going to be me."

Mickey Oswald, all-around athlete and all-around coach, comparing missionaries and athletes: "Only the game is different.... All the boys [missionaries]... have one goal, and that is to preach the gospel of Jesus Christ so something can be brought into the lives of the people. These young elders are just as devoted to their work here as the young men on the teams of East [High] were in their respective sports."

Dick Motta, NBA champion coach: "I think my size has helped make me a battler. Little people always have to work harder.... There's a place in this world for a little guy—in sports as much as any place else."

Rex Berry, the "Carbon Comet" and all-pro gridder: "I was the only member of the LDS Church on that team [San Francisco 49'ers].... I was different, and that difference in personal philosophy and actions caused much comment by my team members. The comments didn't bother me. I did my job and probably worked harder than most. I did not force my personal philosophy, religion, or habits on anyone, but I lived them and went out of my way to be friendly and helpful to all team members. As a result of how I lived and acted, which of course was related to my LDS background, my team members elected me their captain. They wanted me—the different guy—to represent them."

Cec Baker, legendary Utah coach: "I was conscious of my example of good sportsmanship to my ballplayers in how I reacted to what I thought were bad calls by officials. Intimidating officials and calling players for mistakes can arouse a whole studentbody to unsportsmanlike responses. In good conduct I could not bring myself to yell, swear, drink milk publicly, prance on sidelines, or cuss the officials. To me these are plays used to get reactions favoring one team or distressing another. Though the best team does not always win, and officials make mistakes, each player should have the opportunity to do his best. In forty-two years of coaching I had one technical called on me, none on my players."

Unfortunately, many of the outstanding Mormon athletes I have studied have not been included in this and the previous volume, but at least some of their great lives and accomplishments have been brought to light in condensed form.

DANNY WHITE

All-American Quarterback and Pro Football Player

Most Valuable Player,
football, basketball,
baseball, track,
Westwood High School
(Mesa, Arizona), 1969-70

All-state in basketball, baseball,
and track, 1969-70

Arizona State University, 1970-74:
Two-sport letterman
(football, baseball)

All-WAC first team quarterback,
1973

All-WAC punter, 1973

Most Valuable Player in football,
1973

Winner of the WAC Annual Football
Award as the best back, 1973

All-American, 1973

Arizona State University Hall of
Fame charter member, 1975

Professional football, 1974-82:
WFL, 1974-76

Dallas Cowboys, 1976-82:
Cowboys' number-one punter
Cowboys' number-one quarterback,
1980-82

As one of the top high school athletes in the state of Arizona, national collegiate football leader, and current Dallas Cowboys number-one quarterback, Danny White, at six feet three inches and 182 pounds, "casts a tall shadow." The imprint of his athletic ability has been felt dramatically wherever he has performed.

As in so many instances where athletic ability seems to pass from father to son, this outstanding athlete walked in the footsteps of his famous football-player father, Wilford "Whizzer" White, who helped instill within him a desire to participate in athletics. He attributes his success to his family, "the driving force in my life." Danny says, "For as long as I can remember, whichever sport was in season, we'd be out playing with my dad. We'd be playing basketball on the driveway, or out throwing the football or baseball, or playing ping-pong—or something like that all the time."

Whizzer, Danny's father, is regarded by many as one of the greatest athletes ever produced in the state of Arizona. He was all-Church in basketball, softball, and volleyball, and was all-state in three sports (football, basketball, and track) three consecutive years (1943-46). He was a three-sport letterman at Arizona State University from 1947 to 1951, achieving some remarkable records during his career. As ASU's first all-American in football in 1950, he was also the University's first athlete to win NCAA statistical championships by leading the nation in rushing and all-purpose running. He set over seventy ASU football records and was declared Arizona's most outstanding athlete two years in a row (1949-50). He played in the East-West All-Star Football Game (1950) and the College All-Star Game (1951). He was a finalist (top five) in the 1950-51 National AAU Decathlon. His jersey was retired in 1950. After college he played professional football for the Chicago Bears. He is a charter member of the ASU Hall of Fame and was elected to the Arizona Sports Hall of Fame.

2

From 1967 through 1970, Danny was a four-sport letter-man in football, basketball, track, and baseball at Westwood High School in Mesa, Arizona. He was acclaimed the Most Valuable Player in all four sports. He made the all-state team in three of those sports, basketball, baseball, and track. As a long jumper he took second place in the Arizona State Track Meet with a jump of 23 feet 2 inches. He was also a high jumper and leaped 6 feet 4 inches. In baseball he played first base, shortstop, and had a 16-0 winning high school pitching record. He was named all-district covering several western states as a senior. At the conclusion of his senior year, he was given the E. R. Brimhall Award as the outstanding scholar-athlete.

While attending Arizona State University from 1970 to 1974 (majoring in bioagriculture), Danny set some phenomenal records. Although he lettered in both football and baseball as a college athlete, he excelled in football—the one sport in which he was not chosen all-state as a high school player. In college he was one of the top collegiate quarterbacks in the country, and set over one hundred ASU college records, twenty WAC records, and seven NCAA records. As a senior he ranked number one in such categories as total offense, total yardage in passing, and touchdowns. As a junior he was seventh in the nation in total offense, and as a senior finished second in the nation in the same category. He was first team all-conference in the Western Athletic Conference both as a quarterback and punter in 1973. He was an outstanding punter throughout his varsity career. In the Western Athletic Conference he achieved records in such categories as career passing, total offense, touchdown passes thrown, yards per pass attempt, yards per pass completion, and others. In 1973 he was the winner of the Western Athletic Conference Annual Award as the best back in football. He was also named all-American first team (Football Writers, *Time*, NEA) and second team (UPI, AP). He was ASU's Most Valuable Player and received the McBurney Community Achievement Award for distinguishing actions on and off the field.

Danny really had a break during his collegiate career as a sophomore while playing for the Sun Devils in 1971. After having missed some games as the result of a shoulder separation, he received a chance as a starter. He threw six touchdown passes and was named the Associated Press

3

Player of the Week, gaining him national recognition. From that game against the Lobos he rocketed into national prominence. During the next years of his collegiate competition, ASU unofficially changed its school colors from Maroon and Gold to Green and White in respect for the great Arizona State halfback Woody Green and quarterback Danny White. This backfield duo chalked up incessant winning seasons, racking up such point totals as 56, 59, 55, and 60.

While achieving local, regional, and national statistical fame, Danny served as a part-time missionary at the visitors' center at the Arizona Temple. He never failed to put his family and Church first in his life. At that time he said, "A quarterback is a team leader and he has to have respect....I feel the Church has given me confidence. I never go into a game without a personal prayer, and this helps me considerably, knowing that help is there if I need it. I feel very confident that when I'm on the field that any time I need any extra help—if I'm not feeling well or something—I know that I can pray about it, and it gives me all the confidence in the world. It's just a feeling that you're going to do your best." He has never hesitated telling his teammates about the Church, but has done so in an easy manner: "I'm not a pushy guy. I try to be a quiet example without being a nuisance. We talk about the Church, and they know a little about Mormonism."

Before the Fiesta Bowl in 1971, when Arizona State beat Florida State 45-38, Danny and Junior Ah You, a member of the Church from Hawaii and defensive end for Arizona State, were driving back to their hotel room from their training room. Danny relates that Junior "started singing a song in Hawaiian. It was a tune that I recognized, and I asked him where he learned the song. He replied that he learned it in Primary in Hawaii years and years ago. I asked him what was the name of the song. He replied, 'There is Sunshine in My Soul Today.' Here I was just shaking in my boots because we were getting ready to play the Fiesta Bowl in just a few hours, and here he was just as calm and relaxed as he could be. It had a real calming influence on me, and I thought a lot about it since then, and came to the realization that the one thing that stays the same wherever you go is the Church." Danny guided his team to victory in the Fiesta Bowl for three consecutive years (1971-73), and during that period ASU amassed a 32 won-4 lost record.

Danny was drafted by the Cleveland Indians to play professional baseball, but had his heart set on pro football. Since 1974 he has had a professional football career. He spent two years in the World Football League until 1976 and then joined the Dallas Cowboys. He was that team's number-one punter and backup quarterback through 1979. In the 1978 Super Bowl, in which the Cowboys defeated the Denver Broncos 27-10, Danny punted five times and saw minimal play as quarterback backup to the great Roger Staubach. During that Super Bowl game there were two Mormon athletes playing for the Cowboys—Danny and Golden Richards, offensive wide receiver—and two Mormons playing for the Denver Broncos—offensive right guard Paul Howard

5

and fullback John Keyworth. In 1979 the Cowboys again played in the Super Bowl in Miami against the Pittsburgh Steelers. Danny again punted five or six times during the game, and again warmed up on the sidelines, trying to stay loose in case something should happen to Staubach. In the final game of the 1978 season, against the New York Jets, when Staubach was resting from an injured foot and hand, White completed fifteen of twenty-four passes for 156 yards, leading the Cowboys to a 30-7 victory. In the playoffs Dallas met the Atlanta Falcons, but was behind 20-13 with less than a minute to play in the first half, when Staubach was knocked unconscious. Again Danny headed the Cowboy offense. He performed almost flawlessly, moving the Cowboys to two touchdowns and squeaking into the conference championship game against Los Angeles with a 27-13 victory. White was featured in an article in *Sports Illustrated* after that impressive win.

In 1980 Danny's long backup career ended as the fabled Staubach announced his retirement. Danny became the first Mormon to start as a National Football League quarterback—the number-one signal caller for the Cowboys. During the past two seasons he has earned much respect by bringing Dallas to the playoffs both years and by breaking some of his predecessors' passing records.

A recent article in the *Church News* reflects this great athlete's thoughts on the principles of football being applied to life: "Think of yourselves as quarterbacks. Your friends and neighbors are the wide receivers and running backs, and your family and relatives are the offensive line. As quarterback, you are the most important player on the team, and it will never be any stronger than you are. You must make things go."

Danny also likens the premortal existence to the preseason games: "We've proven we have what it takes to play in the game of life. The scriptures are our game plan, and we must communicate with the coach (God) and follow His guidelines if we want to be successful. If you persevere and never give up, you've always got a chance to make your life a success."

Danny urges knowledge, self-discipline, and concentration, which lead to consistency in life as well as on the football field. He maintains that only careful and sound preparation will produce the results we want from life. His long line of successes, patience in preparation in a backup role, and persistence and dedication are a good example of this philosophy.

Danny has been involved in athletics as long as he can remember. During football season, he has daily workouts with the team. During the off-season, he plays basketball and racquetball, and is involved in a strength program and anaerobic and aerobic training. He says, "I think of my body as a tool used by my spirit to perform necessary mortal duties. The stronger and cleaner that tool is, the more my spirit can accomplish with it." About being a Mormon in athletics, he comments, "It has given me a sense of perspective, in that I realize that there are things in life much more important than sports, such as family and a good, spiritual relationship with God. Therefore, I don't feel it's the end of the world when I lose a game. I feel I can cope with the emotional ups and downs of professional sports. It is important to me every day as I strive to improve my relationship with my Father in Heaven. It is of value everywhere I go, but most importantly in my home." In spite of being on the professional football travel schedule, Danny has served as an elders quorum president, a Sunday School teacher, and a seminary teacher, and is presently a stake missionary. He is constantly reminded by a personal letter from President N. Eldon Tanner to "strive for the kingdom of God first."

He comments on athletic success, "Always be alert to temptation. Athletics is a great teacher of the fundamentals of life. Hard work, dedication, teamwork, pride, self-discipline, and mental and physical self-control are all important factors. A young man or woman can become as great as he or she wants to be, but along with athletics goes the constant temptations that come with success in a field that is so closely monitored by the press. One must recognize these temptations and always *very* carefully consider decisions involving them. One must always remember the problems of participation on Sunday, attendance at cocktail parties, and association with certain types of individuals."

Danny White, outstanding Arizona high school all-around athlete, formidable collegiate gridiron star and setter of numerous records, professional football player for the Dallas Cowboys, has set a fine example as a faithful member of the Church.

DANNY VRANES

United States Olympian and All-American Basketball Star

Skyline High School (Salt Lake City), 1974-77:
All-state, 1975-77
All-southwest, 1976-77
All-American, 1976-77

National Prep magazine's Junior of the Year, 1976

Class 4-A Most Valuable Player, 1976-77

University of Utah, 1977-81:

First freshman in modern Ute history to start every game, 1977-78

1979 U.S. Pan American gold medalist

WAC rebounding champion (10.1), 1979

1st native Utahn named to the United States Olympic Basketball Team, 1980

All-WAC and All-region Seven First Team, 1979-81

University of Utah Most Valuable Player, 1980-81

Deseret News Athlete of the Month, January 1981

Multiple Sclerosis Society's Male Inter-collegiate CoAthlete of the Year, 1980

All-American (USBWA, *Sporting News*, AP, UPI, NABC, and *Basketball Weekly*), 1981

Seattle SuperSonics' number-one pick, 1981

Unquestionably one of the greatest basketball players to come from Utah, Danny Vranes, Utah's first native to be selected for the United States Olympic Basketball Team, has methodically built one of the finest cage records imaginable. He has been praised as a "certified basketball hotshot and local hero since his sophomore year at Skyline High,...the living definition of tall, dark and handsome."

At the culmination of his collegiate basketball career, the Redskins' Danny Vranes (along with the Cougars' Danny Ainge—previously praised together as "a double Danny dandy" by *Sports Illustrated*) was named to the Basketball Writers' Ten-Man All-American Team. *Deseret News* sports editor, Lee Benson, commented about Danny's early basketball career: "For Vranes, the all-American distinction comes approximately 15 years since he became hooked on basketball. When he was a second-grader at Salt Lake's Beacon Heights Elementary he used to watch his older cousin, Jeff Judkins, play on the hoops at recess. He was inspired to ask his dad for a basket at home and, since Danny was only slightly taller than four feet, his dad responded with a 7½-footer in the driveway. Thus, Danny Vranes started his above-the-rim career. A few dozen burned out floodlights later and it was off the driveway and into Skyline High's gym, where the hoops were 10 feet and Danny was closing in on 7½ feet himself. He never has looked up to a rim, and he looks back at the driveway 7½-footer as a confidence builder.

'I could have shot at a 10-footer all day,' he recalls, 'and never made a thing.'" That's how it all started.

At Skyline High in Salt Lake City, Danny was touted by many as the best prep performer in Utah history. For three years he was first team all-state and averaged better than twenty-two points and fifteen rebounds a game. He totaled over a thousand rebounds, shot 63 percent from the field, and led his team to two state 4-A championships and a second place finish while compiling a 68-8 record. He distinguished himself in the McDonald Classic and the Sharon (PA) Tournament. He was named Junior of the Year by *National Prep Magazine* and was the 1976 and 1977 class 4-A Most Valuable Player. He was a two-time, all-Southwest, first-team cager and all-American, both as a junior and a senior. He was also named to the Utah All-Star Team as a senior.

Vranes comes from good athletic stock. His cousins Jeff and Jay Judkins were both high school and university cagers of note. His sister Shauna Vranes was an exceptionally versatile Utah high school and collegiate athlete (three-time high school track and field champion; state record-holder in the long jump, 18 feet 10 inches; state champion in the 100-yard dash, 220, and high jump; 1979 Female Athlete of the Year in Utah; University of Utah records in the 60-yard and 440-yard hurdles and high jump; first place in the Mt. Sac Relays, high jump, 5 feet 9 inches; and volleyball team spiker and blocker). His grandfather Lou Vranes was an outstanding athlete and coach.

In launching his collegiate career, Danny chose the University of Utah in order to join his cousin Jeff Judkins, the Redskin star (now a professional basketball player). Duke coach Bill Foster, previously the head man at Utah, tried to lure Danny away from the Redskins but was unsuccessful. As a freshman Danny hit 55 percent of his shots and wowed the WAC with his terrific jumping ability. He became the first freshman in modern Ute history to start every game. He was named to the 1978 Freshman All-American Team (*Basketball Weekly*). He earned a slot on the 1978 United States basketball team that played in the Yuri Gagarin Games in Russia. While in Russia, Danny had a sudden attack of appendicitis and had the unusual experience of leaving his appendix with the Russians. He chalks up the experience of the cold hospital, lumpy bed, and the unusual post-operative diet (the first meal was a bowl of mayonnaise and a raw egg) as one he would like to forget.

With interesting statistics (the highest field-goal shooting percentage—54.7; the highest rebound average and the highest number of blocked shots—16), and as a second team all-WAC performer, Danny continued a stellar performance as a super soph. He was named a 1979 first team all-district seven and all-WAC, led the WAC in rebounding (10.1), and set a new WAC record in field-goal percentage for conference games (.691). He also set a new Utah record in field-goal percentage for all games (.616) and conference games (.691). He was named to the 1978 Rainbow Classic All-Tournament Team and for his second year in a row joined the Redskins in the NCAA playoffs. He was a co-winner of the Jack Gardner Most Valuable Player Award and was named to the 1979 United States Pan American Team. As only one of two sophomores on the team, he worked out against the national team of Italy and then performed as one of the top six players at the Pan American Games. In Puerto Rico he became a gold medalist under the controversial Bobby Knight, playing with some of the finest collegiate basketball players in the United States.

As a junior Redskin performer, Danny was named to the Ten-Man Collegiate All-American Team by *Playboy* magazine, was the Utah Classic Most Valuable Player, and garnered all-district-seven-first-team and all-WAC honors. One of his greatest attributes has been his tremendous attitude in disregarding his own statistics, caring only about the team. With that attitude he became the first native Utahn ever to make the United States Olympic Basketball Team, and for the third year in a row was a United States Basketball Team member. Although the boycott of the 1980 Olympics did not allow him to compete in Moscow, he did shine as the Olympic team defeated the NBA All-Stars.

Not enough can be said about Danny's senior year with the Redskins. He again garnered all-WAC and all-district-seven-first-team honors, was named to the Far West and Utah Classic all-tournament teams, was named to the NABC All-District Team, and was given distinctive All-American-Team honors (USBWA, *Sporting News* Second Team, AP Second Team, UPI Third Team, *Basketball Weekly* First Team, NABC Second Team). He was a star performer in the Pizza

Hut Classic and Aloha Classic. With his senior talent, fire power, and experience, he was praised by Ute head basketball coach Jerry Pimm as "the best basketball player I ever coached." Coach Dave Gavitt of the Olympic squad said, "He was an outstanding member of our Olympic team last summer. He did an excellent job in his role on the team and was one of our strengths up front. Not only does he have tremendous talent, but also, he is a tremendous individual and certainly is one of the premier players in the country." He joined Tom Chambers, Carl Bankowski, Pace Mannion, Scott Martin, and Craig Hammer to lead the Redskins to one of the finest seasons in Utah history. As co-champions of the WAC, they racked up a 25-5 record, and Vranes became the school's career leader as the most accurate shooter, the second leading rebounder, and the fifth leading scorer. As the Ute Most Valuable Player and team cocaptain, Vranes was

12

also given the Best Field Goal Percentage Award (59.5) and the Best Free Throw Percentage trophy (79.6) for the Ute awards in 1981.

Although this great all-American hoopstar kept the Utah Redskins in the top ten national rankings throughout his senior year, his team bowed out in the NCAA West Regional Semifinals against the North Carolina Tarheels. Danny then shined at the thirteenth annual Aloha Basketball Classic in Honolulu, where he was named to the All-Tournament Team.

Behind Danny's brilliant cage career is his well-rounded character. He talks frequently to Scout and church groups, participates in basketball clinics, and has been a member of his Sunday School presidency. He is an avid outdoorsman. He loves to water-ski on Lake Powell, backpack and fish in the Uinta Mountains, and hunt deer, elk, and duck. In addition, he is noted for his remarkable sense of humor. Doug Robinson, *Deseret News* sportswriter, characterized him, as he was named Deseret News Athlete of the Month in January 1981, as a "first-team, all-world practical joker." He called him the "all-time king of shenanigans." He pointed out that as team leader, Vranes's shenanigans are actually more an act of affection for his teammates than anything else. His constant practical jokes and pranks have helped unify his team.

The dazzling career of Danny Vranes continues. As the fifth player chosen in the NBA draft in 1981, the number-one pick of the Seattle SuperSonics, the talented all-American signed a four-year contract for a 1.4 million dollar total, with expectations of becoming Seattle's starting small forward in the 1981-82 season. He was the first Salt Lake City native to be drafted by the NBA since his cousin Jeff Judkins was taken by the Boston Celtics in the second round three years previously. His Redskin jersey number 23 was retired in 1981. His quickness, coolness, and shooting ability may lead him to be an instant star for the SuperSonics.

KIM TAYLOR

National Gymnastics Champion

Five-time Utah state gymnastic champion, 1975-80

Member of AAU National Elite Gymnastic Team, 1978-79

Member of the United States National Gymnastic Team, 1978

AAU Elite Nationals, 1979:
ninth all-around
fourth uneven bars
seventh floor exercise

USGF senior national uneven bars champion, 1980

Deseret News Athlete of the Month, June 1980

National High School Invitational (McDonald's) all-around champion, 1980

Twenty-first All-Around USGF USA Championship, 1981

Member United States National Gymnastic Team, 1981

National champion, uneven bars, floor exercises, High School Invitational (McDonald's), 1981

The first Utahn to make the United States National Gymnastic Team, 1981

A phenomenal and beautiful young lady, Kim Taylor, age sixteen, has been on a remarkable march toward the United States Olympic Gymnastics Team (for 1984) for the past seven years. This Salt Lake City native is one of the brightest stars in Utah gymnastics history.

Kim has practiced for five hours a day, six days a week, since she started gymnastics. She has never once considered dropping out of the grueling regimen. Along the way she has chalked up some outstanding records. In 1975, at the class 3 state meet, she took first place in all-around gymnastic competition. Since then she has excelled in local, regional, and national competition. She has been a member of the Utah Academy of Gymnastics' Nuggets since 1974, receiving both individual and team honors. As Utah's youngest ever elite (Olympic class) gymnast, she has been a four-time Utah bars and floor exercise champion. She has said, "I'd rather do gymnastics than go to school any day." No wonder she has been so successful. Her coaches, Paul Hunt and Michelle Pond, see to it that Kim does not relent in her studies, because any of their students who fall below a B average in school are automatically out of gymnastics.

During her gymnastic career, Kim's strongest event has been the uneven parallel bars, because she has the swinging ability to move from one trick to the next without relying on strength, but one of her more spectacular stunts is on the floor—a side somersault with a full twist. She is one of only four girls in the world able to do it.

Kim was a member of the 1978 Nuggets team, which won the National AAU Gymnastic Championship in Houston, Texas. In 1979 she led her team to second place in national competition, where she finished fifth in the floor exercise and ninth in the all-around, qualifying her for the USGF championships.

In 1980 her star was rising higher. She was the Utah state champion in the vault and the balance beam and the USGF junior regionals champion in all-around and uneven bars competition. She then "vaulted" into first place as she became the United States Federation senior national uneven bars champion at the Junior Olympic Nationals in Tulsa, Oklahoma. She finished second in the floor exercise, topping sixty women. She then went to the Sixth Annual McDonald's National High School Gymnastic All-Around Invitational in Chicago, having been picked as one of the nation's six high-school-aged girls to perform in this showcase competition. She won first place in the uneven parallel bars, floor exercise, and all-around. Interestingly enough, her chief competition was a member of her own team, Wendy Whiting, who took second place. Between the two of them, they took four national gym titles. Kim tied with Wendy for first on the bars with 9.25, won the floor exercise at 9.45, was second at 9.2 on the vault, and third at 8.6 on the beam. Her all-around score was 36.50. Wendy, who had 36.0 all-around, won first place (9.25) on the bars and vault, was second with 9.15 in the floor exercise, and was fourth on the beam at 8.35—both Mormons winning first and second place in the USGF National Championships. Kim was named Deseret News Athlete of the Month for June 1980.

Although Kim was the youngest gymnast ever to attain elite ranking from Utah, she was not to be outdone in 1981. She qualified for the United States championships and was named a United States National Gymnastic Team member (the first ever from Utah) and won twenty-first place all-around in the United States championships. She was one of twenty-one young ladies selected from a field of thirty-two competitors at the National Elite Gymnastics Meet in Bethlehem, Pennsylvania. She again repeated as the 1981 McDonald's National High School All-Around Invitational champion in the uneven bars and floor exercise. As a member of the United States Gymnastics Team, she was selected to participate in the National Sports Festival in Syracuse, New York. This sports festival is an intense clinic run by the United States Olympic Committee to assure the success of the United States teams in the 1984 Olympic games. Only the top twenty-four women gymnasts in the country are invited.

Kim has remained active in the Church despite rigid training schedules, and attends Church meetings whenever and wherever she can. She credits her parents with helping her accomplish her gymnastics goals and says, "Without their help and support I could never do it. Because they have all the faith in the world in me, they are always helping to build up

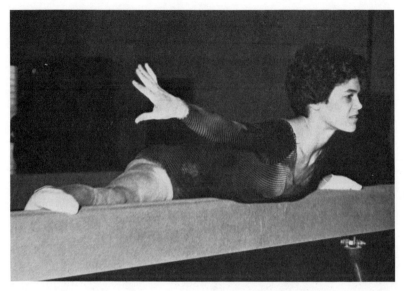

my confidence." She is aware of many blessings in her life and says, "I have been blessed with an exceptional athletic body. The structure is small, but the coordination and ability are there. I give thanks daily for my body and health and pray it will continue. My silent prayers build the spirit needed to excel. Without prayer, the testimony I have gained in the Church, and the Guiding Spirit that directs me, I could not succeed."

Kim recommends the following for other gymnasts or athletes desiring to achieve: "I would tell them that there is a time for play and a time for work, and when it is time to work you have to put your mind to work and start striving for your goals. Also, you have to give up a lot of things that your friends can do. It takes much time and work. If you have a downfall, you have to come right back. You can't let it hold you down for the rest of your career or future."

Kim's crossroads came after a state meet in 1980. She said, "I was trying to decide whether or not to continue gymnastics in the state of Utah or move to another state and gym to further my development. After a great deal of thought and meetings with my coaches and parents, I made the choice. I had to seek help and guidance, for the decision I reached was to continue on with the same coaches and to stay home with my parents and friends. The decision was helped greatly by the thought that life is too short to be away

17

from parents, family, friends, and Church activities. I have seen many gymnasts who thought that life in other parts of the country and other gyms would help their progress in the gymnastics world. In reality it created loneliness and poor results in school, church, and their gymnastics. Their spirits were dampened and in many cases broken. Without the spirit to drive them on, they soon quit and were out of gymnastics. Yes, the spirit is reinforced daily by association with your parents, family, school, and church friends." Presently Kim is helping younger children learn gymnastics. She hopes someday to be a gymnastic coach herself.

Kim Taylor is eyeing 1984 Olympic gold. She recognizes that she still has a long way to go to achieve her gymnastic goals, but as the only member of the United States Gymnastic Team ever to come from Utah, she has a new burst of enthusiasm and is motivated by the continuing competition.

DOUG PADILLA

NCAA Indoor Two-Mile Champion and American Indoor Record Holder (Two-Mile and 5,000 Meter)

Brigham Young University, 1976, 1978-81

Sixth place NCAA 5,000-meter, 1980

Fifteenth place NCAA cross country, 1980

Sunkist Invitational two-mile champion, 1981

San Francisco Examiner Games one-mile champion (3:56.6), 1981

Los Angeles Times-Mirror Games two-mile champion (8:26), 1981

WAC one-mile and two-mile champion indoors (1500 meter and 3,000 meter), 1981

NCAA second place one-mile (4:01.6), 1981

NCAA two-mile indoor champion (8:26.52), 1981

NCAA outdoor fourth place 1500 meter and 5,000 meter, 1981

BYU Invitational one-mile champion
(4:02.9), 1981

United States National Track and
Field Team, 1981

World University Games 5,000-meter
champion (Bucharest, Romania),
1981

Los Angeles Times mile champion
(3:56.3) (personal best, 1982)

Wanamaker Millrose Games
5,000-meter champion "Fabulous
Five-Thousand" (13:20.55)
(new American indoor record,
February 1982)

Jack-in-the-Box Invitational (San
Diego) two-mile champion

New American indoor record
(8:16.8), February 1982

San Francisco Examiner Games
3,000-meter champion (7:46.0), 1982

Two-time Deseret News Athlete of
the Month, February 1981,
February 1982

Brigham Young University eight-time
all-American

Brigham Young University record-
holder (two-mile, three-mile,
3,000-meter and 5,000-meter)

American record holder indoor, two-mile and 5,000-meter

First American to win an NCAA distance crown since 1972

First American ever to beat Suleiman Nyambui

Doug Padilla is the "best indoor distance runner the U.S. has ever produced." He has not only distinguished himself by beating such international track superstars as Alberto Salazar, John Walker, Steve Scott and Suleiman Nyambui, but in 1982 has already had the fastest times in the world for the two-mile, 3,000-meter, and 5,000-meter races. He set new American indoor records in both the two-mile and 5,000-meter distance races.

Although Doug took thirteenth place in the two-mile California state championships in 1974, he certainly didn't make any of the universities drool. From San Leandro, California, he came to Brigham Young University in 1975 after competing for a year at Chabot Junior College and being crowned the "Northern California Junior College Mile Champion" (4:10.7). As a walk-on for the Cougars, he failed to make the cross-country team his first year. Then he made one of his best moves ever—by filling a mission to El Salvador, maturing spiritually and physically. Upon his return, his sensational career closely paralleled that of former teammate and national record holder, Henry Marsh. They both had insignificant first years at BYU. They both went on two-year missions. Both then developed into all-American runners and set national records.

In Padilla's junior year, he finished eighth in the Olympic trials, sixth in the NCAA 5,000-meter (1980), and fifteenth in the NCAA Cross-Country Race (1980). Although he ran a mile leg of the distance-medley relay team that took second place at the 1979 NCAA Indoor Meet and ran respectable races in 1980, it wasn't until January 30, 1981, that the embryo star began carving his place in the world of track champions. At the Sunkist Invitational he upset Suleiman Nyambui in the two-mile event with a time of 8:28.1. Everyone wondered where he came from. They thought he was another non-

21

American distance runner. Bob Wood, head of the Second Sole Track Club, which sponsored Padilla during the summer, had attempted to enter him in the Los Angeles Times Invitational, but was rejected. After the Sunkist Invitational, the people at the *Los Angeles Times* changed their minds. He had "stunned the track world by defeating Suleiman Nyambui, two-time defending national champ, world record holder and Olympic silver medalist, and suddenly meet organizers everywhere were changing their tune."

When he was proclaimed Deseret News Athlete of the Month (February 1981), Doug Robinson, *Deseret News* sportswriter, aptly described what happened: "Certainly nothing in Padilla's past ever indicated such talent. 'All the girls used to beat me in junior high,' he recalls. 'I was never a good runner.' Later, when Padilla entered high school an inch under five feet, opponents would say, 'You're not varsity, are you?' But when the race was over, they'd say, 'You're varsity alright.'" The same article then made this excellent observation: "Indeed, looking at Padilla, few would guess that he's a world-class athlete. With boyish features and a pile of thick wavy brown hair stacked neatly on the top of his head, he looks straight out of 'Happy Days'. And his frail build (5'9", 132) defies all explanations for his powerful, stinging kick at the end of the race. And he does have a kick."

He next won the Los Angeles Times Invitational by defeating former indoor-mile-world-record-holder, Dick Buerkle, while recording the fastest two-mile time in the world for the season (8:26.0). Then, at the San Francisco Examiner Games, he tried the mile at the national-class level. He had never broken four minutes officially, but went on to defeat America's top miler, Steve Scott, with a time of 3:56.6, ranking him in the top ten internationally. Just before the Western Athletic Conference races, Doug blistered the Smith Fieldhouse mile time by clocking a 4:02.9 record at the BYU Invitational. Coach Robison declared that record equivalent to a 3:55 anywhere else and said no one else had ever broken 4:05. Cougar distance running coach Sherald James prophetically stated, "Doug's greatest years are ahead of him. If he can find time to train, he has the potential to break American and world records."

After making headlines against the famous distance runners, Padilla again met Nyambui at the WAC races. If

Suleiman thought Doug's victory at the Sunkist Invitational was a fluke, he soon discovered an error in his thinking, as he was defeated twice again in both the 1,500-meter and 3,000-meter events. Later at the indoor NCAA meet in Detroit, Nyambui was looking forward to a third straight year of winning both the mile and two-mile races, but his winning streak was in jeopardy. In the two-mile, Padilla fell behind at the first part of the race, but burst into the lead and held on to defeat Nyambui at the wire (8:26.52), just .06 second ahead of the former champion. He was the first American to win an NCAA indoor distance crown since 1972, and the only American *ever* to beat Nyambui. The one-mile race turned into a duel between the two distance runners with Padilla losing by .11 second.

In the summer of 1981 Doug was named to the United States National Track and Field Team and then competed in the World University Games in Bucharest, Romania, where he won the gold medal in the 5,000 meter. Track coach Clarence Robison has said that he is impressed by Padilla's natural ability more than anything else: "He's a very gifted young man who has natural running talent and ability. It's going to win him a lot of races."

When Padilla won the Sunkist meet, he said, "You should have seen Nyambui's face when he finished. He looked like the boy caught with a hand in the cookie jar—'Oh, oh, I wasn't supposed to do that.'" Suleiman had a similar look at the WAC meet and was obviously concerned after the NCAA races.

Retrospectively Doug describes his feelings about his NCAA triumph: "I feel that if I do things the way I should—live up to my responsibilities in Church callings, school, and so on, and put in the best preparation that I can in running (with the time that is left over)—that the Lord will help me make up for my deficiencies as I prove my worthiness. I have been most impressed with the hand of the Lord in my life in directing me how to run a race. For example, in the NCAA two-mile against Nyambui, I felt quite strongly that I should make my move with five laps to go (almost a half-mile). That was hard because it would make it an extremely fast finish, and it would be very difficult to hold Suleiman off for five laps—but it proved successful. The Lord has helped me greatly."

At BYU, Doug Padilla was an eight-time all-American and set Cougar records in the two-mile, three-mile, 3,000-meter and 5,000-meter races. Although the NCAA two-mile title was, according to Doug, the "biggest race of my life," what follows in his career is certainly fantastic.

In January 1982 Padilla was actually lapped by Salazar and Nyambui in the Olympic Invitational 5,000-meter run. A week later, however, at the Sunkist Invitational two-mile run in Los Angeles he again began his surge. He shifted into high gear and came home with a personal best time of 8:24.5. Later during the month he out-kicked New York marathon record holder Alberto Salazar by .2 of a second at the Oregon Indoor Track and Field Meet (8:25.05). Salazar called him "the best two-miler in the country." He then competed at the Los Angeles Times Games in the mile run against the heavy-weight field of Steve Scott, the American record holder, and John Walker, the first man to break 3:50. Meet officials did not want Padilla to race the one-mile, because they felt he was best in the two-mile. They finally relented, and he went on to win the race at 3:56.3, a personal best and currently fifth fastest in the world. At the Millrose Games a week later he was featured in the "Fabulous 5,000." The race was supposed to be "a rematch between Nyambui, the Olympic silver medalist, and Salazar, the marathon world record holder. A year earlier in the same event, Nyambui set a world record and Salazar an American record in a thrilling race." Unpredictable Padilla was scared, but in the process set an American record with a time of 13:22.55, shaving more than two seconds off the American record and missing the world record by a scant .15 of a second. A week later, on February 19, 1982, he set another American indoor record in the two-mile championship race at the Jack-in-the-Box Invitational in San Diego (8:16.8), almost four seconds under Prefontaine's record. One day later, at the San Francisco Examiner Games, he just missed Steve Scott's American 3,000-meter record of 7:45.2 with a time of 7:46.0. Kenny Moore of *Sports Illustrated* wrote, "Now as Padilla leaned into the steep San Diego turns with an ease that seemed uncanny for one with his long, high-kicking stride, it was clear that here was the best indoor distance runner the U.S. has ever produced." Doug Robinson of the *Deseret News* noted that Padilla's humility "sounds just plain ridiculous." After his Millrose victory he said, "It's kind of hard to put myself in a class with these guys." Perhaps Moore's description of the crowd's response to Padilla is indicative of things to come: "His display of power so late in the race changed the crowd's response from a shrieked appeal to the low, involuntary moan of the deeply impressed."

This long-distance elite runner is convinced that being a Mormon has given him perspective in his athletic career. He says, "You can't have physical health without spiritual health. This really comes through when it comes to competition. To be able to perform well, I think that you need the confidence that comes from faith in God. It would be difficult for me to handle pressure without it." He elaborates, "Winning is important. You strive to do your very best, but you never do anything dishonest. Always be on good terms with your competitors. They are some of my best friends. *Winning is not always placing first.* Winning is giving your best performance. It's giving your all. It's not giving up. Maybe it is just finishing. If you do your best, you are a winner. If nothing else, never give up!"

Doug states that "the most important thing in my life is knowing that I am a child of my Heavenly Father and that He loves me. So I have a lot to live up to. Then, I know that the talents I have are God-given and I have a responsibility to develop them. I must always try to carry myself like He would want me to. I relate this to the Law of Consecration."

Doug was a district leader as a missionary. He has served as a Sunday School teacher and in various elders quorum offices. He is a student in electrical engineering at BYU.

Doug is a champion who started from humble beginnings, has maintained a humble attitude, was thrilled to be classified with the great runners of the world, gave willingly of his time as a servant for God as a missionary, and has developed into one of the great world-class tracksters.

DEVIN DURRANT

The Best Prep Cager in the United States and Cougar Basketball Star

Provo High School (Utah) basketball, 1975-78

Captain 3-A Bulldog Championship Team, 1978

Deseret News 3-A Most Valuable Player, 1978

All-state, 1978

Leading prep scorer in Utah, 1978

All-American, 1978

McDonald All-American All-Star Games, 1978

Most Valuable Player, Kentucky Derby Classic, 1978

Hertz Number One Award for Utah, 1978

Derby Classic one-on-one champion, 1978

BYU first team varsity as freshman, 1978-79

WAC Freshman Basketball Player of the Year, 1979

U.S. Basketball Team touring China, 1979
BYU basketball 1982

Devin Durrant, one of the finest basketball players groomed in Utah, has been called "the best prep basketball player in America." (*Deseret News,* May 9, 1978.) After a brilliant basketball career at Provo High School, he was recruited by multiple colleges in the United States.

As captain of the Provo Bulldogs, he led his team to an undefeated season (26-0). They went on to win the state 3-A championship. As the leading scorer in the state of Utah while leading Provo to the title, he averaged 31.5 points and fourteen rebounds per game. He shot 59.8 percent from the field and 82 percent from the free-throw line. In the championship game he scored thirty-eight of Provo's fifty-two points against Box Elder, and was voted the Most Valuable Player of the tournament. He was named to McDonald's twelve-man all-American team, participated in the McDonald All-Star versus Capitol All-Star Game in Washington, D.C., and also the Kentucky Derby Classic (U.S. All-Stars vs. Kentucky-Indiana All-Stars in Louisville). He was also named the Most Valuable Player of the Derby Classic, in which the nation's twenty best prep players participated. Besides winning the MVP award, he won the Derby Classic One-on-One Championship featuring the twenty highest-rated players in the country. Devin also garnered the Hertz Number One Award for the state of Utah. The Hertz corporation recognizes the top athletic performance by a high school student during each school year in each of the fifty states, the District of Columbia, and Puerto Rico. Devin was also named an Adidas all-American and a second team all-American by *Basketball Weekly* and the *St. Petersburg Times.* He was honored by *Sports Illustrated's* "Faces in the Crowd" column, equivalent to the magazine's all-American team of 1978.

Commenting on his high school athletic successes, Devin lists as one of his greater achievements an extraordinary claim: "I made many new friends." What a great observation! He also found time to be the assistant in his priests quorum and serve as seminary president.

At 6 feet 6 inches, 185 pounds, Durrant set an image for his college career. He is a great passer and "has the ability to put the ball on the floor and create things," said his Provo High coach, Jim Spencer, who also said, "I've never coached another man that was a better all-around player than Devin. He dribbles, shoots, rebounds and passes extremely well." Carrying a 3.5 GPA in high school, Devin is studying prelaw and business in college. He finally decided to attend BYU because he felt that after looking over the whole spectrum, it was the right place for him. He said, "I needed more than just a basketball program in my life."

During his freshman year at BYU, Durrant was a varsity starter as forward. Paul James, television and radio sportscaster, said, "Durrant plays like a senior, not a freshman." Assistant coach at BYU, Harry Anderson, said before Devin's first scoring outburst of the season, "I told Devin he was like a time bomb just waiting to explode." Known as the Doctor by his teammates, Durrant is a polished player, one of the top fifteen scorers in the WAC in the 1978-79 season, averaging 13.4 points per game and shooting 54 percent from the field. He was also his team's third leading rebounder. He was named WAC Freshman of the Year. He was also chosen as a member of a United States basketball team to tour China.

Devin's sophomore year for the Cougars indicated that he would also be a college whiz, as he matured with a calm assurance and smooth, unhurried style. His relaxed and composed floor play and shooting ability earned him a 55 percent field goal accuracy and a 13.0 scoring average. His attitude is noteworthy: "There is room for intelligence on a basketball court. If you're smart, it makes up for any physical limitations you might have. There are a lot of intangibles in basketball. You can't do it all with talent. I'm not going to be out there gritting my teeth and killing myself. A lot of players get uptight about things and it hurts their play. I think I'm very intent, even though it may not look that way."

Durrant has always tried to have some physical activity each day: "It didn't necessarily have to be playing basketball—just anything that taxed the body a little. I think your physical and mental well-being are interrelated, and through physical exertion each day, my mental capacities were always high. The spirit can't be at its full potential unless the body is put in a situation to strive to reach its full potential." Admonishing athletes aspiring to excellence, he says, "Find

29

something you are good at and something that you really enjoy, and then concentrate on it. I would still advise that you play other sports such as football, baseball, tennis, and as many other sports that you enjoy, but still let basketball (or another major sport) be number one. Then when you enter high school just play basketball (or another sport) year around and make yourself the best player that you can possibly be."

He feels that the most important thing that has brought him success is the knowledge that the only way to achievement is hard work and putting in the necessary time:

"Someone once told me that no matter how hard I worked, there would always be someone, somewhere out there in the world, who would be working harder. So often I would practice just out of fear that someone was getting ahead of me, and that was the last thing I wanted, because I wanted to be the best." He is proud of the fact that he has been raised a Mormon and has been taught that the body is a temple and should be cared for in that way: "Through things like the Word of Wisdom, I have gained a desire to always keep my body in the best condition that I could. To excel in athletics, your body must be in the top condition possible at all times."

Devin has a practical philosophy about prayer and athletics: "Many times I have entered athletic contests after talking with my Heavenly Father, and I think it has been an all-important part of my life. Who else could help you more with anything you do in life than your Father in Heaven? So I have made it a practice to always ask my Father in Heaven for His help in all that I do."

One of eight children, he says, "My older brother was my inspiration all my life. I tried to keep up with Matt—I just grew taller than he did and that gave me the advantage." He also says, "My family has been behind me all the way. I get my competitive spirit from my mom (Marilyn) and my relaxed attitude from my dad (George)."

As an intelligent cager, Devin recognizes that basketball is not the most important thing in life, that it is only a vehicle to greater things. Being selected as a member of a U.S. basketball team to tour China is that type of vehicle.

After two great years of college basketball, Durrant's decision to go on a mission was not unexpected. It was something he had wanted to do all his life. He said, "It's the best thing for me at this time of my life. I have made two great decisions in my life the last two years. The first was to attend BYU. The second was to go on a Church mission. I think they were both good decisions." He explained his decision further in an interview with Chuck Gates, Daily Universe sportswriter: "I've had so much given to me. I just want to give something to someone and the gospel is so important. It's what Heavenly Father wants me to do." He focused on the crux of the matter with this summary: "Basketball is only 10 years of a lifetime and a lifetime is only a dot in the eternities....It's nice, but...life will go on."

From the mission field Dev's father reported, "Devin said

31

it was a great thrill to have his name in the sports page, but it's an even bigger thrill to have his name in somebody's heart whom he helped bring into the gospel. But he does still have an intense desire to play basketball." With that tempered philosophy and spiritual dedication, it will be enlightening to watch the future performance of this cage star after his return from his mission in Spain.

The best American prep cager, Devin "Doctor" Durrant, is continuing a great career on the hardwoods for the Cougars with his feet on the ground athletically and spiritually.

TINA GUNN (ROBISON)

National Women's Collegiate Basketball Scoring Champion and National Player of the Year

BYU basketball, 1976-80

All-conference, 1978-80

National Scouting Association all-American, 1978-79

National scoring runner-up (30.9), 1979

Wade Trophy Finalist, 1979-80

Member United States Basketball Team, Spartacade, Soviet Union, 1979

Amateur Athlete of the Year (Florida), 1979-80

Kodak all-American first team, 1980

National collegiate scoring champion (31.2), 1979-80

Deseret News Athlete of the Month, March 1980

Leading scorer and rebounder in BYU history (2,759 points; 1,482 rebounds), 1976-80

National Player of the Year Award, American Women's Sports Foundation, 1979-80

The parents of Tina Gunn told her to always stand tall and be proud, and that she did, a towering 6 feet 5 inches in physical stature and a giant in women's basketball. She acknowledges that she was destined to be tall, but to those who have had the privilege of being acquainted with her, she is not only tall as an athlete, but also in spirituality.

As a young girl Tina attended private Catholic schools and played volleyball, basketball, softball, and other sports. Her parents insisted that she maintain at least a B average, but she fooled them and graduated from high school with a perfect 4.0 GPA and valedictory honors. Although she played competitively in high school sports during her freshman and sophomore years, she did not participate during her junior and senior years in organized high-school sports. She did, however, attend summer basketball camps, and she wore her driveway thin shooting a couple of hours each night. She also played one-on-one against her 6-foot-4-inch brother. The boys' high-school basketball coach, Joe Patton, gave her a special amount of attention and sharpened her techniques. Her girls' high-school coach, Rose Ann Benson, alerted Brigham Young University about the possibilities of this young girl. She was invited to BYU and was impressed with the Latter-day Saints and their standards. Tina assured her parents (who were concerned about her attending a Mormon school) that she wouldn't change unless she found something better than what she had.

At BYU she had an amazing career. She shot over 60 percent for most of her career for the Cougars. Along the way she has claimed every school and conference record in scoring and the vast majority of rebounding records. She played in 101 games, averaged 74 percent from the free-throw line, scored 2,759 points, and had 1,428 rebounds. She led her team to three conference and regional championships and had scored in double figures seventy-three games in a row. As a junior she was named a National Scouting Association all-American and was the national scoring runner-up (30.9 points per game). She was named to the All-Tournament Copper Classic Team three years (1978-80) and was named Most Valuable Player of that classic as a senior. She was chosen to the All-Tournament Team of the Region 7 Tournament and was a Kodak all-American nominee three years. She was first team all-American as a senior, set the Las Vegas Convention Center scoring record (56 points) against UNLV (January 27, 1979), and set the Pauley Pavilion scoring record for women (45 points) against UCLA (December 16, 1979). She capped her college play by achieving status as the national scoring champion (31.2 points per game), National Player of the Week two consecutive weeks (American Women's Sports Foundation Award), and National Player of the Year by the American Women's Sports Foundation. She was also the Florida Amateur Woman Athlete of the Year (*St. Petersburg Independent*), Deseret News Athlete of the Month (March 1980), BYU Female Athlete of the Year, and the Multiple Sclerosis Society Intercollegiate Athlete of the Year for women. Besides leading the nation in scoring, she was fourth in the nation in rebounding and fourteenth in field-goal percentage. During her career she scored over fifty points in two games, over forty points in thirteen games and over thirty points in thirty-two games (84 games considered). She has been considered by many to be the greatest shooter in women's basketball. She has not only set an example as an excellent athlete, but as an excellent student with high moral standards and determination.

Although Tina never played competitive high school basketball, she always had the goal to make the American National Team. It was her dream. She believed that hard work and adhering to the standards and rules set by her college coach were important in her achievements. She appreciated her BYU coach, Courtney Leishman, because he was consistent in his two-hour practices. She confesses, "I knew that if I worked really hard in those two hours, the time would go by tremendously fast; whereas if I tried to loaf, the time would drag. We did not do any additional running or conditioning during the season because we ran for the entire practice." She also gives another reason for her great accomplishments: "Mentally I was able to gear myself, knowing that you could only do in a game what you had done in practice. Coach used to say, 'You can only play (in a game) as well as you practice.' My physical fitness was taken care of by practices. My mental preparedness was taken care of by a great deal of contemplation."

Raised as a Catholic, Tina says, "I have been taught ever since I was a little child that my body was a very special gift, if you will. It was something God-given that I should not abuse or misuse. As a result I never even thought of using drugs, tobacco, or alcohol. I could not conceive of anyone knowingly or willingly harming their bodies and minds. I also know now that the spirit will not dwell in an unclean body or mind. After having been in top physical condition—to know how your body can feel physically—every other aspect of our being—our emotional, spiritual, and intellectual beings—are open and receptive to newer and higher degrees of success. I know that our bodies must last us a lifetime. I see no reason not to make this life the greatest spiritual experience that we can. By detracting from our physical well-being, we unknowingly put a damper on our spiritual growth."

Tina acknowledges that priorities and goals have been responsible for her achievements: "My parents stressed the importance of being a good young lady. No matter what happens, I was to remember to be a good girl. As I began competing in the junior-high grades, they knew how much athletics meant to me. I realized that athletics would only be a part of my life for a limited number of years, and that it was important also to get a good education. I was allowed to be on as many teams and in as many sports as I desired, as long as I maintained a B average in school. In looking back now, I am grateful that my parents had the insight and love to help me realize what my priorities should be. I was somewhat hesitant upon entering college that perhaps the institution I would choose would try to make athletics the most important thing in my life. In contemplating where I would go to school, I kept this foremost in my mind. Not being a member of the LDS Church at the time, as I looked at BYU I knew that they had very high moral standards and that there was a good education program available, as well as a strong athletic department.

"After choosing BYU I felt very good about my decision. I believed that what I wanted from life was available, if I were willing to work hard to achieve it. After arriving at BYU I certainly was not disappointed. The first thing that my coach told me was that he expected the following priorities: (1) a good young lady; (2) a good student; (3) a good basketball player. If the first two aspects of our lives were not straight, we were not allowed to pursue the third. He helped us to recognize that we did not need to sacrifice our values in life to become a good athlete in life."

She further says, "I believe everyone should set priorities early in life. As you set them and as you grow and mature, you come to realize that there is nothing in this world valuable enough that you should be willing to sacrifice those priorities. Along the same line, I believe in setting goals. Goals give you a purpose in life—something to work and strive for. These goals must be set in harmony with the gospel. If we have our priorities set correctly, our goals will fall along these lines. We will be striving righteously for desires that will help others as well as ourselves. After setting these goals, you must be willing to work to achieve them. Upon graduating from high school, I had two main goals in life: one was to graduate from college, the second was to compete for a major college—and if I did well and perfected my skills enough, to compete for the United States. When I started college I was about as far from these goals as anyone could be, but I was willing to work to achieve them. I spent four years of my life studying and preparing myself in my chosen field of study. In December of 1980 I graduated from BYU with a B.S. in chemical engineering that fulfilled my first goal.

"My second goal was also fulfilled to become the best person that I could be. After being at BYU I realized that there was something else I needed or wanted to pursue in my life. That something else was the restored gospel of Jesus Christ. I believe this knowledge was obtained because of my desire to seek after the truth. It was also made possible because a young boy of six asked me, 'Tina, how come you don't go to church like I do?' After prayerful contemplation I was able to grasp the meaning and significance of making the gospel a part of my life.

"During the period of preparation for my baptism, I had the opportunity of a lifetime in playing and competing as a representative of the United States in the Spartacade Games in the Soviet Union. This opportunity fulfilled my second goal, but more important than that, it taught me the true value of prayer. Prior to leaving for the Soviet Union, I spent one week in Iowa practicing and preparing. I knew no one. I was scared to death. When I got there I realized that the people that I was with had a completely different set of standards, goals, and ideals. I would pray to my Father in Heaven and ask Him for the strength to stick it out. I prayed that I might be a good influence on those individuals with whom I was associated and that I might be safe from any harm or injury. As I felt the strength of the Spirit with me, I knew beyond any doubt that the Lord does hear and answer our prayers. I am thankful that my parents helped me to recognize what my priorities should be and in turn help me to work and achieve my goals. I am also thankful for the many people who guided and instructed me, thus enabling me to keep the priorities and goals that I set."

Tina entered BYU as a freshman from St. Petersburg in Florida on a U.S. presidential scholarship for academics. She was one of several non-LDS players on the team until she was baptized in September 1979 at the beginning of her phenomenal senior year. After achieving honors as the Women's National Basketball Player of the Year and the national scoring champion, she was drafted by Milwaukee in the fourth round of the women's pro-basketball league, but she had no future plans to turn professional. She married Scott Robison, son of the famed Cougar track coach, Clarence Robison, a former Olympian and collegiate track star. She is currently employed at Hercules in the aerospace division as a chemical engineer on rocket propellants. She is the women's stake athletic director for the Provo Utah East Stake and does a good deal of speaking at firesides.

Coach Leishman has praised Tina for her almost uncanny shooting ability, saying that he would match her as a pure shooter against any of the male players out to fifteen feet, including the free-throw line. In all of her athletic accomplishments, she has never sacrificed femininity to play a good game of basketball, nor has she sacrificed her spirituality. She has studied the gospel of Jesus Christ intensely and is impressed with the Book of Mormon because it is so closely tied to the life of Christ. She has set and maintained her goals to be a good student, a good athlete, and above all a good girl. Tall spiritually and athletically, this national scoring champion has fulfilled dreams and is accomplishing childhood goals.

CURT BRINKMAN

Boston Marathon
Wheelchair Champion

Para-Olympiad (Wheelchair Olympics, Toronto, Canada), 1976:

Gold medalist, 100-meter sprint

Bronze medalist, lawn bowling and discus

Fourth place, shot put

Silver medalist, wheelchair division, Boston Marathon 1977-78

Four-time Deseret News Wheelchair Marathon champion, 1977-81

Named as one of the outstanding young men in America by the U.S. Jaycees, 1977

Governor's Golden Key Award on behalf of the handicapped, 1977

One-hundred-fifteen-mile wheelchair marathon around Utah Lake, (16 hours, 45 minutes), 1977

World record, Long-Distance Wheelchair Marathon (275 miles), 1978

National champion, 1,500 meters, 1980

Boston Marathon wheelchair champion, 1980

Deseret News Athlete of the Month, April 1980

Curtis Brinkman is one of those fantastic individuals who, with cheerful determination and strong faith, overcame a life of pain, illness, and depression to become an optimistic and productive person and athlete. At the age of sixteen he lost his legs in an electrical accident in Shelley, Idaho. Initially, all he could do was depend on the Lord to keep him alive, and it was thought for a long time that he might die, but after two special blessings he became well. He then attended Boise State College for a while, but returned to Shelley when his mother died. He said, "I was upset at the Lord about my accident and about my mother's death." Later, after enrolling at Ricks College, he met the "greatest roommate in the world. He really got me going in the Church and in school and I've been going up ever since." Hard work and dauntless faith helped him not only to maintain a positive attitude, but to become an outstanding wheelchair athlete.

In 1976 Curt was invited to join the Utah wheelchair basketball team, the Rimriders, by fellow wheelchair athlete Mike Johnson. He has been involved with the Rimriders ever since. He has also become prominent as a track champion. In 1976, in regional competition with the national Wheelchair Athletic Association in San Jose, California, he became a double silver medalist in the mile and 100-yard dash, and a double bronze medalist in the mile relay and the javelin. In national competition the same year, he took sixth place in the 100-yard dash and seventh place in the mile. In the 1976 Para-Olympiad (Wheelchair Olympics) in Toronto, Canada, following Montreal's Summer Olympic Games, he captured the gold medal in the 100-meter dash and was a bronze medalist in lawn bowling and the discus. He also took fourth place in the shot put. Competing in Class V (the least handicapped), this formidable wheelchair athlete entered the National Wheelchair Games in 1977, where he was a bronze medalist in two events, the 100-yard dash and the mile. He took fifth place in the discus. Then, in the eighty-first running of the fabled Boston Marathon, he covered the twenty-six-mile, 385-yard distance in two hours, forty-three minutes, and twenty-three seconds to earn second place among the wheelchair participants. He was runner-up to Bob Hall, the predicted winner and holder of the world wheelchair record. He was only three minutes behind the world champion in that grueling race. That same year he was the Deseret News Wheelchair Marathon champion and was named one of the outstanding young men in America by the U.S. Jaycees. He was given Governor Scott M. Matheson's Golden Key Award on behalf of the handicapped. He then set out, with fellow wheelchair champion Mike Johnson, to encircle Utah Lake as a marathon for the purpose of publicizing a need for a transportation system for the handicapped in Utah County. They covered that 115-mile marathon in sixteen hours and forty-five minutes.

Although he has competed in multiple athletic events and proven himself one of the fine wheelchair athletes of the United States, extremely impressive is the world record he set in 1978 by wheeling a long-distance marathon of 275 miles from Cedar City to Salt Lake City. Although for the second year in a row he was second place in the Boston Marathon, perhaps nothing could compare to that five-day ordeal in which more than nine thousand dollars in pledges were raised through his efforts for the Utah Easter Seal Society. Besides developing the usual blisters and aches, he battled through rain, hail, and wind, and a battle of the mind to complete that extraordinary trek. He made the journey during National Handicapped Awareness Week to help focus attention on the abilities of handicapped persons, rather than their disabilities. The driving force behind such accomplishments is best summed up in his own words: "I just want to prove to others and to myself that there are things you can do in wheelchairs as a disabled person that perhaps others cannot do." "I hope that what I do brings an awareness to people of what can be done in a wheelchair. I can show those that are disabled, and those that are not, that I can do more than sit at home in front of the television. . . . I have accepted my handicap and I think I have a lot of things going for me." His philosophy of sports is interesting: "I'm always nervous before I compete, but afterward, when I've defeated someone or achieved a goal, I want to do it again and again. When I'm in a marathon, I enjoy it until I get near the end. Up until that point, it's almost leisurely as you make long, rhythmic strokes on the wheels.

But when you realize that you have to catch up with someone or prevent someone from passing you, it's a little frightening."

He has been active in the Church and earned his degree at Brigham Young University in 1978. He gives a great deal of credit to his wife for her support: "The best thing I've got with me is my wife. It's unbelievable the way she cheers me on when I'm in events—especially the slalom. She screams and hollers and tells me what to do. Then she runs up and hugs and kisses me. When I lose and I'm in a bad mood, she just hangs in there and encourages me." His dynamic personality was shown in the Boston Marathon when at one juncture— the infamous Heartbreak Hill—his chair came close to a standstill: "That's where psychology came into play," he said. "I said to myself, 'There are six miles left. Just do it. Get to the top and then it's mainly downhill after that.'" That attitude implies a lasting set of values for any of life's challenges.

Between 1977 and 1981 Curt was a four-time Deseret News Marathon champion. In 1980 he catapulted to fame by becoming the Boston Marathon champion with a time of one hour fifty-five minutes, breaking the previous wheelchair record by more than thirty minutes, and finishing seventeen minutes faster than Bill Rodgers, who ran the race on two legs. Utah Governor Scott Matheson proclaimed a Curt Brinkman Day. He was Deseret News Athlete of the Month for April 1980. He also garnered a gold medal as national wheelchair champion in the 1,500 meters in June 1980 and earned silver medals in the 400- and 1,600-meter relays.

Curt Brinkman, nationally prominent wheelchair athlete, world distance wheelchair record holder, is an inspiring example of fortitude and positive thinking in athletics and all phases of life for both the handicapped and nonhandicapped.

MERLIN OLSEN

All-American Football Player and Pro Superstar

Utah State University 1958-62:

All-Skyline Conference tackle 1960-61

Skyline Conference Lineman of the Year, 1961

Academic first team all-American, 1959-62

National Football Foundation and Hall of Fame scholar-athlete, 1961

Consensus all-American tackle, 1960-61

Outland Award as nation's best lineman of the year, 1961

Pro-Scouts all-American team, 1961

Helms College Football Hall of Fame, 1966

Professional football, Los Angeles Rams, 1962-77:

First-round draft choice, Los Angeles Rams, 1962

Defensive Rookie of the Year, 1962

Member of the Rams' "Fearsome Foursome"

All-NFL Team fourteen of fifteen
years

All-pro honors, 1965-69

Most Valuable Lineman, Pro Bowl,
1969

NEA All-Time All-America Team,
1969

All-Time Ram Team, 1970

Southern California Co-Athlete of the
Year, 1972

Maxwell Trophy as the outstanding
professional football player in the
United States, 1974

Vince Lombardi Dedication Trophy,
1976

Utah Sports Hall of Fame, 1979

College Football Hall of Fame, 1981

Pro-Football Hall of Fame, 1982

Of all the great Mormon athletes, and of all the athletes to
emerge from the state of Utah, Merlin Olsen has to rank as
one of the all-time greats. His success as a football player is
overwhelming.

Although Magnificent Merlin was active in four sports
(football, basketball, swimming, and track) at Logan High
School from 1955 to 1958, his gravitation toward his football
specialty and his accomplishments in that field were like an
irresistible force. One of his finest awards as a young man was
the Outstanding Junior Citizen of Logan Award in 1956,
between his sophomore and junior years of high school. He
was subsequently named an all-state football tackle two years
in a row, in 1956 and 1957. From 1958 through 1962, he
attended Utah State University, where he was a four-year

letterman in football. His collegiate football honors were unprecedented, but he also took time to participate in the junior all-Church program in 1959, at which time he was named to the all-Church basketball team. This rugged gridder, 6 feet 6 inches and 270 pounds, was all-Skyline Conference in 1960 and 1961, and was named Skyline Conference Lineman of the Year in 1961. He was a consensus all-American tackle two years in a row, in 1960 and 1961, his junior and senior years. He was given that honor on eight all-American selections as a junior and was selected on every all-American team during his senior year. To top off his collegiate football honors, he was named winner of the Outland Award, the highest football honor awarded any collegiate lineman. This award was given by cosponsors *Look* magazine and the United States Football Writers' Association. Each year, the Outland Award is given to the top interior lineman in collegiate football. Postseason honors were also bestowed upon Olsen as he was a participant in the Gotham Bowl Classic between Utah State and Baylor; the Hula Bowl in Honolulu, Hawaii; and the East-West, Coaches, and College All-Star Games. He was named Lineman of the Game at the Hula Bowl. He was named an all-American three years, the first Skyline player to make the team. He was named a Football Foundation and Hall of Fame scholar-athlete during the 1961-62 school year.

His college honors were not only athletic, but academic. His 3.69 GPA and busy involvement in school activities were outgrowths of his sterling character. He was junior-class president and a candidate for student-body president; winner of the Department of Army Superior Reserve Officer Training Corps Cadet Award; a member of Blue Key, Scabbard, and Blade; a member of the student senate and Sigma Chi social fraternity; and a member of Phi Beta Kappa, the national scholarship honor society. He graduated in finance and economics as an A student. As a consequence of his numerous collegiate accomplishments, he was named to the Pro-Scouts All-America Team; his jersey, number 72, was retired; he was the recipient of the Dale Rex Memorial Award as the Utahn who had contributed most to athletics during the preceding year; and in 1966 he was named to the Helms College Football Hall of Fame.

This great Aggie tackle was the first-round draft choice of the Los Angeles Rams in 1962 and spent the next fifteen years as one of the great stalwarts in professional football. In his first season, he was named Defensive Rookie of the Year. His talent, strength, enthusiasm, and endurance throughout his career were impressive. He consistently led his club in unassisted tackles. It is significant that despite his imposing size, he relied more on quickness than on strength to do his job. By 1966 the Rams developed one of the most impressive defensive lines, led by the front four, Olsen, Deacon Jones, Roosevelt Grier, and Lamar Lundy, known as the "Fearsome Foursome." Olsen's play was so spectacular that he was a chronic member of the all-NFL team and for fourteen of fifteen years a perpetual player in the Pro Bowl games. He was selected to the All-Pro Team many times and to the NEA All-Time All-America Team. He was named the Most Valuable Player of Ye Old Rams (the team's alumni group), recipient of the Vince Lombardi Dedication Trophy, the Bert Bell Trophy as the NFL's Most Valuable Player, and in 1970 to the All-Time Ram Team in conjunction with the Memorial Coliseum's golden anniversary in Los Angeles. In 1972 he was named the Southern California Co-Athlete of the Year by the United Savings Helms Hall Board. In 1974 he received the Maxwell Trophy as the outstanding professional football player in the United States. He retired from pro football in 1977. He started in 198 consecutive games and played a total of 208 regular season games—both Rams' records. He captained the Rams from 1972 to 1976.

Olsen graduated from Utah State with the highest scholastic average in the college of business and later earned his master's degree in economics. This ironman of the Rams' defense was once described by *Time* magazine as a "home-grown giant who boasts brains as well as brawn." That description never ceased to fit. In 1979 he was elected to the Utah Sports Hall of Fame and in 1981 to the College Football Hall of Fame. In 1982 he was given the great honor of membership in the Pro Football Hall of Fame.

With many interests and superior intellect, Merlin's non-athletic life has also been eventful. During the 1960s and 1970s he was a Hollywood movie and television actor. He worked with John Wayne in the movie *The Undefeated,* and with Dean Martin in *Something Big.* He has been a regular in the television series *Little House on the Prairie.* It has been said that he displays a natural flair for light comedy and that he possesses the intelligent and native intuition necessary for

success as an actor. He and fellow Rams quarterback, Roman Gabriel, cohosted a filmed television interview show, *Man-to-Man*, syndicated throughout the country. He was known for his "facile ability to discuss a widely diversified range of subjects beyond the realm of sports and an easy, affable manner which enhances the presentation."

Merlin Jay Olsen has eight brothers and sisters. His brothers Phil and Orrin have also made their marks in collegiate and professional football. Phil (6 feet 5 inches, 265 pounds), the smaller brother of Merlin (6 feet 6 inches, 270 pounds) and the bigger brother of Orrin (6 feet 2 inches, 240 pounds) contributed "heavily" to the 775 pounds of Utah beef. He was also a consensus all-American defensive end (1969) and a professional gridder (Rams, Denver Broncos, and Buffalo Bills). Orrin also achieved all-American honors and played professionally (Kansas City Chiefs, Baltimore Colts).

Father and Mother Olsen have to beam brightly as they recall the great accomplishments of their athletic sons. The three brothers have also been involved in the Olsen Brothers Sports Camp in Logan. Although Mother Olsen is extremely proud of her gridiron sons, she wanted one of them to be a dentist. When Phil came along, he let her down easy when he told her his hands were too big to get into a patient's mouth. It was a first-class argument! Then when Orrin came along, she tried to get him to be a dentist, but he had learned from Phil and told her his hands were about the same size.

After his retirement from professional football, Merlin signed a contract with the National Broadcasting Company as a color commentator. He covers football broadcasts, post-season bowls, and other sporting events. He is one of the finest commentators in the business. One sportswriter commented, "He is not particularly glib, and that is his strength. He is a refreshing breath of restraint and reason in a world filled with rhetoric. Most impressive is the first-hand knowledge of the sport and sense of history he brings to his observations. This...is a man who has done his homework well." Merlin, the Gentle Giant, currently stars in *Father Murphy*, a hit television series.

This phenomenal athlete has exemplified the teachings and standards of the Church both on and off the playing field. As a young boy he served in presidencies of his deacons and teachers quorums, and was athletic director in his ward YMMIA program. He participated in the softball and basketball programs of the Church and received five individual priesthood awards and his Duty to God Award. His father once said, "If anyone has lived the Word of Wisdom, it is Merlin." He gives credit for his speaking ability to the experience he received in the auxiliary organizations of the Church, where he has spoken in ward and stake conferences and before Aaronic Priesthood groups. The head coach of

Utah State University, John Ralston, once commented that Merlin is "a real fine leader, who is continually setting ideals and high standards for the entire ball club. He is a tireless worker who enjoys football to the utmost and is continually trying to improve himself. His high academic background gives him an opportunity to achieve the highest as regards to the mental aspects of the game....He is a tremendous inspiration and an excellent football player."

Merlin has been civic minded and involved in various community projects, such as Easter Seals and the March of Dimes. He and his wife, Susan, have been honorary chairmen in the Primary Children's Hospital fund drive for several years.

Merlin Jay Olsen is one of the greatest high school, college, and professional football players of all time.

JOHNNY MILLER

All-American and
Golf Superstar

National Junior Champion, 1964

Most Valuable Athlete of 1964
Award, Abraham Lincoln High
School (San Francisco)

Low Amateur U.S. Open, 1966

All-WAC first team, 1966-67

All-American first team, 1967

BYU's first all-American golfer

California Amateur Open champion,
1968

Pro Golfer 1968-79

Second place masters, 1971

U.S. Open champion, 1973

World Cup champion with Jack
Nicklaus, 1973

Hickock Professional Athlete of the
Year Award, 1973

Eight major pro titles, 1974

PGA Player of the Year, 1974

College Golf Hall of Fame, 1974

Gillette's Calvalcade of Champions
Outstanding Athlete of the Year,
1975

Sports Father of the Year, 1975

British Open Champion, 1976

Golf's youngest millionaire, 1976

BYU Hall of Fame, 1978

Twenty-one major tour victories,
PGA Tour, 1969-82

The dazzling story of Johnny Miller is awe-inspiring to any golfer, athlete, sports enthusiast, or follower of success stories. Sports headlines have proclaimed his name throughout the world. From the time he picked up a golf club, he was headed down the road of success.

When Johnny was five years old, his father started him golfing with a sawed-off golf club, driving balls into a canvas bag set up in the basement. At the age of seven, he started playing at the San Francisco Golf Club and had the opportunity of being tutored by the club's pro, John Geertsen, a friend of his father. Both his father and Geertson believed he had a great future in the golfing profession and encouraged him to that end. As he progressed, Geertsen helped him polish his game, often working with him in the evening from five o'clock until dark. Johnny credits his father with helping him develop a healthy attitude toward life in general and golf in particular. Teaching him the necessity of positive thinking, his father said, "You must never learn to think the negative. You can become a professional, but if you want to become a champion, you are going to have to do more."

He started his competitive golf career when he was ten, and as a junior golfer began accumulating some impressive titles. Lifting weights and squeezing a rubber ball to strengthen his thin wrists, he won the San Francisco City Golf Championship in 1963 and the same year won the Northern California Junior Golf Championship. In 1964, at the age of seventeen, he won the San Francisco City Prep Golf Championship and the Block Letter Award at the Abraham Lincoln High School. He also won his high school's Most Valuable Athlete of 1964 Award, the Northern California Amateur Medal Play Golf Championship, the California Junior Golf Championship, and topped these off by winning

the USGA National Junior title. The USGA *Golf Journal* proclaimed him "the best golfer and the best competitor of this year's junior crop." By winning the USGA Junior Championship at Eugene, Oregon, he was considered the top junior golfer in the nation. Besides maturing in the golf world, he was already beginning to develop his philosophy of life, particularly as a Mormon. At that time he was a priest and had already garnered four individual awards. He was his ward YMMIA sports director.

Considered the most sought-after junior golfer in the nation, Johnny decided to enroll at Brigham Young University. Having been a mid-year graduate of his high school, he started at BYU at the beginning of the second semester and was not a competitor as a freshman. At the 'Y' he achieved first team all-WAC honors in 1966-67, was honorable mention all-American in 1966, and was first team all-American in 1967, the first golf all-American from Brigham Young University. He also won the Dale Rex Memorial Award (sharing this honor with Phil Odle) during his junior year and was ranked the greatest golfer to come out of the collegiate ranks in Utah. While at BYU he qualified for the U.S. Open in 1966 and was honored as the low amateur in that tournament, achieving an overall position of eighth.

Missionary-minded, Johnny met his wife, Linda, in college and baptized her, later marrying her in the temple. Always active in the Church, he had considered going on a mission. Even though his mother always wanted him to fulfill a mission, they both decided that if he could be a good golfer, he could do tremendous missionary work for the Church. He knew this was especially true if he could live the kind of life he should and express the things he knew to be true. Johnny feels that if he had not gone to BYU, he wouldn't be where he is today. He credits his golf coach, Karl Tucker, with helping him to mature both in the Church and in golf and feels that BYU was a step up the ladder that he needed. Because of his positive experience at BYU, he plans on sending his children there.

Miller was not able to compete during his senior year at BYU because of an NCAA ruling declaring him ineligible to compete on the collegiate level, so he set his sights on the professional tour. In 1968 he won the California Amateur Open and was declared the Northern California Golfer of the Year. He entered the PGA tour in 1969 and gradually became one of the leading golfers on the tour. His earnings increased yearly, his image as an all-American boy skyrocketed, and his ability as a golf ace became more recognized by the leading golfers. In 1972 he was touted by *Golf* magazine as "The charismatic new bright light of golf."

In 1973 he won the U.S. Open, setting a course and Open record of 63 for one round, and setting a course and Open record of 279 for the tournament. In spite of this tremendous victory, he still recognized that the eternal things were the most important. He said, "Golf is very important to me, but the family and Church come first." He also continued to be missionary-minded by recognizing an important fact: "When people find out you're a Mormon, they expect you to know a lot about the Church. Players on the tour especially ask a lot of questions."

Johnny said this soon after winning the world's number-one golf honor at the U.S. Open at Oakmont. There was perhaps no greater finish in the history of golf. In that seventy-third U.S. Open, Johnny was in a three-way tie for third place with Jack Nicklaus and Bob Charles at 140. Gary Player held the thirty-six hole lead with 137, and Jim Colbert was in second place with 138. On the third day John Schlee with a 67 and Arnold Palmer with a 68 moved into a tie for the lead with 210 scores after fifty-four holes. Miller shot a 76 for a 216 total after his third round. All the leaders of the second day had dropped back. In the final round Johnny birdied the first four holes, parred the next three holes, and had a bogey the eighth hole, and birdied the ninth. After nine holes he had a score of 32, four stokes under par. He parred five and birdied four of the last nine holes for a 31 on the final nine, giving him an eight under par 63. This was the lowest round ever played in any round of the U.S. Open. He surpassed Arnold Palmer, Jack Nicklaus, Gary Player, Julius Boros, and many others. Billy Casper said it was one of the greatest eighteen holes of golf ever played: "It was a 63 that could have been a 59 with a couple of breaks. To shoot like that in the final round of the U.S. Open, well, that was doggone near superhuman." He overcame a six-stroke deficit to win that astonishing tournament. In 1973 he was also chosen a member of the eight-man *Golf* magazine All-American Golf Team. The same year he teamed with Jack Nicklaus to win the World Cup for the United States in Marbella, Spain, and was given the Hickock Professional Athlete of the Year Award.

The pro-golf tour was dominated by Johnny Miller in 1974. He won eight tournaments and a staggering $353,021, setting a new one-year record earnings. He became the first golfer to win eight matches in a single season since Arnold Palmer in 1960. His golf success also earned him many personal appearances, exhibition fees, and media endorsements of MacGregor sporting goods, Sears clothes, and other products. He was named the PGA Player of the Year and to the College Golf Hall of Fame in 1974. In 1975 he was named the Outstanding Athlete of the Year in Gillette's Third Annual Cavalcade of Champions. He received a total of $15,000 for that honor, which he donated to BYU ($12,500) and to the

Johnny Miller Camp in Scotland ($2,500). He was a member of the Ryder Cup Team, also.

In 1975 Miller was voted Sports Father of the Year by the National Father's Day Committee, which noted that he was not only an outstanding athlete, but a "devoted husband and father, symbolizing the virtues of American family-ness." That recognition showed his emphasis on family life. Miller has often said, "In my life, there are three things. First my family. Then my Church. And finally, there is golf. If I ever have to give up one of them, it'll be golf." He has also said, "I try to enjoy the game, but I don't live and die with it. At home I never play golf."

In 1976 Johnny's victory in the Bob Hope Desert Classic made him the youngest golfer ever to win one million dollars in a career on the golf tour. He also won the British Open.

In 1976 Johnny experienced a deep slump in his golf career. His tournament victories ceased and his earnings plummeted, perhaps due to an increase in weight and strength, a different swing, competing business interests, his growing family, and conflicting priorities. Whatever the reason, it was a dry season for Miller. The champ stuck with it, however, until mid-1980 and declared, "Maybe everybody needs a slump to go through, not necessarily in golf, but in some aspect of life." In 1978, during the slump, he was elected to the BYU Hall of Fame. Then in 1980 he won the Inverrary Golf Classic and in 1981 climbed out of his four-year golf bunker to be the twelfth-place money-winner on the tour as he won the Tucson and Los Angeles Open and let Tom Watson know he was around by runner-up recognition in the Masters Golf Tournament.

He started 1982 by winning golf's richest-ever prize of a half-million dollars in Sun City, Bophuthatswana (South Africa), in a sudden-death playoff against Steve Ballisteros, as Nicklaus, Player, and Trevino in the elite five-man field were out of the title chase. Subsequently he captured the San Diego Open and then lost in a sudden-death playoff against Watson at the Los Angeles Open.

Since his entry into the PGA Tour in 1969, golf has been good to him. He has won honors, earned money, gained world-wide recognition, and been highly esteemed by sports-writers and fans, as well as his own golf gallery. In spite of this recognition, he has remained humble in declaring the source of his success. He has given credit to his mother and father;

his golf mentor, John Geertsen; his golf coach, Karl Tucker; to BYU; the Church; and to his Heavenly Father. He acknowledges great examples in the golfing world, such as Billy Casper, Arnold Palmer, Jack Nicklaus, and others. He also realizes, however, that he put a lot of hard work into his golf game: "I feel like success is a by-product of the foundation I laid before." In spite of outstanding records achieved on the pro tours and in the amateur golf world, he has had a down-to-earth set of priorities which has enabled him to view golf's setbacks as relatively minor things in his life. He generally keeps his mind uncluttered with worldly pursuits. He has built his life around his family and Church and enjoys simple pleasures such as fishing and hunting. He says, "Spending time with the family is really my favorite activity. In the end, how good a parent you are has got to be more important than whether you shoot 68 or 71.... Golf isn't my whole life, and I'm not going to die if I miss a short putt. If I ever reach that stage—or get bored with it all—I'll quit."

In his busy life, he has always felt that it is important to make everyone around him feel important. With the ups and downs of a golf career, he has tried to mask his emotions and treat his fans to autographs and smiles. Perhaps the great golfing pro, Billy Casper, who has had an influence on Miller's life both professionally and personally, helped him with this philosophy: "Billy told me to wait it out: that there would be good days and bad ones, but never look back on the bad ones. He could see I was a little on the frustrated side when I had a bad round. He leveled me off and was a steadying factor in my first golf play. I learned from Bill that when you have that bad day, which I have had many times, the next one might be brighter—and bright enough to win."

A profound tribute was paid to Johnny at his election into the Cougar Hall of Fame: "Johnny Miller...has always represented his church, his sport, and his school at the highest level. He is a dedicated family man. He has never compromised his principles to win money or tournaments. He has contributed time, money, and effort to golfing programs here and in other areas to help young golfers. He has helped to make the BYU golfing program synonymous with excellence. And he has demonstrated that success can be coupled with integrity."

JEFF JUDKINS

Pro Basketball Player

All-around athlete at Highland High
School (Salt Lake City):

All-region football, baseball, 1973-74

All-region, all-state, all-American
basketball, 1973-74

Basketball star, University of Utah:

All-WAC first team, 1976-78

WAC scoring leader, 1976-77

All-NCAA district seven first team,
1976-78

Academic all-American, 1977

Fourth leading scorer (career),
University of Utah

Member U.S. World University
Games Team (gold medal winners,
Bulgaria)

Deseret News Athlete of the Month,
October 1978

Pro basketball, 1978-82

First native of Salt Lake City to play
in the NBA

Jeff Judkins is one of the most brilliant basketball players
to come out of Utah. Even at eight years of age he set a goal
to make the pro ranks for an NBA club. He became the first
Salt Lake City native and the first Utahn in thirty years to play

in the NBA. (Before Jeff, University of Utah athletic director Arnie Ferrin made it to the NBA with the Minneapolis Lakers in 1948.) After brilliant high school and college basketball careers, Jeff was drafted by the Boston Celtics in 1978 as a second-round draft choice in the June NBA draft.

At Highland High School in Salt Lake City, he lettered in three sports. He earned three letters in basketball and baseball and two in football. In basketball he was a prep all-American, all-state, and all-region. In football and baseball he was all-region. He was also his senior-class vice-president.

In college he became one of the premier forwards in the nation. He finished an amazing four-year college career at the University of Utah by starting in eighty-two games during his sophomore, junior, and senior years. He led the Western Athletic Conference in scoring during his sophomore and junior years and was fourth in scoring during his senior year, shooting 55 percent from the field, 81 percent from the foul line, and finishing as the fourth-highest scorer in the school's history (1,740 points). He scored in the double figures in his last fifty-six straight games. He averaged thirty-eight minutes of playing time per game and was truly one of the real ironmen in the collegiate basketball ranks. Not only was he the leading scorer during his final three years at the University of Utah, but he led the team in steals and was third in rebounding. He was the first-team WAC selection in 1976, 1977, and 1978. He was first team NCAA district seven during the same three years, and was the all-district seven Most Valuable Player during 1978. In 1976 he made the Utah Classic All-Tournament Team and in 1977 was a member of the All-Tournament Wolf Pack Classic. He was the Most Valuable Player of the Kentucky Invitational and the Most Valuable Player of the Volunteer Classic. He was a member of the U.S. World University Games Team in 1977 (gold medal winners). He also led his team for two straight seasons into the NCAA championships. He was academic all-American during his junior year. Jeff was also named Deseret News Athlete of the Month for October 1978.

As a rookie in the Boston camp, Judkins had a make-good contract. Although he was nervous, the coaches kept a close eye on him, noting his ability as a polished shooter and his excellent hands and anticipation. Because of his excellence as a ball player, Judkins made the Boston Celtics team. The coach at the time, Tom Sanders, remarked, "Judkins has

an instinct for the ball and he's a fundamentally sound basketball player. He has a tremendous amount of poise for a rookie. He has handled the transition from forward to guard with ease." Jeff earned his spot in the pros as well as the respect and confidence of Boston players, fans, coaches, and the news media. He was called by many Baby Hondo, a genuine compliment comparing him to the all-time Celtic great, John Havlicek. He has been seen to be the perfect swingman of the future, alternating between forward and guard. What a thrill it has been for Jeff Judkins to see his boyhood dream of playing with an NBA ball club come true. After starting his pro career with the Celtics, Judkins spent time with the Utah Jazz and is presently with the Detroit Pistons.

While playing for the Utah Redskins, Judkins was one of only a few Mormons on his team. He said of this experience, "In my four years here, I've grown closer to the Church. Being in the minority made me want to do my best and be at my best. The guys on the team never teased me or bothered me about being a Mormon and it's been a great experience associating with them. I know that my testimony has grown."

Although this great basketball star has known the thrills of athletic competition and the acclaim of the world, he has also enjoyed the thrill of being married in the temple and helping young people strengthen their testimonies. Not neglecting his spiritual health in his rigorous training and playing schedule, Jeff has spent many hours talking to youth groups and firesides, and teaching and coaching young members of the Church. He says, "Kids watch me pretty close to see if I'm living Church standards." He has recognized his responsibility to set a good example. He wants the young people to know, "You can be a good athlete and still honor the priesthood." His advice to young people is to keep their goals high, to set goals that will take hard work to achieve. He says, "When you try to do something, do your best and be satisfied with yourself. If you can't love yourself, you can't love anybody else."

Jeff has worked hard during his years as an athlete, kept the Word of Wisdom, and enjoyed confidence in himself and his teammates. He deeply appreciates the support of his wife, his parents, and his Heavenly Father.

He has recognized the power of the priesthood in his life and looks back with humility on spiritual experiences with the priesthood. In high school, just two days before a big game for the regional championships, he had a tubing injury requiring forty-five sutures in his leg. Even though the doctor initially told him there was no way he could play in the game, Jeff called upon his coach for a priesthood blessing. When he returned to his doctor for a checkup, the leg was so much better that he was allowed to play. During college he had a knee injury that kept him out of a game the following week. Two of his brothers-in-law gave him a blessing. Because of the remarkable improvement, again the doctor allowed him to play. Jeff felt the Lord was watching over him and gives credit where credit is due.

His reputation as a team player and hard worker on the playing floor has provided much inspiration to young people. He once received a letter from a high school boy who didn't feel he could accomplish anything. This boy said he had struggled with inactivity in the Church and went to his priesthood advisor for help. His priesthood advisor wisely used Jeff as an example. He told the young boy to watch the basketball star, Jeff Judkins, because of his hard work as a player. He said that Jeff didn't always make points, but that he was always out there working. When Jeff received this letter he was pleased that someone would use him as an example to help this young man.

Jeff Judkins, Baby Hondo, has achieved his goal to play in the NBA, but he is achieving a more mature goal to help others in the Church by setting a good example.

JEAN SAUBERT

National Ski Champion and Olympic Silver Medalist

Two-time national junior champion, slalom and combined events, 1957, 1959

Champion, Senior National Giant Slalom, 1963-64

Champion, Senior National Slalom, 1964

Champion, Senior National Downhill, 1963-64

Olympic Ski Team, 1964

Champion, Swiss International Women's Giant Slalom, 1964

1964 Olympics at Innsbruck, Austria:

Second grand slalom, silver medalist

Third slalom, bronze medalist

Declared second-best woman skier in the world by International Ski Federation, 1964

Ski Hall of Fame, 1976

During active skiing competition, Jean Saubert was the best American woman skier and one of the best skiers in the world. She was said to be "intense, serious, hardworking, dedicated and quick to smile." This famous athlete, a powerful and compact skier of superlative style, was not only a champion on the American slopes, but a consistent winner against Europe's best women skiers. Bob Beattie, in *Sports Illustrated*, commented, "The tougher the race, the tougher she'll get." A teammate, Starr Walton, said, "She's so good-natured and even-tempered all the time. And when she's on her skis, nobody in the whole world can beat her in any event."

Jean grew up in the small town of Cascade, Oregon, and since there weren't many things to do, she worked hard to reach the top of the skiing world. She says, "I skied because I loved to ski. I loved to practice, and I got a great deal out of it." She loved to travel and made many wonderful friends. She was a "'little girl' who was the big girl of American women's skiing."

Raised at a ranger station near a ski resort, Jean began skiing at the age of six. With parents who helped her along, faith in God, and a desire to win, Jean fought the battle of champions. In 1957 and 1959 she was the national junior champion in the slalom and combined events. She was a member of the 1962 USA FIS (Federation of International Skiing) team that competed in the World Skiing Championship in France. She placed sixth in the giant slalom. In 1963 she won the slalom and giant slalom and combined titles in the prestigious Roch Cup at Aspen, Colorado, and the slalom, downhill, and combined at the Sun Valley Harriman Races. She was the senior national giant slalom champion and downhill champion in 1963 and 1964, and the national slalom champion in 1964. She also won the Vail Cup, the Broadmore Slalom Derby, and many other skiing awards.

In 1964 Jean became the United States' hope for the Olympics in Innsbruck, Austria. Before the Olympics, as one of the fourteen members of the U.S. Olympic Ski Team, she spent the summer and fall in exhaustive activity by tumbling into sawdust pits, skipping rope, racing up steep hills, and generally giving her all in preparation. In competitive preparation she won the Swiss International Women's Giant Slalom Championship, her third victory during the U.S. team's European tour. Then at Innsbruck she became a two-medal winner, capturing a silver medal in the giant slalom and a bronze medal in the slalom. In the women's slalom Jean placed third behind the two Goitschel sisters, Christine

and Marielle. In the giant slalom races the Goitschel sisters again captured medals. Marielle took the gold medal, and Christine shared the silver medal with Jean.

Jean felt bad about losing the gold medal in the Olympics, but admitted that she defeated herself by entering the race with a negative feeling, one of the few times in her life that this had happened. She says, "I wouldn't change the past. True, I didn't get the gold medal, but the experience of the discipline, of being able to have that kind of control over yourself, is worth it. The added honors are nice, but learning self-control is so much more important."

Jean has had a wonderful philosophy about competition: "I have always believed it was me against the course, not against the other skiers. That is one of the reasons I love skiing, and that's the way it ought to be."

In 1964 Jean was rated the second-best woman skier in the world by the International Ski Federation in the three events—slalom, giant slalom, and downhill races.

After the Olympics she continued in competitive skiing for a short time. She won the near-mile-long giant slalom course in the Twenty-fifth Annual Snow Cup Classic and the combined slalom and giant slalom in the Lowell Thomas Ski Classic. Jean ended her racing career with a fourth place in the slalom and tenth in the downhill races of the World Championships at Porterville, Chile, in 1966. She was a commentator for ABC television in the Winter Olympics in 1968. Jean Saubert was inducted into the Skiing Hall of Fame in 1976.

She received her bachelor's degree in elementary education from the University of Utah after having previously completed most of her undergraduate studies at Oregon State. She also completed some graduate school study at the University of Utah with enough hours for a master's degree.

This former Olympian, who is now an elementary school teacher, has also been a ski instructor at the Sundance ski resort and at Brigham Young University.

She has been active in the Church as a genealogy instructor, an activity counselor in the YWMIA program (both on a ward and stake level), and a member of the General Athletic Committee of the Church.

Jean continues to ski for fun and has a daily regimen of running, rope-jumping, bike-riding, tennis, and racquetball, as well as calisthenics.

Her own great success in skiing she attributes to "faith in God. Knowledge that whatever happens, God still loves me; my grandmother's advice, 'God helps those who help themselves'; 'The faith of a mustard seed can move mountains'; God will not test beyond a person's ability to handle the problem at hand." To be successful as an athlete, she recommends the following: "(1) Set goals within reach and don't reach too far too soon. (2) Compete against yourself and not others. (3) Know what price success takes and be willing to pay for it. (4) Read *The Heart of a Champion* by Bob Richards." She also believes that "one who can't keep the physical in control doesn't have 100 percent of the spirit under control."

Jean has been particularly impressed by *Thoughts on Skiing* by Alton C. Melville, father of Utah Olympian Marv

Melville. (Alton served as both vice-president and president of the U.S. Ski Association.) She quotes from his philosophy: "Ask not for smaller mountains. We make the mountains seem smaller by our increased proficiency. Do not expect all falls to be eliminated. We only hope to control mishaps, then go again."

Jean also believes Vince Lombardi's philosophy. She says, "Winning is not everything, but wanting to is. I will demand a commitment to excellence and to victory, and that is what life is all about. I think that a boy with talent has a moral obligation to fulfill it, and I will not relent on my own responsibility. Fatigue makes cowards of us all. The harder you work, the harder it is to surrender. The will to excel and the will to win, they endure. They are more important than any events that occasion them."

With such philosophy incorporated into the life of this great skiing champion, it is understandable how Jean Saubert became one of the world's greatest skiers, and how she is competing for righteousness in her personal life.

KEN SHELLEY

Outstanding Sportsman
in the Winter Olympics
1972

Pacific Coast figure-skating pairs
champion (with partner Jo Jo
Starbuck) four times

U.S. National junior pairs champion,
1967

United States Olympian, 1968, 1972

United States national pairs
champion, 1970-72

United States national men's
champion, 1972

Outstanding Sportsman in the
Winter Olympics Award, 1972

First American in three decades to
be a national figure skating
champion in two skating events

First American to qualify for a U.S.
Olympic Team in two figure-skating
events

Professional ice skater with
Ice Capades

Kenneth Shelley, former United States national men's
figure-skating champion and star of Ice Capades, has
contributed substantially to sports as a Mormon skater. While

establishing his remarkable records, he was not only a splendid performer, but a missionary.

Ken started skating when he was six years old, and for the following seventeen years had one of the most rigorous and intense schedules that any athlete might imagine. His coach, John Nicks, a world pairs champion from Great Britain, was a great example of concentration and discipline, which helped Ken not only in skating but in other areas of his life. His family has also been extremely interested and helpful in his career, watching and following his performances and encouraging him in his skating talents. His sister, Pat, was also a fine skater.

He and his partner, Alicia (Jo Jo) Starbuck, both hail from Downey, California. In competition they trained about six hours a day, six days a week, and competitions were quite frequent. If dedication is a prerequisite to athletic success, Ken exhibited that trait in abundance. During training he arose at 5 A.M. each day and was on the ice by 6 A.M., skating until 8:30 A.M. He then attended school, returned to the rink for a few hours, went back to class, and then came to the rink after school to finish up a total of six hours of training. He said this schedule was not only monotonous, but tiring. He did manage to relax on Sundays, the one day in his life that was relatively normal. Even though he was on the road much of the time, he attended Church whenever possible, in Japan, Germany, England, all over the United States and Canada, and elsewhere. In spite of his grueling nation-hopping and full schedule, he has been active in Church activities, recognizing his responsibilities as a Mormon competitor and acknowledging his dependence on the Lord. An article by Rodger Dean Duncan in the *New Era* in 1973 described how Ken coped with touring: "The tour is a lonely way of life. You go from city to city, from hotel room to hotel room. I take a record player and records with me, photographs of my family and friends, and a few posters to liven up the hotel room. And I have several Church books. When I'm down in spirit, I read and it gives me a lift. I'm also taking a correspondence course in the Book of Mormon. Of course, another lift is when I attend Church on Sunday mornings." Commenting on his role as a Mormon among competitors, Ken says, "They've [fellow athletes] been great, and I've had no problems with anyone on the tour. I discovered early in the show that there are many people with different kinds of moral standards and

ideas about life. But I found that the only way they'll respect me is if I respect them. You can't be an effective missionary by condemning the other fellow. Even though I may think their standards are unusual, they probably think the same of mine. But the mutual respect is still there. I've never been much of a talker, and I'm not a salesman. But I know I'm being watched, and I try to let my conduct speak for what Mormonism represents."

In 1972 Ken won two United States senior figure skating titles, an accomplishment that hadn't been done in thirty-one

71

years. He said about his success, "I really believe it was due to my observing the Word of Wisdom. In doing two events you must be in particularly good condition. My body was always clean; I worked hard, rested well, and stayed in shape. The first things that go bad on a competing skater are his legs and his wind capacity. Some skaters, particularly professionals, deliberately start smoking to keep from gaining weight. But, of course, they're running the risk of doing serious damage to their bodies."

A former bishop described Ken in these words: "Ken is a very intelligent, modest, humble young man who hesitates ever to talk about himself. But he virtually shines as he skates onto the ice and performs there."

This modest champion pays much tribute to his parents: "There's a lot of time involved.... You must have plenty of self-discipline. I was fortunate. My parents always encouraged me but never pushed. They were rarely at the skating rink during practice. Also, they didn't display my trophies and medals all over the living room. I'm grateful that they treated me just like their other children. They've never treated me like 'our son, the skating star.' At home I was just Kenny. No pressure. No pushing. Just encouragement. And that helped emphasize the need to discipline myself."

Ken's athletic feats are inspiring. He and his partner, Jo Jo, were Pacific Coast pairs champions on four occasions. They entered their first national contest in 1966 and earned a medal in every national competition until they retired from amateur skating in 1972. They were standouts in six national championships and competed internationally four years. In 1967 they were named the U.S. national junior pairs champions and in 1968 won a place on the U.S. Olympic team, finishing thirteenth in competition. Also in 1968 they were third in the U.S. National Pairs Competition, but placed first in National Pairs Competition three years in a row from 1970 through 1972.

In 1972 Ken established some remarkable records. Besides winning the National Pairs Championship with Jo Jo for their third consecutive year, he became the U.S. national men's champion. He became the first American in more than three decades to be a national figure-skating champion in two events, and because of his expertise as both a single and pairs skater, he was the first ever to qualify for a U.S. Olympic team in two ice-skating events. While competing in both major divisions in the Olympics (pairs figure skating and men's figure skating), America came in fourth, behind the Russians and East Germany. The U.S. Olympic Committee later presented Ken with an award as the "Outstanding Sportsman in the 1972 Winter Olympics." In the summer of 1973, after an exhibition tour of the United States and Canada, Ken retired from amateur competitive skating and joined the Ice Capades, the professional ice-skating show that tours major cities in North America. He had starring roles as both a solo performer and in pairs skating with Jo Jo.

On tour several years, Ken has been a great influence for good among Mormons and non-Mormons alike. He has taught the gospel through personal example. He has found it easy to be at home among Mormons anywhere in the world.

Ken Shelley, champion Mormon ice skater, national pairs and national men's figure-skating champion, the "Outstanding Sportsman in the 1972 Winter Olympics," star of Ice Capades, has mastered not only the great maneuvers in the ice rink leading to national and international fame, but has mastered many principles of true living as a good example to others.

HARMON KILLEBREW

Baseball Superstar

American League baseball superstar
for twenty-two years, 1954-75:
Washington Senators, Minnesota
Twins, Kansas City Royals

Mid-Season All-Star Team eleven
times

American League home-run
champion six times, 1959, 1962,
1963, 1964, 1967, 1969

Leading batter, World Series (tie),
1965

Individual leader in the American
League in runs batted in,
1962, 1969, 1971

Three consecutive home runs in a
game, September 21, 1963

The only baseball player selected for
the All-Star Team at three different
positions—third base, first base,
outfield

American League's Player of the
Year 1969-70

Baseball Writers Association of
America's Most Valuable Player,
1969

Second baseball player in history to hit more than forty home runs for a total of eight seasons (Babe Ruth was the only other such hitter)

David O. McKay Award for Athletic Excellence, 1970

BYU Exemplary Manhood Award, 1970

Eleven grand-slam home runs

Fifth all-time career home runs (573)

Second lifetime career for home runs per times at bat (14.22) (Second only to Babe Ruth [11.76])

Member of the elite 500 Club

Harmon Clayton Killebrew is one of the all-time super-stars of baseball. Even as a farm boy from Payette, Idaho, he was a dedicated athlete. He attached an oatmeal box above a door and pitched a tennis ball into it for hours. He also battled imaginary curve balls by swinging at lilac bushes and anything else that helped him adjust his swing to various levels.

At Payette High School he earned twelve letters, starring in football, basketball, and baseball. He was not only an all-star basketball player, but achieved honors as an all-American quarterback in 1953. His four-year batting average was .500. His jersey was retired.

After high school he played semi-pro Idaho-Oregon Border League baseball, where he batted an amazing .847. Idaho senator Herman Welker convinced the Washington Senators' owner, Clark Griffith, to look at this young Idaho baseball player. Griffith sent out scout Ossie Bluege, who described Harmon as a right-handed Mickey Mantle. He was so impressed that he signed him for $30,000 before his eighteenth birthday. As a bonus baby signing directly with the major-league Washington Senators in 1954, Killebrew found that he was not ready for such rugged competition. After his first two years with the Senators, he was sent to the South Atlantic (Sally) League, where he had a chance to play regularly. He spent two and a half seasons in the minors and then returned to Washington as an accomplished slugger. In 1959, his first year back in the majors, he tied for the most home runs in the league with 42 and had 105 runs batted in (RBIs). From that time on until 1974, there were only four seasons that the "Killer" did not bat more than twenty-five home runs.

During the next decade he was one of the finest baseball superstars of all time. In his twenty-two years of professional baseball, from 1954 through 1975, he played in 2,435 games and was at bat 8,147 times with 2,086 hits. He was the home-run leader six different seasons—1959, 1962, 1963, 1964, 1967, and 1969. He was the fifth all-time leading home-run artist, behind only Hank Aaron, Babe Ruth, Willie Mays, and Frank Robinson. He superseded such notables as Mickey Mantle, Jimmy Foxx, Ted Williams, Ernie Banks, Eddie Matthews, and Mel Ott. All of these players were members of the elite 500 Club, the only men during the entire history of baseball who have hit a total of 500 or more home runs in major-league games. As one of these select home-run leaders, Killebrew was second only to Babe Ruth in home runs per at-bat. He hit a home run in each 14.22 times at bat, while Babe Ruth hit a home run each 11.76 times at bat. He was one of a select few who hit ten or more grand-slam home runs during his career. He was also one of a select number who hit three consecutive home runs in a game (September 21, 1963). His lifetime batting average was .258.

Per 162 game season schedule, he was one of the ten top batters in the RBIs category. He was individual leader in the American League for RBIs in 1962, 1969, and 1971. He tied for the American League's leading batter in a World Series in 1965.

Killebrew was very versatile and was willing to play wherever he was positioned. He played 969 games as a first baseman (his most talented position), 792 games as a third baseman, 470 games in the outfield, and 11 games as a second baseman. He was the only baseball player in the professional ranks to be selected to the All-Star Team at three

different positions—third base, first base, and outfield. He
was a member of eleven American League all-star squads.

In 1966 this famous slugger was baptized into the
Mormon Church. During ensuing years he commented, "The
Church has really been a blessing to me and my family. I'm so
thankful for my membership. We've really been blessed by

having the Priesthood in our home. One of the great things about the Gospel is that it has given me the feeling that baseball is not the most important thing in life." He is highly appreciative of his testimony of the gospel being strengthened all the time. He further said, "Most everybody knows now that I am a Mormon and they respect me for it. The Church has helped me in so many ways in my baseball career."

During the All-Star Game in Houston in 1968, Killebrew stretched at first base, rupturing his left medial hamstring muscle. The team physician thought it might be the end of his career. Killebrew never gave up at home and worked hard to recondition the injured leg. He made a major comeback. In 1969 he played in all 162 games, something no other Twin did, and helped power his team to the West Division Championship. He had forty-nine home runs and 140 RBIs, both of which were major-league highs. He even stole eight bases and had a batting average of .276—sixty-six points higher than the previous year. His forty-nine runs tied his career high, and his 140 RBIs broke the club record. He had twenty game-winning hits during the season, and of his 153 hits, 57 could be counted as key ones. Reggie Jackson said, "If Harmon Killebrew isn't this league's number one player, I've never seen one. He's one of the greatest of all time." His astonishing accomplishments that year garnered him the American League's Most Valuable Player Award from the Baseball Writers Association of America. He was also named Sporting News Player of the Year in 1969. A quiet man, he let his baseball bat do his talking that year and during his career.

In 1970 he was again voted the American League's Player of the Year, and in 1971 he became the Twins' first $100,000 player. Interestingly enough, the Minnesota Twins President, Calvin Griffith, said that he always expected Harmon to be the first $100,000 player. This he did not resent, as he stated, "He is the most unselfish star player I ever have known." Further praising him he has said, "He's the most appreciative player I've ever met. I've never seen him refuse to sign an autograph and he never complains." Commenting on his modesty, this team owner who knew him for so many years said, "The best thing going for Harmon Killebrew is his level head. His early publicity would have gone to a lot of kids' heads. I talked about it when he was 21 and he told me, 'Mr. Griffith, you'll never have to worry; I'll never change.'" Harmon never did change. He probably received more mail than any other of the Twins players and tried to answer it all. He was also one of the most sought-after players by kids hunting for autographs. His manager, Bill Rigney, who won two championships with him in a five-year period said, "Every manager ought to have one Killebrew to manage before he dies."

This famous Mormon athlete received the David O. McKay Award for Athletic Excellence in 1970. It was an outstanding award in memory of President David O. McKay's love of and interest in sports. The same year he received the Brigham Young University Associated Men Students' Annual Exemplary Manhood Award. This award is given each year to a man who has achieved success through his own courage and application, and whose life is considered a pattern for men of BYU to emulate. In accepting that award, Killebrew said, "Baseball has taught me a lot about life. I have felt the need to find a better purpose in life. This can be found in the Gospel of Jesus Christ. I believe in God; it gives me a wonderful dimension in my life." Having had his baseball career threatened twice by injury, he said, "Obstacles in life must be surmounted by a loftiness of spirit. Magnanimity is a quality taught by Jesus Christ."

This Idaho strong-man will long be remembered in pro baseball. The powerful swivel of his hips, the uncoiling of his muscular wrists, and the slugger's reaction to the solid crack of a bat will long live in the memory of the Minnesota Twins fans.

A dedicated family man, Harmon has worked diligently with his wife, Elaine, to do things as a family. They have observed family home evening and taught their children that they are a special part of the family. During all his active years as a busy, traveling athlete, Harmon was active in the Church and taught the elders quorum in his ward. He has served as president of the Salt Lake City firm, Killebrew, Inc. The company manufactures athletic training devices, including a power-stride batting trainer, hopefully to train future Harmon Killebrews. Following in his father's footsteps, a son, Cam Killebrew, was a recent all-American baseball player. He was drafted by the Texas Rangers.

Harmon "Killer" Killebrew, Idaho strong man, Paul Bunyan of baseball, had his jersey retired by the Minnesota Twins as one of the all-time great superstars in the world of baseball. He is also an all-time great Mormon.

AB JENKINS

Champion
Racer—Superman of
Speed and Endurance

Utah's First Citizen Award 1935

Champion of Champions in the 100
Mile Club, 1940

President of the American Racing
Society

Driver of the Mormon Meteor—
License Plate "Utah - 10,000"

Utah Sports Hall of Fame 1970

David Abbott Jenkins, the "uncrowned king of Utah's Bonneville Salt Flats" and internationally eminent speed and endurance racer, a champion of clean and simple living, was one of racing's top professionals. Nephi L. Morris wrote in the *Improvement Era*, "This lone Mormon boy has established more world records than any other man in the history of sport. While many champions are selling their endorsements to cigarette and liquor interests, David Abbott Jenkins gives credit to clean habits and simple living for the endurance that has brought him nearly a thousand records."

At age seventy-three during an endurance run, Ab and his son Marvin broke all existing American unlimited and Class C stock-car records up to twenty-four hours. *Time* magazine (July 1956) noted that Ab held more auto distance speed records than any other man living. He counted as his most important award a presentation made in 1940, naming him the Champion of Champions in the 100 Mile Club, comprised of men who have driven more than one hundred miles per hour in competition.

Many authorities believe that Ab was the most skilled race driver that ever lived. He has also been called the safest driver in the world. At the time of his death this patriarch of the Salt Flats held hundreds of world speed and endurance marks. One writer noted, "During his long career he has broken more than 10,000 racing records." He also made the Bonneville Salt Flats the nation's most famous racing ground.

Ab Jenkins was born in 1883 in Spanish Fork, Utah, and later moved to Salt Lake City. He found pleasure in competitive athletics, and those who knew him say he was never beaten in a foot race. Even as a boy he matched his speed and endurance against other youngsters in the neighborhood by running against them as they relayed each other around a city block (he was a one-man relay team). He also raced around the old Salt Palace Saucer Track on a bicycle. He built his own sleds and sped down the dangerous hills at breakneck speed.

Ab excelled in field events and tests of strength as well as racing. He was never defeated in weightlifting competition, and he matched his strength with that of some of the country's professional strong men. After his father died, when he was fourteen years old, he assumed the place of the provider for his family, as far as his years and abilities would permit. Later he entered motorcycle speed events. His only real injury occurred in a motorcycle accident between Salt Lake City, Utah, and Blackfoot, Idaho, in which he suffered several broken ribs, a dislocated shoulder, a broken nose, and numerous cuts. He was ordered to bed by the doctor, but disregarded the orders and surprised the crowd at the Idaho State Fair in Blackfoot the following day. He appeared on the race track in bandages and splints. He won every event of the day. He also held an unofficial world record in the standing broad jump of 10 feet 11 inches.

He began his auto racing career at the age of eight, when he built his own wagon out of hickory and raced around the streets with a goat and a cart. He became a man of steel and a die-hard competitor. He won nationwide notice in 1926, driving from New York to San Francisco in a shorter time than it took the fastest continental train (he raced the crack passenger train of two railway systems over a distance of 3,200 miles).

Ab popularized the Bonneville Salt Flats as a racer's haven, and he headed a committee to promote the invasion of the European speed kings, including England's Sir

Malcolm Campbell, Captain G. E. T. Eyston, and John Cobb.

In 1935 he received Utah's First Citizen Award from Governor Henry Blood. He has been regarded in his profession as much a superman as was Jack Dempsey at the height of his career as a boxer. His famous Mormon Meteor was his record car for many years. He drove the Mormon Meteor I, II, and III. The third version of the Meteor cost $40,000 to construct, and was later enshrined in the Utah State Capitol. After the Mormon Meteor III, Ab built a new car for $65,000—the Mobil Special. With this car and at the age of sixty-eight, he set several new twenty-four hour records. He was an early proponent of jet power for record cars, and as early as 1947 predicted that jet propulsion was the future of high-speed racing. As President of the American Racing Society he pushed for the kind of experimentation that eventually led to the success of people like Art Arfons, Mickey Thompson, and Craig Breedlove. At the age of seventy-three, the phenomenal speedway king cracked every American unlimited and Class C record up to one hundred miles. For twenty-four hours Ab and his thirty-six-year-old son averaged 118.37 miles per hour and traveled 2,841 miles.

Besides his tremendous accomplishments in the world of racing, Ab was a carpenter, a mason, and active in the building contract business. He also served as mayor of Salt Lake City from 1940 to 1944, and was instrumental in building up the personnel, housing, and equipment of the police, fire, and health departments. He also authored a book, *Salt of the Earth.*

Ab was a man of strong convictions and tremendous energy. As a staunch champion of clean living, he gave hundreds of talks on the Word of Wisdom, and many times attributed his health and endurance to abstaining from liquor and tobacco. His car carried the now-famous "Utah—10,000" license plate, opposite of which (on cross-country tours) was always found a similar plate with the inscription "Yes, I Am a Mormon." Ab was proud of his Mormon heritage and recognized his missionary responsibility as a racer.

Ab paid tribute to his mother, who "gave him a healthy body and taught him to preserve it in highest efficiency. She taught him the value of physical health attained through simple and wholesome living. She set him the example of ceaseless effort in a given undertaking and from her, in a hereditary sense, came the indomitable will-power to achieve and succeed. Through a mother's influence and power—the power of prayer and faith—she kept out of the garden of his soul the noxious weeds and poisons of harmful and evil habits." He proudly said that he never tasted liquor or tobacco. To the Word of Wisdom he attributed his "endurance, steady nerve and imperturbable poise of mind and body, which enable[d] him to drive hour after hour at terrific speeds without visible evidence of fatigue or nervous tension."

As an exponent of clean living, Ab achieved much good and was a worthy example for the youth of America. He was once approached by a tobacco promoter and offered $2,500 for a testimonial for a cigarette advertisement. He refused, saying, "I think too much of the kids."

"Ab Jenkins was an honest man—and an honest man is the noblest work of God." These were the words of Elder Mark E. Petersen at the funeral services of Ab Jenkins. He said, "Honesty was such a great part of Ab. He had to do the thing right. His conscience wouldn't let him do otherwise." He noted that Ab was a staunch believer of the Golden Rule and that his drive for safety became a moral matter, since he felt it was dishonest to drive in such a way as to endanger the lives of others.

Elder Petersen remarked further, "He wanted everything out in the open—no under the table dealings. He wanted everyone to be as honest as he was. He was a great public servant....Ab's word was greater than any bond, because by nature Ab always gave more than he received."

Honest Ab was elected to the Utah Sports Hall of Fame as a charter member in 1970, Utah's great contribution to racing. This great speedway king was a champion racer and a champion of honesty!

DANNY LOPEZ

Featherweight Boxing Champion of the World

Professional boxer, 1971

Professional fight record:

Forty-seven fights (forty-two wins–five losses)

Forty KOs in forty-two victories

Featherweight boxing champion of the world, 1976-80:

Successful defense of title eight consecutive times with eight consecutive KOs

Danny "Little Red" Lopez is one of those outstanding athletes who has truly earned his title as a champion. He is one of those courageous few who has literally fought his way to the top of the boxing world after many hard knocks and not only in a literal sense; from the beginning of his life Danny has faced many difficult challenges. Part American Indian, he grew up on a Ute Indian reservation in Fort Duchesne, Utah. His maternal grandmother was three-fourths Ute, and his maternal grandfather was part Irish. His father was a mission Indian from Northern California who deserted Danny and his six brothers and sisters when he was but a young lad. His mother struggled to rear her large family in a two-room shack. She was eventually forced to place several of the children in foster homes. This instability in Danny's early life influenced him to hang around with the wrong kind of crowd and have slight run-ins with the authorities. Fortunately, he never was in serious trouble.

At the age of sixteen he moved in with a sister in Pleasant Grove, Utah, where some of his aggressive behavior was replaced with the sport of boxing, which he seriously worked at in Stan's Club in Orem. He became more involved when he was taken into the home of Glen Burr, a trainer at Stan's. In the summer of 1967 he sparred with AAU champion Gary Brown. Danny himself never won an AAU national championship for his Orem club, but he did get to the semifinals.

After graduating from high school, Danny moved to California. His older brother Ernie ("Indian Red") had also been an amateur boxer out of Stan's Club and was an eventual ranking welterweight in the Los Angeles area. Danny followed in his brother's footsteps, making a name for himself as he ventured into a professional boxing career in 1971. Boxing out of the Olympic Auditorium in Los Angeles, Danny "Little Red" Lopez, a toe-to-toe slugger, became one of the most popular boxers in the area. He became the proud representative of the "little guys." He won twenty-two of his first twenty-three fights by knockouts. In 1974 he went into the ring against Bobby Chacon for the U.S. featherweight title. Danny was defeated soundly when he was knocked out in the ninth round. He then lost two of his next three bouts, and the experts said that this fighter, turned professional at nineteen, was washed out. But Danny never gave up.

During this time, he turned to the Church. As a priest in the San Gabriel Ward, he became more active. Danny recalled, "God helped me turn myself around. The Church helped me get back on my feet. My wife was baptized—I baptized her—and we started to get active." After that change of heart and with renewed enthusiasm and vigor, Danny won eighteen straight fights, seventeen by knockout. During the process he developed a real reputation in the fighting world. He has been especially noted for his ability to take punishment. He has been knocked down in as many as a dozen fights, and then reversed the course of the battle by knocking out his opponents. His manager, Bennie Georgino, says, "A lot of the experts rate Danny as the third or fourth alltime greatest puncher—based on knockouts—and he ain't finished yet." Don Chargin, veteran matchmaker at the Olympic Auditorium, says, "Pound for pound, Danny is the hardest puncher in all of boxing today." Of his forty-two victories, he knocked out 95 percent of his opponents.

In 1975 Danny lost a split decision to Famaso Gomez. He then had a series of seven wins that propelled him into an interesting title bout against Dave Kotey in 1976. Before that fight in Ghana, Africa, he took an Indian headdress to present to Kotey as a token of friendship. Kotey tossed it aside, however, because of superstition. Lopez was warned before the fight, "You'll never take the title out of this country." Before a crowd of more than one hundred thousand hostile Africans, he won the fight in a fifteen-round decision. Danny remarks, "I remember the end of that fight. I could hear 15 Americans cheering. Otherwise it was silence. I didn't have anybody over there." Lee Benson, *Deseret News* sports editor, made an interesting comment on that situation: "That wasn't anything new. He grew up fighting a few, more than a few, when the odds were a lot worse than Ghana. That fight was a cinch. They had a referee and a ring and rules. You could even lose and not end up in jail." From his tough, rocky childhood, Little Red developed into the featherweight champion of the world. This fighter, who gained a reputation as one who could bounce back from a knockdown to win a couple of rounds later by knockout, did take the title out of Africa. When he later had a return match with Kotey in Las Vegas, his sense of humor prevailed as he entered the ring with his headdress, and Kotey's entourage immediately began drumming and chanting to drive out the evil spirits. Little Red, wearing his deserved chief's headdress, knocked Kotey out in the second round.

As the second native Utahn (besides Gene Fullmer) and the third Mormon (besides Fullmer and Jack Dempsey) to gain a world boxing-championship title, Danny has not found the reign of a champion to be easy. He is the only champion to retire seven straight challengers before the final bell. On two occasions during his title defenses against Jose Torres and Juan Malvarez, Danny was knocked off his feet and in danger of being counted out. With strong will and determination he rose to the occasion and stopped Torres in seven rounds and Malvarez in the second round.

On March 10, 1979, Danny came home to his native Utah to fight Roberto Castanon, the European featherweight champion and second ranked in the World Boxing Council. It was the first championship bout in Utah since Gene Fullmer decisioned Florentino Fernandez in fifteen rounds in Ogden in 1961. It was the fifth world-title fight in Utah and the second indoor title fight in the state. Upon his arrival at the Municipal Airport, Little Red wore the Indian war bonnet to please some two hundred Ute Indians who greeted him at the terminal, including Ruby Black, Ute tribal chairman, and

several tribal singing and dancing groups. Aside from his training program of daily workouts in the Salt Palace, the champion was a crowd pleaser, making various public appearances, including appearances at Primary Children's Hospital and LDS Church headquarters, before the long-awaited championship bout in his own territory. His fans were excited and had the opportunity to get better acquainted with the champ. It was a colorful event with newspaper reporters, television and radio publicity, and general prefight excitement. Not disappointing his home state, Lopez won by a knockout in the second round. *Tribune* sports editor John Mooney, said, "The first round may have equalled any single round of boxing, for boxing action and punching, in Utah's long boxing history." Both boxers fought furiously. Early in the second round, the champion had the challenger down for the count of eight; the second time the European champion was down, he attempted to arise at the eight count, but then slumped back in defeat. The legendary punch of Lopez, the gunshot right arm, had caught Castanon twice and put him away. This skinny Indian kid, deprived in his youth, was again the successful defender as featherweight champion of the world.

In February of 1980 Danny lost his crown to Salvador Sanchez. He also lost the rematch in June and retired with a fine record (forty-two wins and five losses).

Danny believes in the Church. He once even fought for the right to be a Mormon, when an uncle and an aunt tried to persuade him to leave the Church for another religion. He is proud of a younger brother, Larry, who served a full-time mission in Oregon. He also believes that living the Word of Wisdom has helped him maintain the high degree of fitness required of a champion fighter.

Philosophically Danny says, "Everybody needs to lose one fight. It made a better man out of me." His manager, Bennie Georgino, lauds Little Red: "Lopez is the golden boy of boxing. He is a manager's dream—he works hard, takes care of himself, and he is an exciting fighter. Boxing has made a great human being out of him and he has been a credit to boxing."

Danny advises aspiring athletes to find something to hold on to, and then give it everything. He says, "There are no easy fights. When you are on top, you have to fight all the tough ones. I train harder and fight harder each time." Danny included speed-boxing, sparring, and jogging three to five miles as part of his daily routine. He believes in dedication and super conditioning.

Before his Salt Lake City staged championship bout, Danny praised his wife, Bonnie, with these words: "You know, a boxer's wife has to be behind him. She has to understand it's his wish to be a fighter and a champion. She's behind me all the time. This is a break because some fighters are being nagged and whined at by their wives to quit and retire every week. She's a good wife and she'll be coming here for the fight." Bonnie paid him a great compliment when she said, "He really didn't change too much, other than he was floating on a cloud because he'd won the title. His personality hasn't changed much. He's still the same guy."

Danny "Little Red" Lopez, second native Utahn and third Mormon to become a world boxing champion, is a genuine credit and example to the boxing world.

VERN LAW

Pro Baseball Superstar and Cy Young Pitcher

Star baseball pitcher, 1948-67:

Class D Far West League (Santa
Rosa), 1948
Davenport, 1949
New Orleans, 1950
Pittsburgh Pirates, 1950-67

National League Player of the
Month, August 1959

All-Star Team National League, 1960

All-American Team, 1960

Cy Young Award (best pitcher in
major league baseball), 1960

All-Church Award, 1960

BYU Exemplary Manhood Award,
1960

UPI's National League Comeback
Player of the Year, 1965

Sporting News Most Valuable Pitcher
Award, 1965

Lou Gehrig and Babe Didrickson
Awards (both given for courage in
overcoming physical injuries to
continue in professional baseball),
1965

Pittsburgh Post-Gazette Dapper Dan Award, 1965
David O. McKay Award for Athletic Excellence, 1970

Vernon Sanders Law, affectionately known in the world of professional baseball as the Deacon, was a superstar on the baseball mound as a right-handed pitcher and as a well-known Mormon athlete.

Vern attended Meridian High School in Meridian, Idaho, where he was an outstanding athlete in three sports, football, basketball, and baseball, earning twelve varsity letters, four in each sport, before his graduation in 1948. He was a tailback in football, a fine-shooting basketball player, and a star pitcher on his baseball team.

U.S. Senator Herman Welker of Idaho, who put the scouts on Harmon Killebrew, recommended Vern to the Pirates in 1947. Bing Crosby, a Pirates stockholder and a college classmate of Senator Welker, telephoned Vern's mother to ask for her help in influencing him to sign with the Pirates. Upon graduation from high school he signed a contract with the Pittsburgh Pirates and began his baseball career with the Santa Rosa Club in the Class D Far West League in 1948. From there he went to Davenport in the Class B Three-I Loop in 1949 and then split the 1950 season between the class AA New Orleans team in the Southern Association and the parent Pirates. He was then on the Bucs roster from 1950 to 1967, except for a stint in the Army from 1952 to 1953. After returning to the Pirates in 1954, he spent a total of sixteen years with the same national-league team. During those sixteen years he won 162 games and lost 147 for a .524 percentage. His total earned-run average (ERA) was 3.77, indicating the number of runs his opponents were able to score per game. He pitched a total of 2,672 innings in 483 games. He started 364 games and completed 119. During his amazing period of pitching he had 1,092 strike-outs, allowed 597 walks, and had 28 shutout games. In the 1960 season he had a 20 won–9 lost season in leading the Pirates to their first victorious National League pennant in thirty-three years and their first World Series title (against the Yankees) since 1925. That year he had a winning percentage of .690 and an ERA of

91

3.08. His performance earned him the Cy Young Award as the best major-league pitcher of the year.

At the time he was the only member of the Mormon Church playing in the big leagues and was highly respected for his example of clean living and dedication as an athlete. He was the recipient of the All-Church Award from the YMMIA, which he cherishes above all other awards received during his career. At the time he received the awards, President David O. McKay said to him, "You do lots of good. You are the ideal of many of our young people. We're proud of you." He was also honored with the BYU Exemplary Manhood Award for his "achievement in athletics, good sportsmanship and dedicated observance of the principles of the Church of Jesus Christ of Latter-Day Saints." So profound was his example in living the principles of the gospel, even before the completion of that outstanding 1960 season, that he was lauded by Lester J. Biederman (the immediate past president of the American Baseball Writers Association) in an article in the Pittsburgh Press: "If you were to take a vote among the Pirates on the player they most admire for his athletic ability and his stature as a man among men, Vern Law would win by acclamation. Nobody has ever seen Law smoke, drink a beer or ever heard him use profanity. He's the typical All-American athlete, father of four sons and an elder in the Mormon Church."

After his triumphant 1960 season, Law experienced the most trying years of his baseball career. A freak accident occurred in which this rugged athlete sprained his ankle en route to the airport with his teammates. While pitching he found that he had to favor his ankle and that by so doing he put undue strain on his right shoulder, almost ending his career. In 1961 he had three wins and four losses. Because of his problems he was sent back to the minors, placed on the disabled list, had pay cuts, and voluntarily retired. It wasn't until 1964 that he showed any signs of making a comeback. During this time, Vern kept his head high and never lost faith in himself. In the 1965 season he registered a 17 won–9 lost record, pacing his Bucs to third place in the National League. Even more significant, he had an earned run average of 2.16. For that astonishing comeback he was named the National League Comeback Player of 1965 by the United Press International's Board of Baseball Experts. He was given the

Sporting News Most Valuable Pitcher Award. Because of his courage in overcoming physical injuries to continue in professional baseball, he was the recipient of the Lou Gehrig Memorial Award and the Babe Didrickson Award. The Gehrig Award Committee said that Law "possesses an indomitable competitive spirit, as is attested by his refusal to surrender to repeated injury. He has great strength of character and he commands the deep respect of his teammates, his competitors in the National League and baseball fans everywhere." Les Biederman, writing in *Sporting News*, caught a little of the greatness of this outstanding athlete. Speaking about Vern's performance with the Pirates since 1950, he said, "And the only thing that has changed about him in those 15 years is the strength of his character and the esteem in which he is held by teammates, opponents, sportswriters, broadcasters, umpires and fans. Law has survived many mishaps during his baseball career and emerged a bigger man for all the adversity. His philosophy has always been, 'What is to be, will be.'" He then quoted Vern's trainer, Danny Whelan, who said of Vern, "I never saw a fellow suffer as much as he did when he was trying to pitch his way back. He endured every kind of pain, yet never once complained. He often would take a pill or two to ease the pain, but all he ever wanted to do was pitch. He's all man." He further quoted Vern's roommate, Smokey Burgess, who said, "I could see pain written all over his face every time he threw a ball. Many a night he walked the floor after pitching because of pain. Just being associated with a fellow of Law's caliber is one of the most rewarding experiences I've ever had." This same article lauds his comeback: "Player after player, manager after manager and umpire after umpire not only congratulated Law on his comeback, but seemed rather pleased that such a high type of man was doing it." Then the article quotes from Law's small red book of words to live by: "I have never met a man who is not my superior at something." "A good timber never grows with ease. It needs a strong wind and storms to give it strength." "A discouraged man is not a strong man." "Don't be satisfied with mediocrity." "There is nothing wrong with youth. Actually only ten percent are bad and these ten percent get all the publicity." "I shall never criticize my superiors. I will never uphold my opinion to the extent of angering another. I will never forget that I am one of God's

marked men. I will always remember that I am made of the same stuff as the worst sinner, and without God's help I would be worse than he. I will always have a happy smile for everyone, especially those who like me least."

He then quoted Law's true philosophy related to God: "I often bow my head when I am pitching or even sitting on the bench and say a silent prayer. I simply ask for strength to do my best. I don't expect my prayers to be answered in a positive way immediately. I just want to be able to do my best. Prayer doesn't guarantee anything, but a person needs to be humbled once in a while." Biederman concludes the article as follows: "I've known Vern Law ever since he first reported to the Pirates in 1950 and he's become one of my all-time favorite players. And I've seen hundreds of them in Pirate uniforms in the past 28 years. In success and in adversity Law has always had compassion for his fellow man. He doesn't change to any extent whether he wins or loses. The morning after he won his seventh straight game by beating the Giants, 6-0, on four hits, at Candlestick Park late in June, Law came out of the Sheraton Palace Hotel. As he approached the Pirate bus, he noticed a legless man sitting on a stool selling pencils. Law automatically reached into his pocket for some change, dropped it into the cup of the legless man and stopped to chat with him until it was time for the bus to leave for the park. The man without legs recognized Law and congratulated him on his fine performance the night before and also for the season. Law almost blushed and tried to change the subject. Yet he took the time to stand there and talk to a stranger who had no legs while the other players passed up the man and stepped into the bus. This incident is typical of Vernon Law. He has always had compassion for his fellow man; he never has belittled an opponent or embarrassed anybody. This is a man."

The Pittsburgh sportswriter Les Biederman also wrote a small article about Vern Law's dedication to tithing: "Law, a tither with the Mormon Church, missed the team bus last spring when his name was placed on the traveling list at the last minute. The automatic fine is $25. The next day, Law handed Danny Murtaugh, team manager, his check for $25. 'Would you do me a favor?' Law asked Murtaugh. 'The Mormon Church in Fort Myers is having a drive for a building fund. Would you turn this check over to the building fund?' Murtaugh went him one better. The Pirate manager wrote out his own personal check for $25 and handed the $50 to the Mormon Church building fund. This is the esteem in which Law is held by all."

When Law was further honored by receiving the Pittsburgh Post-Gazette's Dapper Dan Award for his 1965 performance, Al Abrams, sports editor, praised the superstar: "I've never met a man, woman or child who knew him who didn't like and respect Vernon Sanders Law. There never has been an athlete honored by the Post-Gazette's Dapper Dan Club in its 34 years of experience who will reflect the popularity of a man who was not only magnificent in his choosen field of endeavor but one who is also a living symbol of all that is good and clean in this troubled world than

Vernon Law. This is a broad statement to make in view of the number of worthy and popular stars of the past and present who have been cited. Nevertheless, it stands, I repeat that no athlete I have ever met better exemplified the kind of man every youngster should aspire to be than the tall, handsome Mormon from Boise, Idaho. Vernon Law is this good that he inspired a fellow we know to say the other day: 'I'm not much of a church goer but Law can make a believer out of me. I've never seen a man in sports whose outlook on life was so ideal, his conduct on and off the field so impeccable.' The rogue who said it meant every word, too."

Perhaps some of Vern's "words to live by" best exemplify his conduct: "If you would rise to great heights, remember you cannot climb on the shoulders of your fellow man, but you must be worthy to be lifted by those about you to this lofty position. No matter what your pursuit in life, or the effort you put forth, there will be others who will rise above you and they deserve your praise. This does not mean that you will step down and give up. It is all right to be content with what you have but never with what you are."

After his very satisfying comeback year, the Deacon pitched two more years and then decided to retire as a professional baseball player. He was a sterling performer, a superstar on and off the baseball diamond, and one of the most outstanding representatives of athletics anywhere. His performance on the mound was matched by his actions out of uniform. He was in constant demand as a speaker throughout his career. Unknown is the amount of time he has given to encourage young people to set their ideals and goals high. He urged others to give their best, as he gave his best while playing. After ending his career as a pitcher, he spent two years as pitching coach for the Pirates, and then returned to Provo, Utah, where he joined the baseball staff at Brigham Young University. He has been an assistant baseball coach there for the past ten years. He has also had duties in high school and college relations, fund raising, public relations, and as a special consultant in development and athletic recruitment. Recently he had a challenging assignment as pitching coach for the Seibu Lions, a team in the Japanese major leagues. Presently he is a pitching coach for a Pirates' farm club.

One of the more outstanding feats of Vernon Law as a pro was an eighteen-inning pitching marathon in 1955 against

Milwaukee. He lost eight pounds during that game. It is likely that he received some of his endurance and talent from his father, Jessie, who also pitched eighteen innings one day in a doubleheader for a semipro team in Boise, Idaho. Vernon also passed on his athletic prowess to his five sons. All have been outstanding athletes, performing well in little-league sports. Veldon and Vance played BYU baseball, and Veryl and Vance were BYU basketball players (Vance is in the pro ranks, playing with the Pittsburgh Pirates). Vaughn quarterbacked Provo High School's football team to the state 4-A championships and played basketball and baseball, and Varlin played football and basketball for Timpview High and basketball for BYU-Hawaii.

In 1970 Vernon Law received the David O. McKay Award for athletic excellence, honoring the great prophet for his love of and interest in sports. He was later honored as a nominee for the Baseball Hall of Fame.

Law has maintained his standards of excellence throughout his sports career. He says, "I took care of myself. I was never blessed with all that ability and I had to use my head. I will always believe that being an active member of the LDS Church helped me in my career." He also said, "Living the Word of Wisdom has helped me compete successfully against the best athletes in the world. It has strengthened me physically. But more than that, good health has improved my mental attitude. When you feel good about yourself, you can compete better. Life is more satisfying." Recognizing the pitfalls that beset athletes, he says, "It [the gospel] has certainly been a life saver for me in all kinds of temptation." He also says, "My Church believes that a Christian must give all-out evidence of his beliefs. That applies to his private life as well as his career. My biggest problem I have regarding my ball playing is Sunday baseball. I'll never really approve of it, but I have to reconcile myself by saying that I can overcome this shortcoming with other good deeds and living within the Church."

Many may never realize the great example that Vernon Law has set, but Church writer Dell Van Orden has told of several times when Vern influenced other lives. Vern once addressed an all-girl Catholic high school, telling of the beliefs and position of the Church. He later received a letter from one of the girls, who said, "When you introduced your wife to the audience, I felt that you two were the happiest people in the world." Another letter from a parent of one of the girls said, "Before you talked at the school, my daughter was unhappy and sullen. But after your visit, her life has changed completely. You have given her something." An eighteen-year-old boy who ardently followed Vern's career was highly receptive to tracting missionaries. He later attended Ricks College and between semesters asked Vern to baptize him. Vern considered his entire baseball career as a mission. Although he was not able to be as close to Church activities as he would like, he went to Church as often as he could. His Church activity was limited, but not his testimony. In addition to speaking at many Church functions and setting a great example as a missionary baseball star, he coached many M-Men teams. Since retiring from professional baseball he has served as a branch president and in a bishopric.

During his off-season as an active baseball player, he worked for the Idaho First National Bank and also as a carpenter. One of his hobbies is playing the harmonica. He has been a member of the Lion's Club and a member of the Greater Boise Chamber of Commerce, and has served in an advisory capacity with the Fellowship of Christian Athletes, a group of many ballplayers who have banded together to work against juvenile delinquency.

Although Vern thinks that young men should pursue their athletic desires, he does not believe that they should neglect their education for athletics. He says, "Get schooling first. I have seen too many cases of starting out in baseball right after high school, just like myself, and spending the best years of their life trying to make the majors." Vern spent many hours taking college correspondence courses while in the majors.

Law always encouraged people. At the Utah Technical College, he said, "You are going to have to produce under difficult circumstances, and when you suffer a setback, don't let it defeat you for life.... When you win, the discouraging moments and setbacks seem small, but at the same time, you can look back and see how important they were in helping you develop the right attitudes for success."

Vern "Deacon" Law, baseball superstar and super-pitcher, courageous missionary and symbol of clean living, has written his own outstanding story in the book of life and sports history, leaving a fine example for athletes and nonathletes to emulate.

ALF ENGEN

National Ski Champion: "Utah's Old Man of the Mountain"

National ski champion sixteen times

National jumping champion eight times, 1931, 1932, 1933, 1934, 1935, 1937, 1940, 1946

National classic champion, 1939, 1941

National downhill and slalom combined champion, 1942, 1947

National downhill champion, 1947

National slalom champion, 1947

National four-way champion, 1940-41

Only skier ever to win the Big Four (National Jumping, National Classic, National Four-Way, and National Downhill and Slalom Combined)

Canadian Jumping Crown, 1937

North American Jumping Crown, 1937

All-American Ski Trophy, 1940

Member 1940 Olympic Games Team (cancelled due to World War II)

Coach, U.S. Ski Team, 1948
Norwegian Ski Association's highest award, 1948
Master Ski Instructor, 1949
Skier of the Century Award, 1950
Helm's Hall of Fame, 1954
National Ski Hall of Fame Award, 1959
Director, Deseret News Ski School, 1948-present

Alf Engen is not only the greatest skier that Utah has ever produced, but one of the all-time great skiers of the world. The records he has set, the trophies he has won, the strides he has made as a coach and a teacher, the contributions he has made technically to skiing and mapping out ski resorts, and the personal influence he has had on skiing locally and throughout the world are so far-reaching that it is difficult to believe that one person could have achieved so much during his career.

At the age of two, this hearty Norseman started skiing under the direction of his father. His father said, "Come Alf, we shall have fun." Alf has not only had a lifetime of fun skiing, but in the meantime has set all of his records. Alf learned to ski on the dim trails in the long Norwegian twilight and to feel his way over the course in the darkest night. He started in his first competition at the age of eight, and won over sixty trophies in his native land and more than eighty European trophies during his career. Many of his native trophies are Queen's Cups.

After Alf and his brothers, Sverre and Corey (Kaare) grew to boyhood, their father died. Finally, Alf left his trophy-filled home in Mjondalen to come to America in the fall of 1929. Later his two brothers and his mother joined him.

Before leaving Norway in the year of the market catastrophe (1929), Alf had also achieved other significant honors as an athlete. Besides skiing, he was an excellent soccer player, boxer, hockey player, speed skater, and swimmer, and was a member of a folk-dancing team. At the age of eighteen Alf had earned a spot on the Norwegian Olympic Team, but couldn't compete because of his youth. He was, however, invited to participate in a ski jump at the famed Konnerud Kollen in the post-Olympic celebration, welcoming home the Olympic jumpers. Alf and his brother Sverre "stayed up most of the night waxing (or tarring) their skis for the next day," and then hiked seven miles to the jumping hill. Even though Alf was suffering from a neck boil and didn't do too well through the first jumps, in the finals he gave it everything he had and beat the whole Olympic team.

Upon arrival in the United States, Alf was not quite sure of himself. In Norway he had been a hero, and in the United States he was just another face. Because of his background as a top soccer player, he began playing pro soccer in Milwaukee. His outstanding success and credentials as a soccer player in Norway afforded him the opportunity to meet Knute Rockne, also a Norwegian, who thought Alf had the potential to convert into an American footballer. He was offered a place in the Notre Dame football program, but Alf decided to stick to soccer.

After a pro soccer match, Alf's coach drove him to a nearby park where some ski jumping was being performed. Even though Alf came to America thinking he might never ski again, he had the opportunity that day. He said, "That was my first time on skis in America, and it remains one of the most memorable days of my life. I had no equipment, but I asked one of the fellows if I could borrow his skis. All I had on was a pair of oxfords. He said that if I could make the skis stay on, I could use them. I strapped them on, climbed up the hill, and went on to break the hill record—several times." Some of the area newspapers picked up the story and started calling him "Ski jumper in the street shoes." From that first winter in America Alf began an amazing story. Wearing oxfords, no gloves, no hat, without practice, and on borrowed skis, he launched into a string of ski triumphs. He said of his lifetime career as an athlete, "I won over a thousand trophies."

In 1931 he set his first world's record. The year before, he had tested the record-making possibilities of Ecker Hill near Salt Lake City. Liking Utah, he chose the state for his own. On January 1, 1931—New Year's Day—he made his famous flight of 247 feet at Ecker Hill. It was later recognized as the world's longest official leap. He was the perennial national jumping champion in 1931, 1932, 1933, 1934, 1935, 1937, 1940, and 1946—eight times in all. In 1937 he won the Canadian Jumping Crown and also the North American Jumping Crown. His accomplishments at this first national ski tournament ever held in Utah brought fame to the skier and the skiing resort. Alf was also the national classic champion two times in 1939 and 1941 (cross-country and jumping combined), winning the titles of National Amateur and Open Champion. He was also the national downhill and slalom combined champion two times (1942, 1947), the downhill champion one time (1947), and the slalom champion one time (1947). His accomplishments as the national four-way champion two times (1940, 1941) were almost unheard of. The National Four-Way Championship includes the cross-country, downhill, jumping, and slalom. No one has ever equaled his record. He is also the only skier ever to win the big four: National Jumping, National Classic, National Four-Way, and National Downhill and Slalom Combined. Alf Engen has been a national champion sixteen times.

Besides all of these amazing feats, Engen won the All-American Ski Trophy in 1940, the Americanism Award in the same year, and was chosen for both the jumping and downhill and slalom teams for the 1940 Olympic Games (cancelled because of World War II). During 1948 Engen was coach for the U.S. Ski Team and received the Norwegian Ski Association's highest award for being an "ambassador of good will and sportsmanship." He received the title of Master Ski Instructor in 1949, captured the Skier of the Century Award in 1950, was named a member of the Helm's Hall of Fame in 1954, and won the National Ski Hall of Fame Award in 1959. The hundreds of ski meets he has won and the numerous hill and course records he has set are legion. He has broken world and American records many times in jumping competitions in the United States and won over eighty trophies in European competition, as mentioned.

From 1935 to 1942, while working for the U.S. Forest Service in the capacity of technical advisor, he helped plan and develop winter sports areas throughout Utah, Nevada, Idaho, and Wyoming. Among these major ski areas are Alta, Brighton Ski Bowl, Snow Basin, Sun Valley, Bogus Basin, Pocatello, Nevada's Kyle Canyon, White Pine and Wyoming's

Jackson area, Teton Pass, and Michigan's Porcupine Mountain Area. He has helped with twenty-nine ski areas. He was sports advisor for Sun Valley, Idaho, from 1937 to 1942, and again from 1946 to 1948. During the years he was in the Forest Service, he conducted ski schools and taught winter mountaineering and rescue training for forest rangers and supervisors.

Alf has also starred in ski movies and has written many articles for national ski magazines. He has written several pamphlets on skiing and was a coauthor of the training program written especially for the 1948 U.S. Olympic Ski Team.

Since 1948 he has been the director of the Deseret News Ski School. For thirty-four years this dean of skiing in Utah has had the great responsibility and joy of teaching people how to ski. As one of the most accomplished powder skiers,

103

he has been responsible for thousands of skiers bearing the "Engen Cup" label. This Old Master of the Waxed Board, Utah's Old Man of the Mountain, has become a legend. In 1965 he was the winner of the first Ski Man of the Year Award, selected as the man who has done the most to gain international recognition for Utah winter recreation.

Abby Rand, travel editor of *Ski* magazine and author of several American and European ski guidebooks, wrote a portrait of Alf Engen in 1973 that depicted the feeling of a student under his guidance: "His teaching system is pure Engen. Snaking down the mountain with metronomic rhythm, his square bulk communicates a mixture of power and grace. The pupil, trying to follow in his tracks, picks up the rhythm and gets the notion that he is skiing like the leader. Soon, by golly, he almost is. Engen's secret is to set his own pace two notches above what he deduces to be the pupil's normal pace. The student becomes exhilarated by the unaccustomed speed and by the fact that he is coping with it. He feels no fear because he is following His Serene Majesty through his personal empire." Such are the feelings of those who have been tutored by Alf Engen. The Deseret News Ski School stands as a monument to his name. Including students from age eight to eighty, it is the largest and longest-continuing school of its type in the nation.

One of the nation's best ski runs at Alta has recently been designated Alf's High Rustler in tribute to this resort's beloved ski figure.

At age seventy-two Alf still believes in regular exercise each day and retiring and arising at the same time each morning and night. He says, "If you are physically fit and have done your homework, you are mentally fit and prepared to win." He believes it is especially important for a person to like himself and live clean, and that it is important for an athlete to pick a sport that he can use all his life and that he enjoys. Alf always wanted to be the best skier in the world and has without question accomplished that. He has been good for skiing, and skiing has been good for him. He believes that skiing is a game that one plays for pleasure.

Besides his full-time responsibilities in skiing, he has a hand in Alf Engen Cosmetic Company, which, among other things, makes suntan oil and ski wax. He has found time to be a merit-badge counselor in the Great Salt Lake Council of the

Boy Scouts of America. His famous skiing brothers, Sverre and Corey, have remained active in skiing. Sverre helps Alf with the Alta Ski School, and Corey heads the ski school at Brundage Mountain in Idaho. Alf's son Alan was a national downhill and slalom ski champion.

Alf Engen, Utah's greatest skier and one of the leading ski figures in the world, has had a profound impact on skiing locally, nationally, and internationally. Claire W. Noall, writing in the *Improvement Era*, captured the champion in action setting a world's record performance: "All motion ceases save his own. The immense throng beneath endures an infinite moment of suspense as he slices the cold, crisp air high above their heads to complete a tremendous arc. Arms circling to catch the hollow of the wind, body bent far forward to greet the angle of descent, skis parallel and perfectly still, at last he clips the hill's incline 247 feet from the jump-off. Down go his knees to receive the blow; up they come, feet well under, body upright, lithe, rhythmic, and in one accord to shoot swiftly forward as he surfaces the snowy apron for a hundred yards or so in a graceful finish. A hill record! A world's record!"

Alf Engen, described as the "Human Falcon," soared not only high as a jumper, but as a champion among champions!

LINN ROCKWOOD

National Public Parks Tennis Champion

Undefeated in Conference Play at BYU 1943, 1947

Intermountain Region champion in Tennis six times

Ranked First in Men's Singles 14 Years in Utah

National Public Parks Men's Singles champion three times (1952, 1956, 1957)

Idaho State Men's Singles champion five times

National Doubles champion 1957 (with Wayne Pearce)

Utah's Athlete of the Year 1952

National Public Parks Hall of Fame, 1964

Utah Sports Hall of Fame, 1974

BYU Athletic Hall of Fame, 1976

Linn Rockwood is one of the greatest tennis champions to come from the state of Utah. His story is personal and touching. As a teenager in the 1930s he and his family lived across from Liberty Park in Salt Lake City. He weighed just over ninety pounds and was just a little over five feet tall, but he learned to play against the court giants of the time.

In assessing his success as an athlete, and particularly as a Mormon, Linn says, "I had a very difficult childhood and often felt much mental anguish, frustration, discouragement, and embarrassment. I found that through success in tennis I could build a more positive self-image and gain the respect and recognition I could not have otherwise achieved." Thankful for his Mormon background, he says, "I feel that it helped me from departing from an ideal course and helped me keep in excellent physical condition."

He actually started his competitive tennis in 1934 when he became active in the "junior high school net wars." He lettered at South High School, then attended Brigham Young University, where he was a tennis standout, helping the team to the title three different years. He was undefeated in Conference play in 1943 and 1947 and captain of the team both of those years.

During World War II, while in the Marines, he won the Marine V-12 135-pound battalion boxing championship in North Carolina in 1944.

Linn was prominent in Utah intermountain and national tennis wars for twenty years. He won the Colorado Springs Invitational in 1943, was six-time champion of the Intermountain Region, ranked first in Utah for fourteen years, won the National Public Parks Men's Singles Championship on three different occasions (1952, 1956, and 1957), and won the Idaho State Men's Singles Championship five times. He won innumerable tournaments in his forty years of activity in tennis, and during the early 1940s was even the Utah table-tennis champion three times.

In 1952 he was named Utah's Athlete of the Year. The "Rock" was given the Distinguished Service Award of Provo in 1956 and the Dale Rex Memorial Award in 1957. Besides his own personal tennis domination, he teamed with Wayne Pearce to win the National Doubles title in 1957, and in the same year won the National Singles championship. He "retired" from competition in 1957, but returned to win the Utah Singles title in 1960. In 1963 he won his last Intermountain Region title at age forty-three. In 1964 he was elected to the Hall of Fame of the Public Parks Tennis Association. He was named to the Utah Sports Hall of Fame in 1974 and to the BYU Hall of Fame in 1976.

He not only received his bachelor's degree from BYU in 1947, but went on to achieve a master's degree in 1952 from the same institution and his doctor of education degree in 1967 from the University of Utah.

He was a sportscaster for a Provo radio station and hosted a nightly KSL television sports program in the mid '60s. He also broadcasted high school football and basketball games. In 1964 he was named director of sports for KSL radio and television.

He was Provo's director of parks and recreation from 1960 to 1964 and managed the Salt Lake Swimming and Tennis Club from 1964 to 1966. He has been associate professor of health, physical education, and recreation at the University of Utah since 1968, specializing in parks and city recreation administration.

Dr. Rockwood has been a member of the National Recreation and Parks Association, Society of Park and Recreation Educators, and the National Association of Sportswriters and Sports Broadcasters.

It has been said of Linn Rockwood that he was toughest against his best competitors. He once told a reporter in Detroit at the National Public Parks Tournament, "I am going to go for every ball, every point of the match until somebody cracks—and it isn't going to be me." That basically sums up his philosophy of athletics and life.

Linn was in excellent physical condition during his prime, running, jumping rope, playing basketball, boxing, and playing tennis. He enjoyed fishing and broadcasting sports for mental relaxation and stimulation. Presently, he has been hampered by a hip operation that has confined him to tennis once or twice a week and a few minor local tournaments, such as the Church tournaments and doubles play. He won a couple of senior divisions this summer in spite of his handicap. He tries to keep in good physical condition by staying with his tennis game. He also renovates homes for resale.

Linn has had many callings in the Church. He has served as a branch president, a ward clerk, and in ward and stake Sunday School superintendencies. He is presently the secretary of his high priest group.

In advising athletes toward successful goals, Linn says: "They must be willing to sacrifice many ostensibly 'fun' things and to devote a tremendous amount of time, effort and mental activity toward perfecting their skills, and putting themselves in the necessary psychological frame of mind—to psyche themselves up into veritable tigers. Use every loss or defeat to learn something that can be turned to your own account in future competition."

One of the great tennis champions and competitors, Dr. Linn Rockwood has gone "for every ball, every point of the match" of life. As a Utah, regional, and national champion, there has been no finer example among Mormon athletes.

KENNETH LUNDMARK

Swedish and NCAA
High-Jump Champion

Member, Swedish Olympic Team,
1968

Three-time Swedish national high-
jump champion, 1968-70

Represented Sweden at twenty-four
international track meets, 1967-71

Swedish high-jump record holder
(7 feet 2¾ inches), 1969-71

European Cup high-jump champion,
1970

Indoor and outdoor WAC high-jump
champion, 1970

NCAA indoor high-jump champion,
1970

NCAA outdoor silver medalist, 1970

Two-time all-American high jumper,
1970

Kenneth Lundmark has earned a reputation as one of the finest high-jump champions in both Europe and the United States. This Swedish national champion has had one of the most active, exciting, successful careers of the world's outstanding jumpers.

In 1964 Ken, the "Jumping Swede," became determined to become a champion as he watched the Olympics. At that time he was seventeen years old, and at six feet eight inches was a skinny, wiry athlete. From the picturesque town of

Skellftea, Sweden, where he helped his father as a carpenter and builder, he saw himself as an Olympic champion while watching the Olympic events on television. During the next seven years the evolution of a colorful champion took place. In addition to his regular occupation, he worked out five hours a day, six days a week, and observed the general rules of good health, including well-balanced meals and plenty of sleep. From 1967 through 1971 he represented Sweden at twenty-four international meets. In 1968 he was a member of the Swedish Olympic Team. The same year he was a member of the European Track Team and was the Swedish national high-jump champion. He repeated as Swedish national champion in both 1969 and 1970 and was the Swedish record holder from 1969 through 1971, his record leap being 7 feet 2¾ inches. He won numerous invitational meets in both the United States and Canada from 1969 through 1971 and was the European Cup winner in 1970. During that season he was unbeaten in European competition.

During the 1969-70 school year Kenneth Lundmark attended Brigham Young University. A friend and another "jumping Swede," Chris Celion, had encouraged Ken to accept a scholarship to BYU. Even though he had read the Bible in school and in his home, he was not especially interested in religion and didn't know much about the Mormons. In Provo, Ken became a part of a BYU "family," holding regular family home evenings. He was introduced to the MIA and other Church activities and was given a Swedish copy of the Book of Mormon. He also met his future wife, Susan, in college. She had a great influence on his personal life.

While at the 'Y' he won numerous track meets while majoring in physical education. He was the 1970 Western Athletic Conference indoor and outdoor high-jump champion and a two-time all-American. In 1970 he was the NCAA indoor champion with a leap of seven feet and was the only participant to clear the 7-foot level. In the outdoor competition he was the NCAA Silver Medalist. He also became the BYU school record holder (7 feet 1½ inches), sharing those honors with fellow countryman Chris Celion. He also shared the WAC record (7 feet 0 inches). He set the new record for the Texas Relays with a leap of 7 feet 1 inch and was the Canada Maple Leaf Games champion at 7 feet 1¼ inches.

Although Ken constantly practiced at the 7-foot 3-inch level and had cleared 7 feet 2 inches in competition, in all of his track meets he was never able to clear the mark he made while in a training camp in Switzerland, 7 feet 5½ inches. The mark he did clear, however, was the exciting step he took on his way to becoming a champion of the gospel of Jesus Christ. After his return to Sweden following his year at BYU, he realized what a great impression Susan and the Church had made on him. Remembering how happy Mormon people are (especially Susan), he decided to seriously investigate the Church. He read the Book of Mormon and contacted a man in Sweden whom he had previously met and participated with in hockey, David Eskil Karlsson, a branch president at Skelleftea. He also began meeting with the Mormon missionaries in Sweden and read everything he could about the Church. He continued his schooling in Stockholm and also continued his missionary lessons. In November of 1970 the "jumping Swede" was baptized and said, "It's just great to be a member of the Church. I really didn't know what I was missing, but now I know what I have. It is how I feel when I am sure of myself, like when I just know I can clear 7' 2"." Later he married his BYU sweetheart, Susan Wilkinson, and decided to take up his permanent residence in Salt Lake City. He is presently an owner-manager of Feminine Fitness World in Ogden. He has been active in the Church as a Young Marrieds' activity leader, a home teacher, and a Sunday School teacher. Although he is not currently active in competitive athletics, he exercises one and a half hours daily, including lifting weights, jogging, playing racquetball, and occasionally skiing.

Although Ken became a Mormon only at the end of his competitive athletic career, his comments on the effects of Mormonism on his life are enlightening: "My athletic career affected my ability to recognize the truths in Mormonism. In man's pursuit of excellence and perfection, the same basic principles operate in both athletics and Mormon doctrine. These doctrines have reaffirmed my belief in the infinite capacity for human development and achievement where appropriate desire and effort are applied."

A hard-training athlete, appreciative of the support of his parents during his many years of training and competition, Ken declares that the most important thing in his own life that has led to athletic success has been his desire to achieve

goals and his belief in his ability to do so. For those who want to be successful athletes, he declares, "Carefully analyze and get to know all about yourself. Set long-range, intermediate, and short-term goals. In your progress toward these goals utilize this self-knowledge to maximize the results of your effort and increase your potential. To aid in this process, keep a daily, accurate diary or record of all aspects of your training and progress. It is important to understand the abilities, potentials, and reactions of your own body in order to progress. Don't allow your mind to limit your efforts or potential. Instead you should use its powerful force to further your progress. Make use of your failures as positive experiences for growth and learning. You can often learn more from a failure than a success." He then uses an example of this type of thinking from personal experience in his training program. He says, "One year as a developing athlete, I worked out five hours daily according to a well-planned, personal schedule. In competition that year my performance had increased by a mere half inch. Defeat seemed near, and I honestly reevaluated and questioned my commitment and potential. I carefully examined my well-kept records and could not find any explanation. It seemed that I had done everything possible and that all of my efforts had been correct and appropriate. At the time, my coach had been considered to be the best high-jump coach in the world. Even he could not find any errors in my training procedures or personal effort. He began to question my inherent abilities. But because of my knowledge of myself and my sports, I maintained a strong enough belief in myself and my ability to make appropriate effort that I continued my efforts for another long winter with the same intensity and determination. Following that second year of concentrated, determined training, I improved my performance by over eight inches—and that was at the second meet of the season."

This remarkable champion high jumper makes an exceptional observation about the relationship of the body and spirit: "I feel they are two equal parts, complexly interrelated, comprising the total person." He has worked long and hard in an attempt to perfect both body and spirit. In his early training years as a tall and skinny athlete, Ken realized that much physical conditioning was necessary to become a champion. He always believed that he had that inherent ability and was not deterred by one of his early observations: "When I turned to the side, I was so skinny no one could see me." Although he believes in innate athletic abilities, he is thoroughly convinced that hard work is one of the most important aspects of becoming a champion.

Kenneth Lundmark, the "jumping Swede," former three-time Swedish national champion, European Cup champion, NCAA champion, and world-recognized high jumper, has soared to exceptional heights both in the athletic world and in the wonderful world of the gospel.

DALE MURPHY

Professional
Baseball Player

Wilson High School (Portland,
Oregon):

Three-sport letterman (football,
basketball, baseball)

All-city baseball, 1974

All-state Oregon baseball, 1974

Professional Baseball, 1974-present:

Atlanta Braves number-one pick in
the 1974 baseball draft

All-Star Team, Western Carolina
League, 1975

All-Star Team, Southern League,
1976

All-Star Team, International League,
1977

Topps Bubble Gum AAA All-Star
Team, 1977

Atlanta Braves, 1978-present

NL All-star Team, 1980

Home run and RBI leader
(National League), 1982

Dale Bryan Murphy, outstanding professional baseball
player and hard-hitting outfielder for the Atlanta Braves, has
enjoyed an exciting life in athletics. His life as an athlete,

however, has changed because of a change in his religious philosophy.

At Wilson High School in Portland, Oregon, he was a three-sport letterman, including all-city and all-state as a catcher in 1974. He was the Atlanta Braves number-one pick in the 1974 baseball draft. Directly out of high school, he went to the minor leagues and played baseball in South America during his off-seasons. In 1975, in the Western Carolina League, he earned a spot on the All-Star Team. In 1976 he made the All-Star Team of the Southern League, and in 1977 made the All-Star Team of the International League. He also was named to the Topps Bubble Gum AAA All-Star Team in 1977. Although he came up to the majors for a few weeks during both the 1976 and 1977 seasons, it was not until 1978 that he played the full season for the Atlanta Braves. He was switched to first baseman from his position of catcher in order to fill a hole in the Braves' lineup. Although his hitting average lagged somewhat (.220), he was a real slugger (hitting twenty-three home runs) and had seventy-nine RBIs for the season.

In the 1979 season Dale was setting the pace in National League home runs before being sidelined for half of the season with a knee injury. He slammed nine homers in one month (April), two short of a major-league record. Braves manager Bobby Cox claimed that Dale had all the tools to be one of the dominant hitters in the game. He further said, "Dale is the best all-around athlete on this club." Home run king Hank Aaron, farm-league director for the Braves, concurred on the compliment with this remark: "I think he has the best talent, based on potential, in the National League."

During 1980 this budding superstar hit .281, was third in the National League with thirty-three home runs, and tied his Club lead with eighty-nine RBIs. He was named to the All-Star National League Team with fellow Mormon Ray Knight of Cincinnati. Through four seasons Murphy hit ninety home runs (through 1981) and was a leader in RBIs. Thus far in the 1982 season, he is the National League leader in home runs and RBIs.

Murphy had a change in his life when he met outfielder Barry Bonnell, an active Mormon, while the two were teammates on the Braves' Greenwood South Carolina Farm Club. After talking with Bonnell about some of the great

116

Mormon principles, Dale decided he wanted to join the
Church, and was baptized by Bonnell in August 1975. He
claims that since then his life has been changed for the better
by strict adherence to the Church's principles. He says, "I
think the Church has improved my attitude toward the game
of baseball as a career and life in general. I think I have a
better outlook on life, a better purpose for being here. I don't
take things for granted because I know I'm here for a
purpose." With that change of heart, he further says, "Being a
Mormon has greatly enhanced my athletic career in many
ways, but there is one specific reason: playing baseball now
has a deeper meaning than just trying to make a lot of money

and to get on television. I feel I have a special message to share—that of the Church of Jesus Christ being restored in these last days—and I want to use my career in getting that message to as many people as I can." With that remarkable attitude he has been a part of several "Mormon Nights." In Atlanta, Kansas City, and other areas, such "nights" have been organized to emphasize the LDS concept of family unity and to admonish the fans to follow the teachings of Christ, and in so doing, to be unafraid and valiant. Thousands of Mormons have attended these events. Dale Murphy, Barry Bonnell, Paul Dunn, Hartman Rector, Jr., Vern Law, and others have participated on these extraordinary occasions to reach millions of people by radio and in the stadiums in the great missionary cause.

Commenting further on the change in his life after becoming a Mormon Dale says, "It keeps me at a constant emotional level. Baseball is an emotional game and an everyday thing. Some nights you're on top of the world when you get the winning hit, but you can't drain yourself emotionally on the bad nights." One of the factors he has found to be important in his new way of living is self-discipline. He says, "Self-discipline is difficult to master, and there are times when temptation to stray from the Church's lofty principles can be great. Some of the things took a little adjusting to on my part and some of the things I'm still working on. But it's not that difficult [to live clean] once you know there's a higher reason for doing it. Once you know it's a commandment you have a better incentive to do it."

Murphy does his best to avoid temptations that come in the way of athletes. He dated LDS girls before his temple marriage to Nancy Thomas in 1979 and avoided going to places where living as a good Christian would be difficult. He says, "I think the moral and spiritual code that is followed as a member of the Church teaches one discipline. I've noticed that good hitters are disciplined hitters. They don't swing at very many bad pitches, and when they get a good pitch to hit, boy, watch out! They let it go! I believe the gospel teaches us that discipline. We are taught not to pursue the material things extensively or engage in things that will harm ourselves or others; but when there is good to be done, watch out! Go after good with all your heart and all you've got. Discipline in the gospel helps me, because without it control over one's self is impossible. An athlete won't be able to use his physical energies in the best possible way. Instead of channeling his energy toward a goal, the lack of discipline will gradually drain that energy away."

As an active major-league player, Dale finds that it is important to keep in good condition both physically and mentally. He says, "Mentally I try to relax. I think there are a lot of pressures, and if one lets these pressures build up, it is hard to be happy, to be yourself, and to perform to your best capabilities. It is important to read good, uplifting literature to be inspired and to get that 'good' feeling. LeGrand Richards has a great saying: 'For every worry under the sun, there is a remedy or there is none; if there is one, go and find it; if there is none, never mind it.'"

Dale confesses that his body is in much better shape most of the time than his spirit. He says, "Sometimes I have to think twice about how important I make my physical exercise programs. I tend to give my spiritual exercise program second billing."

As a successful athlete he counsels that there are three major factors that are important for achievement: "(1) Have a positive mental attitude. (2) Work hard! I once heard someone say, 'You shouldn't have hired out, if you didn't want to work.' (3) Gain the desire to succeed." He also feels that it is important to take care of the body, eat right, and stay in good physical condition. He advises listening to people of experience and wisdom. In assessing his own personal accomplishments, he says, "The realization of the power of one's attitude toward the accomplishment of a desired goal is all important. It has been said, 'Athletics (or anything for that matter) is 90 percent mental and 10 percent physical.' I'd wager it's more than 90 percent. It's your mind that controls anything you want to do. It's those guys with the mental 'toughness,' the calmness, the concentration, and the thought control who will succeed. I've learned the importance of that truth. Now it's up to me to develop it to the fullest extent."

Thankful for his own conversion, Dale has gained the spirit of missionary work and was instrumental in the conversion of Ray Knight, Cincinnati Reds third baseman.

Dale Murphy, outstanding baseball player and outfielder for the Atlanta Braves, is using his athletics as a great missionary tool in the accomplishment of newfound goals in his profession and life.

LELEI FONOIMOANA

All-American and Olympic Swimmer

California Junior Olympics champion, fifty yards, backstroke, 1972

California Junior Olympics, second place, one hundred yards, backstroke, 1972

National Junior Olympics, second place, backstroke, fifty yards, 1972

Fifteenth place nationally, 100-meter backstroke, 1973

American record, 400-meter medley relay team, 1974

Third place Olympic trials, 100-meter butterfly, 1976

Seventh place, Olympic Games in Montreal, 100-meter butterfly, 1976

AIAW Regionals:

Champion, 100- and 200-yard butterfly, 200- and 400-yard individual medley (IM), 1977

Champion, 200-yard IM and 200-yard butterfly, 1978

Champion, 50- and 100-yard butterfly, 1979

AIAW Nationals: Eleven all-American citations, four years:

Five all-American citations, 1977
Three all-American citations, 1978
Two all-American citations, 1979
One all-American citation, 1981
First BYU woman point winner at a national meet

BYU Olympian, Lelei Fonoimoana, is the first woman athlete from Brigham Young University to win all-American honors each of her four collegiate years.

This remarkable Olympic swimmer received her start at home under the training of her father, Alio. He carefully tutored all of his family in swimming and other sports as they were growing up. Lelei and her family won multiple trophies in athletics. As a thirteen-year-old in 1973, Lelei won first place in three separate events during an annual international surf festival at Manhattan Beach, California. At that time she beat fifty other participants in the two-mile rough-water swim from Hermosa Beach to Manhattan Beach (her fifteen-year-old sister Debbie placed second and her mother placed third in the senior women's category). Besides the rough-water victory, during the same afternoon she took first place in the quarter-mile open-water event. Then, with a boy teammate, she won the quarter-mile race for inflated "surfmats." Earlier during the day she had broken a bone in her foot when alighting from a bicycle.

In 1972 in Junior Olympics and AAU competition, she placed first and second in the 50- and 100-meter backstroke for California and second and fifth nationally. In junior high, she and her sister Debbie won decathlon honors four consecutive years.

Lelei's great-grandfather, a Samoan gentleman named Opapo, was one of the first two Islanders to be converted to the LDS faith over two generations ago. His great strength, conviction, and faith in the gospel passed on to this great competitor.

In 1973 Lelei took fifteenth place in the nation in the 100-meter backstroke. During the same year she went to the United States Volleyball Nationals in Hawaii. In 1974 she swam one leg of the 400-meter medley relay team that set an American record. In 1976 she took thirteenth place in the nation in the 100-meter butterfly. She placed third in the Olympic trials in the 100-meter butterfly. She then competed in the Olympic Games in Montreal in this same event to become the seventh-best in the world with a 1:1.95 finish. She missed winning a medal by five-tenths of a second. In 1977, as a freshman at BYU she was the AIAW regional champion in the 200- and 400-yard individual medley (IM) and the 100-and 200-yard butterfly. At the AIAW National Swimming Championships in 1977, Lelei entered five events and won an all-American citation in each one. She placed third in the 100-yard butterfly, eleventh in the 200-yard butterfly, third in the 100-yard IM, second in the 200-yard IM, and third in the 400-yard IM (breaking the AIAW record). She won a total of sixty-four points for BYU—the first points ever won by a BYU woman swimmer at a national meet. She is credited with helping her team to finish eighteenth out of 120 teams entered.

In 1978 she won the 200-yard IM and 200-yard butterfly at the regionals and won three more all-American awards at the College AIAW Nationals. She placed second in the 100-yard butterfly with a clocking of 55.38 (breaking the national record of 55.68), first in the consolation 200-yard IM (this was an outstanding achievement, since she swam the 100-yard butterfly and the 200-yard IM back to back), and sixth in the 200-yard butterfly.

Lelei majored in physical education while establishing an enviable record for the Cougars. Through 1981 she earned eleven all-American citations. As a junior at the Nationals she won seventh place in the 50-meter butterfly (25.66) and tenth place in the 100-meter butterfly (56.19), after winning both the 50- and 100-yard butterfly in the regionals. During the 1979-80 season she was absent from the Cougar team while training for the 1980 Moscow Olympics, a dream that faded because of the world political problems, but in 1981 she captured another all-American citation in the 100-yard butterfly in the AIAW Nationals (53.4 sec.).

Lelei generally trained as much as six hours a day, swimming sometimes three times a day, with long rests in between. While at BYU she swam at least two hours six mornings a week and two hours or longer in the afternoons—about eight miles a day. She also ran from four to six miles or did jazz dancing exercises one and a half hours per day. She usually did 200 sit-ups a day and stretches for at least half an hour.

Lelei thinks an athlete should eliminate all negative self-talk, concentrate on reaching goals, eat a well-balanced diet, and get sufficient rest at night to maintain physical excellence.

Lelei's strong spirit and determination have convinced her that through the work of her mind, she can make her body do amazing things. She credits much of her success to the influence of her Heavenly Father. She says, "Anything you want to achieve is possible if you want to sacrifice for it. It's important to have a high self-esteem, to believe in yourself. You must have a strong self-motivation or you will never succeed."

Her mother and her Olympic coach Jim Montrella have had much faith that Lelei would someday set American records and do great things. She credits much of her success to them.

Lelei feels that being a Mormon has kept her from getting involved socially with the wrong people, which might have ended her athletic career. She says, "Ninety-eight percent of those around me smoked dope, took drugs, sniffed cocaine, and drank. Swimming kept me so involved I never had time to get into anything else."

A personal conviction has pierced Lelei's heart and soul since she received further direction from her patriarch. She says, "I know now since I received my patriarchal blessing that my talents of swimming come directly from my Father in Heaven. He meant for me to succeed, and so I did. His Spirit has been strong with me since I was very young. I love my Heavenly Father more than anyone else, and know that it's through His will that I succeed. As long as I do my part and try to work hard, He helps me endure the pain and pressures. I am promised that if I live righteously, I will always succeed, and therefore I strive that much harder to be an example for Him and to all the world."

Lelei Fonoimoana is an all-American girl and gold-medal Mormon.

BOB RICHARDS

National Steeplechase Champion

Bloomfield Hills High School (Michigan), 1961-64:

Regional and conference champion, 880-yard run, 1962-63

Regional and conference champion, one-mile run, two-mile run, 1963-64

Michigan all-state champion, cross-country run, 1963

Michigan all-state champion, one-mile run (4:16), 1964

Detroit News Award as the most outstanding high school track athlete in Michigan, 1963-64

Brigham Young University, 1964-68:

Beehive Invitational cross-country champion, 1964

Annual Colorado Relays champion (mile team and distance medley), 1965

U.S. Track and Field Annual Federation 3,000-Meter Steeplechase champion, 1966

National (NCAA) all-American 3,000-meter steeplechase champion (8:51.6), 1966

Kenner Kartchner Award as the highest-rated track man by the NCAA, 1966-67

BYU's "most inspirational track man," 1967-68

WAC champion, three events (three mile, one mile, 3000-meter steeplechase), 1968

Participant, U.S. Olympic Trials, 1968

BYU touring European track team, 1965, 1968

115 Races (78 track meets), 1964-68:

42 first-place victories

83 percent first-, second-, or third-place victories

BYU Hall of Fame, 1977

Robert L. Richards was not only a national champion and one of the greatest middle distance and distance runners in Cougar history, but was a spiritual champion as well. He was known as an "individual who has the rare gift of giving you an emotional lift,...a person who through continuous association makes you smile privately upon sight and elevates a saddened spirit."

This track star, who was born in Detroit, Michigan, became one of the Automotive State's best prepsters as a runner. As a sophomore and junior at Bloomfield Hills High School, he was the regional and conference champion in the 880-yard run in both 1962 and 1963, and the regional and conference champion in the one-mile and two-mile runs in 1963 and 1964. As a senior he was the Michigan all-state champion in the cross-country run and also the all-state champion in the one-mile run (4:16). Competing in the

National Senior AAU Cross-Country Run in 1963, he won twelfth place. He was voted the Most Outstanding Athlete at Bloomfield Hills High School during his senior year and was also given the Detroit News Award as the "Most Outstanding High School Track Athlete" in his state. Although he had already been named the state champion in the cross-country run during the fall of his senior year, and was senior class treasurer and high school representative to the Birmingham City Council, he also served as his seminary class president.

He was looking forward to the state track meet, but three days before that championship meet he came down with the flu. Disappointed at the time, he later said, "I remember thinking, how could this happen to me? I have done everything that is right.... In this weakened condition I thought for sure I had lost my chance to compete. But with all my anticipation and strong desire to represent my school, coach, parents, and Church, I just couldn't give up. While searching for a way, I recalled the power of the priesthood and the privilege of a father's blessing. The very thought gave me new strength—how good it felt. This was the first time I had ever needed a blessing, for health and strength had always been mine." Bob approached his father and received a blessing that he might have health and strength and perform his best. Although he gradually improved, he was still weak just before the race. With a prayer in his heart that he might perform his best, he became the state champion in the mile run—still running a fever. He remarked later, "I was extremely happy that day while also realizing that there was power in the priesthood. It was not in having a miracle, but by understanding a simple principle, that through faith and effort one will be strengthened and guided."

Although the University of Michigan had offered this brilliant high school state champion a full-ride scholarship, this nephew of Michigan's Governor George Romney accepted a scholarship at Brigham Young University and became one of the Cougars' outstanding champions. During his four years at BYU from 1964 through 1968, he ran 115 races in 78 track meets. Of those many enduring distance runs, he was the champion 42 times. Not only that, but he took either first, second, or third place in 83 percent of his races. His performance eventually propelled him into national recognition. His wins, places, and shows are too numerous to enumerate, but his major achievements are significant. As a freshman he became the Beehive Invitational cross-country champion and was a champion in the Annual Colorado Relay (mile team and distance medley). As a sophomore he was the Intermountain AAU cross-country champion and also the WAC cross-country champion. He blossomed as a steeple-chase runner, though most of his experience had been in the 880, one-mile, two-mile, and cross-country events.

In the spring of 1966 he competed in the United States Track and Field Federation Championships in Terre Haute, Indiana—only his third time to compete in the steeplechase. Although he had some difficulty judging his pace because of the hurdles, he ran his heart out and became the champion. In that unfortunate race, however, he struck his right knee on a hurdle and developed water on the knee. He was informed by the physician that, because of internal bleeding, it would be at least a month before he would be able to run again. With the NCAA meet only a week away, he was sick at heart. He said, "The whole thing weighed very heavily on me, as heavy as any experience has in my life. I can even remember the disappointment on Coach Robison's face when the doctor told him....I wanted to be in the NCAA meet more than anything in the world. I loved BYU and highly respected and admired my coaches. I just had to run for them!" The following Sunday he had much time to meditate about his predicament. He recalled, "I spent that Sunday walking along the banks of the Wabash River thinking about my life, my parents, the Church, my Father in Heaven. I tried putting it all together, thinking about the principles I had been taught through Primary, Sunday School, MIA, and Priesthood. Then it confronted me so strongly that one more time I needed the help of that priesthood. But it seemed now, being a university student, more difficult to ask for a blessing. I don't know if I didn't have as much faith or if I was just questioning every-thing. I knew I couldn't fool myself or be a hypocrite by asking for a blessing and not believing in it. I couldn't just say that's the thing to do, go ask coach for a blessing and this will keep a good Mormon image. I had to believe it was right. More than that, I had to know I would be blessed from it. So I was really calling upon myself to come up with substantial faith. It was a real testing period for me as I spent that morning meditating and praying. I questioned and chal-lenged myself, asking my Father in Heaven for strength and understanding. I grew and gained belief as I came up with my

answer. I knew that no matter what would happen, having a blessing was what I wanted most of all.

"I returned to the motel and asked Coach Robison if he would give me a blessing, and of course he answered yes. What a fantastic experience to be on a university team and be able to turn to your coach, a man who has the power and priesthood of our Father in Heaven, and ask for a blessing. As far as I was concerned, that made our track team a very special one. I asked two other team members to assist our coach."

Bob recalls distinctly the words of the blessing: "Heavenly Father, bless Bob that he will be a fine representative of the

Church, university, of himself and family. If it be Thy will, we pray that he will be returned to full health and strength and be able to compete." Bob later commented, "Basically this blessing put the responsibility back on my shoulders." The next several days he meditated, prayed, and walked. The day before the race he went walking. He later said, "I could hardly feel the pain and just had to try to jog. Though it hurt, I could do it and maintain control. I went into a full run. Oh, did it feel great to move fast! I wanted to run and train that whole day. I will never forget that night. I ran the steeplechase so many times in my mind, I could hardly count. They were for real, as I would be covered with sweat and I won them all. To help my hurdling, I had come up with a good mental picture of the form I needed with a verbal phrase to remind me of each movement: 'kick, bend, drive, snap.' I kept repeating it over and over."

Just before the finals he had victory on his mind, but in his heart he was grateful just to be running. He was ready to compete and to give his all. He planned to run the whole race fast and not leave victory to a sprint at the end. He told his coach to yell when he saw him falter or when his competitors started to gain on him. He was not going to look behind no matter what. Later, he exclaimed, "It was the greatest moment of my life. I started a little fast, then settled into a stride as I took the lead. My first hurdle, could I do it? Oh it felt good. I had form and could follow through. I kept it going, keeping myself alert, thinking every moment. With less than a mile to go, I called out to Coach Robby, 'Are they gaining on me?' He answered, 'No, you look fine.' The next lap the same reply. I couldn't believe it, they had to make their move now. Then I thought, if I were a coach I would say you look fine also. Even if it wasn't true, it would keep one psyched. The next lap I yelled out, 'Tell me the truth,' but it was the same reply. Running on a rubberized track, I couldn't hear or feel how close they could possibly be. It was my final lap, and I picked up my stride a little—not having any unusual kick as I recall. Then it was the homestretch, finish line, national collegiate champion, all-American! This thrill became even greater when I turned around to see my nearest competitor, Jack Bacheler, coming off the final turn, some eighty yards behind me.

"Stardom, with all its glory, unfolded. Newspaper reporters, picture-taking, offers of free track shoes from various companies became my new experience. It was all very exciting, but still I kept my thoughts on my parents, Church, and university with an expression of gratitude to my Father in Heaven. I think sometimes we wish life would stop at these happy moments, but not so, for it continues with its challenges."

Bob Richards became the 3,000-meter NCAA steeplechase champion (8:51.6)!

As a junior, Bob captured the Mount Sac Relays and Compton Invitational 3,000-meter steeplechase, was the WAC cross-country champion, and won many meets. As a senior he was the Beehive Invitational mile and 880 champion and captained the Cougar track team. He received the Wayne Hales Award as the athlete that "most exemplifies spirituality, leadership, and academics." He also won the Cougar Club Memorial Scholar-Athlete Award. As a junior he was BYU's high-point track man, and as both a junior and senior he was BYU's "most inspirational trackman" (awarded by the team) and the Downtown Coaches' "outstanding trackman." During his junior year, while competing in the NCAA finals held in Provo, he had a disappointing accident. The "leather-lunged defending champion of steeplechase" was winning his race, when one and a half laps before the finish he injured his knee, costing him the championship. He finished the race, however, just barely able to walk over the last hurdle. At that championship meet he was featured on the NCAA Track and Field Championship program with such greats as Jim Ryun, Bob Seagren, Randy Matson, and Tommy Smith. He was unable to compete in the 1968 NCAA meet because of a ruling that disallowed competition more than three years.

He capped his career in college at the WAC championships in Laramie, Wyoming, by competing in three events. He won first place in all three events, the steeplechase, the mile run, and the three-mile run, a phenomenal and exciting conclusion of four great college years.

While in college Bob had the opportunity to compete with the BYU touring European track team in both 1965 and 1968. He was also a participant in the U.S. Olympic trials in 1968, but did not make the final team. One of his most prestigious honors was the Kenner Kartchner Award, which he was given as "the highest rated trackman by the NCAA" during the 1966-67 year.

Richards was graduated in geology from BYU in 1969. Two things might be said of his college experience: (1) His father, a Tahitian mission president, and BYU were thrilled that he attended BYU; (2) Michigan State University lost one of the greatest potential tracksters possible. The champion's own words best clarify his feelings: "I will always be appreciative of the fine people I met in athletics for their example and unique personalities. I was always proud to represent BYU in competition because of the support of the students and professors. My desire to win and pride for BYU were greatly enhanced by my respect and admiration for Clarence Robison and Sherald James. They are two of the finest coaches, but more importantly two of the finest men, I have ever met."

After college he spent five years in the Air Force. His achievements continued. He was the wing chapel representative and in charge of the spiritual activity of fourteen hundred men and women. He received national recognition for a fund drive to "have a heart" for the purpose of helping Sung Won Kim receive open-heart surgery. He was a pilot and instructor of pilots. While at Williams Air Force Base in Arizona, he dated and baptized his wife, Argene. He also had the opportunity to participate in some degree in track. In 1972 in the Air Training Command Championships he became the champion in the 880, mile, and three-mile run and took second in the steeplechase. With only three months to get into shape, he participated in the Olympic trials, winning his heat in Eugene, Oregon, but finishing eighth in the finals, which was not sufficient to go to Munich for the Olympics. He commented later, "This was soon forgotten with the birth of our son Aaron Robert." He also participated in the AAU Championships.

Bob's best times in the many events in which he competed throughout his track career were remarkable. He ran the mile in 4:01.2 (1962), the 880 in 1:52.1 (1972), and the steeplechase in 8:38 (1972). In 1977 he was honored by being named to the BYU Athletic Hall of Fame.

As a production geologist with Union Texas Petroleum (Allied Chemical Company), Bob still believes in active exercise, doing warmup and stretching exercises, running one to two miles, and playing tennis whenever he can. He has reduced his exercise schedule from his prime, in which he exercised and ran six to ten miles a day before breakfast and worked out three hours each afternoon in a personalized track program. He has always believed in taking care of his body. He says, "My body is a barometer to the well-being of my spirit. Learn physical discipline and you will gain spiritual freedom. Care and respect for my body develops a spiritual pride. The reverse is also true—be spiritually in tune and you will want to be physically fit."

He maintains that the most important element that contributed to his success was having parents who taught him love of life and instilled in him the understanding that "self-discipline is freedom and great joy." He declares, "Being a Mormon had a great effect on my athletic experiences. I developed in wanting to stand up for the physical, ethical, and moral principles of the gospel, and living these principles has made me a better athlete. I had confidence in knowing how I would act and perform regardless of the circumstances. My greatest asset in being a Mormon was having peace of mind. I knew who I was, where I was going, and that my Heavenly Father cared. My athletic experiences have made me a better Mormon."

Addressing would-be champions, he says, "My personal counsel is: (1) Gain an understanding of one's Divine origin and great self-worth. This does not mean an attitude of 'I am the greatest,' but instead, a foundation of *wanting* self-discipline. It also develops the understanding that failure or defeat can never destroy you. (2) Learn to develop standards and set goals. Work on implementing your goals into a daily program. (3) Be honest with yourself and uphold priorities."

Mindful of the need for continuous spiritual control and development, Bob has maintained his activity in the Church. In high school he was a seminary president for the Pontiac Ward, but college kept him active as an elders quorum group leader, Sunday School teacher, MIA president, instructor of the teacher development course, and a counselor in the elders quorum presidency. While in the Air Force, as a result of his activity in the Church (Sunday School teacher, elders quorum advisor, deacons quorum advisor, Scoutmaster), his military activity, and his athletic participation, he was named the Williams Air Force Base Junior Officer of the Quarter, the highest honor bestowed on any junior officer at Willie. He has since served as an elders quorum president and is presently one of the seven presidents of seventy in the Odessa Texas Stake.

This great athlete faced the same challenges most athletes face, as well as the more spiritual challenges that arise in the life of a Mormon athlete. Bob has done his own thinking about running on Sunday. He was once faced with the decision to compete in the AAU Championships on a Sunday. He later said, "I told them I would have to think about it and call them later...I spent the next day trying to decide and make a commitment about running on Sunday. I had always respected the Sabbath Day and even felt strong about training on Sunday. In a discussion with my parents, they had said the decision was between me and my Father in Heaven and they would give me all their support. It was my responsibility to decide." Facing that dilemma, he sought the advice of a good friend of the family, President N. Eldon Tanner. The president answered his query, "Young man, that is between you and your Father in Heaven. But if you were my son, I would ask you not to run." He then made the decision not to compete on Sunday and feels that he has been respected for that decision ever since.

Bob says about the valuable experience he has had as an athlete, "Without a doubt the most valuable thing I have acquired would have to be the understanding I have gained about my relationship with my Father in Heaven and Elder Brother Jesus Christ. Just to know that there is a Father in Heaven is a great source of strength, but then to know of the principles of eternal life and exaltation which gives an unlimited value to self-discipline and dedication, life becomes quite a pleasant challenge.

"To do as one whims or act on a dare is a sign of a wandering and weakened self, but to carry out what your intellect or spirit has testified is true is the expression of direction and strength, and I must say, the foundation of happiness."

A spiritual and inspiring athlete, Bob Richards has won the hearts of track competitors and fans everywhere as an endurance runner with a champion's attitude and a champion's performance.

MEL HUTCHINS

All-American Basketball Player and NBA All-Star

Brigham Young University 1947-51:

Three years all-conference basketball, 1948-51

All-district seven, 1951

Consensus all-American, 1950-51

Member NIT championship team, 1951

NIT all-tournament team, 1951

Most Valuable Player, East-West Game, 1951

Professional basketball, 1951-58:

NBA number-one draft choice, 1951

NBA Rookie of the Year, 1952

NBA Rebounding Crown (tie), 1952

NBA All-Star Team, six of seven years

437 professional games, 11.1 average, two years Milwaukee, four years Ft. Wayne, one year New York Knickerbockers

Listed in *Who's Who in Basketball*

BYU Athletic Hall of Fame, 1976

National Association of Basketball
Silver Anniversary All-American
Team, 1976

Mel B. Hutchins has rightfully earned a reputation as one of the most colorful of all basketball players ever to grace Brigham Young University. The name "Marvelous Mel" describes his play and expertise.

Interestingly enough, at Monrovia High School in Arcadia, California, Mel was hardly interested in basketball. He lettered in both football and track during his junior and senior years as an outstanding player. As a trackster he could high jump 6 feet 3 inches and was a high hurdler. He was a first-string end in football during his junior and senior years, and won a football scholarship while averaging two touchdowns per game, during his senior year. Although he sincerely intended to play football at BYU, his course changed rapidly. He began shooting basketball on the courts while waiting for a football injury to heal. Coach Floyd Millet recognized the potential of this 6-foot 6-inch 205-pound embryo hoopster. Mel decided to give basketball a shot and ended up solely as a basketball player. The next few years Marvelous Mel created an impressive image of BYU basketball. He was all-conference from 1948 through 1951, capping his senior season by being named a consensus all-American by all major wire services, Helms Athletic Foundation, *Look* magazine, *Sporting News* and Converse. He teamed with Roland Minson to lead the Cougars to the NIT championship in 1951 and a fourth-place finish in the NCAA National Tournament. During his four years of BYU basketball, his team won the conference championship three times. In Skyline territory he was affectionately known as the Big Elf, but opponents probably knew him by less endearing names. As he was picked for the NCAA all-district seven team and given all-American honors, *Look* magazine reported, "Probably the most stylish player in the country is Mel Hutchins. Tricky in the pivot, accurate from outside, facile underneath the basket, the Brigham Young ace moves with a graceful, self-contained change-of-pace and takes charge of a game. For example, against Niagara in Buffalo, he caged 12 field goals in 25 attempts, and broke up three Niagara rallies

by his defensive maneuvers." That description of his play describes the gifted and graceful Hutchins precisely.

In 1951 he became the NBA's number-one draft choice and then went on to excel in professional basketball for seven years. His first year, 1952, he was named the NBA Rookie of the Year and tied for the NBA Rebounding Crown (with Larry Foust) with a 13.3 average. He was named to the all-star team six times in his seven years of play. He spent two years with Milwaukee, four years with Ft. Wayne, and one year with the New York Knickerbockers. Hutchins was one of the best defensive players in the league, and was the Pistons' second-best scorer and rebounder with a 12.4 scoring average and 571 rebounds. The New York Knickerbockers had been trying to lay their hands on Hutchins, the great all-around player, ever since he joined the pros. While with the Ft. Wayne Pistons (Detroit Pistons) his team won the Western Division title three times. In April 1957 the Knicks and Pistons finally confirmed one of the most important player trades in league history. During the 1957-58 season, Mel injured his knee in the thirteenth game of the year and retired from pro basketball at the end of the season. His excellence in basketball earned him a place in *Who's Who in Basketball.*

Although Mel didn't really begin his basketball career until college, hard work and desire proved to be substitutes for his lack of previous experience in basketball. He spent at least two hours every day working on his sport. Understanding what it takes to be a winner, he now comments, "The spirit drives the body, and a healthy body enjoys a healthy spirit." He relates his own athletic success to "the sheer love of competition against the best—both in athletics and life itself." Admonishing others to succeed, he says, "Strive for the best competition possible, for this is the only way to better oneself. Enjoy and learn defeat, because unless we taste defeat we are not in strong enough competition. We use such a minute part of our physical and mental strength that we have to learn to draw on the portion that is unused or virtually dormant."

About his membership in the Church, Mel says, "This aspect of my life helped my competitors to respect my beliefs and trust in my honesty, thereby allowing us to enjoy competition on a much cleaner and more honest basis. This has been true of all sports in which I competed."

Presently Mel is a real-estate developer in the Los Angeles area, plays tennis, is active in basketball, and enjoys water skiing and jogging. A highly competitive golfer, he is one of the outstanding linksters in northern California with a handicap of one. Mel's competitors respect him highly. He says, "I play golf with a group of sixteen low-handicap golfers. Many of them cheat because they play for high stakes. I am the only one who is allowed to write down scores on the sheet and distribute any winnings or losses." That tribute alone is worth all of the athletic honors one might achieve.

A great honor was bestowed upon Mel in 1976—he was chosen for the National Association of Basketball Silver

Anniversary All-American Team. He was also elected to the BYU Athletic Hall of Fame in 1976.

Most of Mel's activity in the Church has been related to teaching, and he is presently first counselor in his ward Sunday School presidency. Two of his children are on missions. He is proud of his family members, who have accomplished some remarkable things. His sister Colleen has won many honors: BYU homecoming queen in 1947, Miss University of Utah in 1950, Miss Utah in 1951, and finally Miss America in 1951. She married another great professional basketball star, Dr. Ernest Vandeweghe, and their son Kiki was a star for UCLA. Colleen was an excellent swimmer, and her daughter, Tauna, competed for BYU and was an Olympian in the 1976 competition at Montreal. Mel's son, Matt, averaged twenty-two points a game as a high-school cager before filling a mission.

Mel Hutchins, great Cougar, all-American, and professional basketball player, is a fierce competitor in athletics and upholds morality and honesty in his personal life.

WADE BELL

National 880 Champion and Pan-American Games Champion

Ben Lomond High School (Ogden, Utah) track star, 1960-63:

Region II 880 champion (1:57.0), 1963

Region II mile champion (4:24.5), 1963—new record

Utah State 880 champion, 1963

Utah State mile champion, 1963

Oregon State University 1963-67:

NCAA 880 champion (1:47.6), 1967

National AAU 880 champion (1:46.1), 1967

National 1,000-meter champion (2:18.7), 1967—new American record

First Mormon to break four-minute mile (3:59.8), 1966

Pan-American Games Olympic gold medalist, 800 meter run (1:49.2), 1967

National AAU 880 champion (1:45.5), 1968

1968 Olympian

Wade Bell was one of the fastest middle-distance runners in America. He also holds the distinction of being the first Mormon athlete to break the four-minute barrier in the mile run.

Bell was a star track performer at Ben Lomond High School in Ogden from 1960 to 1963. His high school track coach, Chic Hislop, predicted that Wade would become the state's greatest prep miler. As a senior in Region II performance, Bell set a new mile mark in 4:24.5, fulfilling that prediction. At that same meet he was also the 880-yard champion, finishing in 1:57 flat. A week later he was again the state champion in both races.

In the fall of 1963, Wade entered the University of Oregon. He was told by his track coach, Bill Bowerman, that it would be necessary for him to train on Sundays. The Mormon freshman said, "I'm a Mormon boy and I don't train on Sunday." His coach replied, "Sorry, we do here." Undaunted, this courageous athlete answered, "If you'll allow me to have my Sundays to attend Church, I'll be the finest half-miler Oregon ever had." Wade fulfilled that prophetic statement by becoming not only the finest half-miler Oregon ever had, but a national champion and one of the fastest athletes in the world. Along his way to great achievements in 1966 he broke the four-minute mile, establishing his lifetime best in that event at 3:59.8. He was the fifty-ninth track star to break the four-minute barrier. As a senior in 1967, he set several new records. In the 880-yard run (half-mile) he set a new record of 1:47.6 for the Athletic Association of Western Universities (Pacific Coast). It was the fastest time for this run during the 1966-67 collegiate track season. He won the 880-yard NCAA Track Meet at Provo, Utah, to become the national champion (1:47.6). A week later he won the National AAU 880-yard Championship in Bakersfield, California, in 1:46.1, the third-fastest 880 run in history. His time was second only to Peter Snell of New Zealand (1:45.1) and Jim Ryun of Kansas (1:44.9) and was only 1.2 seconds off the world record in the half-mile run. He also established a new American record in the 1,000-meter run (2:18.7), only two seconds behind the world record. As the American champion he competed in the Pan American Games in Canada in 1967, where he was a gold medalist in the 800-meter run with a time of 1:49.2. He had previously run this race in 1:45 flat. In competition in the 1968 Olympics in Mexico City, he failed to

win a medal. In 1968 he clocked the fastest 800-meter race in the world with a time of 1:45.5.

Wade described his philosophy of running in an interview published in the booklet, "Oregon Today." He said, "Track is a recreation and a proving ground. It's a place where my mind can make my body do something it doesn't want to do, where I can say I did ten 440's today in 60 seconds each, that the last four were so hard I thought my legs would drop off, but that my mind kept me going. It gives me great satisfaction knowing I have mind over matter." He was noted for his famed kick, which was like a passing gear in an automobile.

In concluding his race he would keep up a fast pace for half a lap, and then would sprint for the final 220 yards. This tended to demoralize the other runners, because they were being passed so fast and suddenly found themselves with a huge gap to overcome.

Bell participated in numerous track meets thoughout the world and has spoken to young people in various meetings of the Church, explaining how being a Mormon has helped him in athletics. While establishing his record performances, he was graduated from the Institute of Religion. He served as president of the LDS Student Association during his senior year. The director of the Institute of Religion at the University of Oregon said, "Wade is a tremendous young man who never shirks from his testimony or desire to be active. If a conflict develops in his mind, the Church is always first." That is an outstanding tribute to a Mormon athlete. Bell has stressed the importance of prayer in competition and asked the Lord for help before each meet and thanked him for his goodness after each meet. He says, "The faith and knowledge I've gained in the Church, knowing there is a God and that he blesses us, have been a great comfort to me."

C. Wade Bell, one of the fastest middle-distance champions of the world, the first Mormon to break the four-minute mile barrier, has proven that following gospel principles can enhance athletic attainments and inspire respect in competition.

MIKE YOUNG

National and Pan-American Games Wrestling Champion and Wrestling Coach of the Year

Idaho Falls High School:

Undefeated high school wrestler

Idaho State High School champion, 1960-62

Utah State Golden Gloves boxing champion, 1962

Western regional boxing champion, 1962

Brigham Young University 1962-66: Wrestling

WAC champion (137 pounds), 1963

WAC champion (145 pounds), 1966

Pan-American Games gold medalist (138 pounds), 1967

Third place, world championships, 1967, 1970

National AAU champion, 1969-70

Third place, World Invitational Tournaments, 1971-72

United States Federation champion, 1973

Wrestling Coach of the Year, Big Sky Conference, 1973-77
BYU Athletic Hall of Fame, 1977
Coach, United States Wrestling Team, World Games, 1978

Michael M. Young, now the wrestling coach at Boise State University, has one of the most enviable records in wrestling as an Idaho prepster, a Brigham Young University collegian, and a post-collegiate competitor.

Mike started his wrestling career at Idaho Falls High School when he was fifteen years old. Earl Lindley, the football and wrestling coach at the time, tells of a time in the autumn of 1959 when the grappler entered the wrestling room, looking around with bright brown eyes. The coach said, "Did you ever wrestle?" Mike said, "Yeah, some." Lindley answered, "Would you like to come out and wrestle for us?" Mike said, "I might." Two weeks later the young sophomore won his first match and then forty-one straight matches without a defeat to become the Idaho State High School champion in his weight all three years.

Attending BYU on a wrestling scholarship from 1962 to 1966, Mike was one of the best competitors in BYU wrestling history. He was an inspiration to his teammates, winning the WAC 137-pound title as a freshman in 1963 and the WAC 145-pound title as a senior in 1966. Unfortunately he was unable to compete in the conference championships two years because of injuries, and also was unable to compete in the NCAA finals three years because of injuries and a conflict between WAC and NCAA rules. As a senior he was the first BYU athlete to receive the Most Competitive Athlete Award.

Mike was not only a wrestler, but during the interim between wrestling seasons, he boxed for Stan's Club in Orem. He won many boxing bouts and became the Utah Golden Gloves champion and the Western regional champion in 1962. Although he had a broken leg, he still competed in one tournament while dragging his broken leg and cast around the ring, and he won! Of course, everyone present was thoroughly impressed—especially the opponent.

While with the Cougars, Mike was the Arizona Invitational champion in addition to his WAC honors, but after leaving

145

BYU (having majored in advertising and public relations) he continued his wrestling career. In 1967 he entered the Pan-American Games in Winnipeg, Canada, and took home the gold medal. The same year he wrestled in the World Freestyle Wrestling Championships, where he garnered third place. In 1969 and 1970 he was the National AAU champion in his weight division, and again during 1970 was third in the world championships. He also won third place in the World Invitational tournaments in 1971 and 1972 and was the Federation champion of the United States in 1973.

Mike earned his master of science degree from BYU in 1969 and later accepted a job as wrestling coach at Boise State University. He was named Wrestling Coach of the Year in the Big Sky Conference four years in a row, from 1973 to 1977. Along the way he competed for six United States teams, served as a member of the U.S. Olympic Committee and National Wrestling Coaches Association, and was named to coach the United States wrestling team in 1978 for the World Games. In 1977 he was voted to the BYU Athletic Hall of Fame.

Mike has always been an ardent believer in physical conditioning. He has been a constant worker, dedicated to success. He was faithful in good eating habits and getting adequate rest. As an active competitor he ran five miles a day, lifted weights, and wrestled daily, trying to work with three or four fresh wrestlers per session. As a university coach he still wrestles, plays badminton, and participates in casual weight training. He maintains that both the body and the spirit need to be cared for in order to feel good about the "total self." His own self-imposed set of rules for achieving athletic success is commendable. He advises: "(1) Set goals—you must have something to reach for. (2) Develop a workout schedule and try to follow it. (3) You must learn to push yourself—you can't depend on someone else to provide the drive needed to become a champion. (4) Learn to be mentally tough. I believe to a certain degree you can train yourself in this area. The mind is the most important part of being a champion." He credits his own success to "an inner feeling—a very strong desire to succeed."

Presently Mike serves in the Church as a home teacher and an assistant Scoutmaster. His philosophy of success is succinct: "Do the best that you can, live the best that you can, and put your total efforts into achieving your goals."

Mike Young, Idaho Prep and WAC wrestling champion, Golden Gloves boxer, National AAU and Federation champion, Pan-American Games champion, outstanding wrestler in world championships, is an ardent competitor, a fine representative of sports, and one of BYU's all-time favorite athletes.

ELDON FORTIE
("The Phantom")

All-American and
Pro Football Player

Brigham Young University 1959-63:
Freshman and varsity football four
years

All-Conference Scholastic Team,
1961

Selected as outstanding back in
eight out of ten games, 1962

Outstanding back of the Western
Athletic Conference, three weeks,
1962

Associated Press Back of the Week,
November 6, 1962

Sports Illustrated Back of the
Week, November 12, 1962

All-WAC quarterback, 1962

WAC Back of the Year, 1962

Cougars' first bonafide first team all-
American in football, 1962

Fifth leading all-time total yardage
gainer, 1962

Sixth place, National UPI Player of
the Year poll, 1962

Tenth place, Heisman voting, 1962
Dale Rex Memorial Award, 1962-63
BYU Hall of Fame, 1976
Utah Sports Hall of Fame, 1980

Eldon Fortie, the Phantom, will always remain one of Brigham Young University's legendary sports heroes. He earned his unusual nickname because of his knack for darting through holes, shifting direction, and bouncing off tacklers. His name and fame spread through the gridiron world. It is interesting that this nationally recognized athlete was once described in *Sports Illustrated* as a "scrawny 158-pounder who could pass for the water boy."

Eldon played many sports as a young man, and was always a rather thin, freckle-faced, red-haired kid. He has been described as having a heart as big as a football. At Granite High School in Salt Lake City he weighed only 145 pounds as a senior. He was an outstanding athlete, lettering in both basketball and football from 1956 through 1959. As a senior he was cocaptain of the football team and was a good gridder, but was relatively unknown. College recruiters weren't too impressed with him, partly because of his size—six feet 150 pounds—but the girls were impressed, and made him their "Gridiron King." In actuality, his football coach at Granite, LaVell Edwards, was impressed by him and recommended him for college play. He never made all-state, but played on a losing team and had not mastered his full football potential. What he accomplished after his entry into the college scene is a phenomenal story, when one considers that he began as a relatively obscure high-school player and overcame many obstacles.

At age twelve, Fortie was in a severe auto accident, in which he was thrown from a car. Not expected to live, suffering from a severe concussion complicated by internal injuries and significant loss of skin, he fought his way back to health and achievement. His father died when he was in junior high. Later, his own two-month-old child died, and he was plagued with injuries during college. He enjoyed only mediocre success during his first two years, but as a junior began to spark as a tailback in Hal Mitchell's modified single-wing. He

149

had some great games and then was injured while playing against the Utah Redskins, putting him out of commission for four games.

As a senior he came into his own. BYU's "galloping phantom" began making ghostly runs through opposing lines, appearing to be nowhere and everywhere at once. His mere appearance on the football field was enough to send the BYU crowd into a frenzy. His offense became the best in college football. He developed an attribute on the field which few football players master—the ability to cut. His deception as a runner was unprecedented. One opposing player said, "Fortie wouldn't be so hard to stop if you only knew what he was going to do." But the phantom of Provo replied, "Tell the guy not to feel too bad. I never know what I'm going to do. If I see daylight I run. If I see a receiver open, I pass." Coach Hal Mitchell was also impressed and stated, "If Fortie were playing for a big-time team, they'd say he's the greatest player since Jim Thorpe. And that's exactly what he is." Wyoming coach Lloyd Eaton said, "When he's carrying the ball, you better figure on six or eight men getting in on the tackle. He'll wiggle away for sure if you don't."

Although Fortie was a smart player, having made the All-Conference Scholastic Team as a junior, his play seemed to be instinctive. The honors he achieved were innumerable. He was selected the outstanding back in eight out of ten games and was named outstanding back in the Western Athletic Conference three different times (September 22, October 29, November 4). He was chosen Associated Press Back of the Week on November 6, and *Sports Illustrated* Back of the Week on November 12. He led the nation in total offense through most of the football season and ended up second in the nation in total offense (1,963 yards), the fifth leading all-time total yardage gainer. He set twenty-one new BYU records (five single game, eight season, eight career), three conference records, and was selected all-WAC first team quarterback and WAC Back of the Year. He was also chosen to be the WAC Honor Team captain. Because of his many records he became BYU's first bonafide first team all-American. He placed sixth in the national UPI Player of the Year poll and was tenth place in the Heisman voting, just behind Oregon's great quarterback Terry Baker. He was invited to play in the North-South Game in Miami, the All-American Game in Tucson, the Hula Bowl in Hawaii, and the

Coaches' All-American Bowl in post-season play. He was given the Dale Rex Memorial Award for his contributions to Utah athletics, and his jersey, number 40, was formally retired. Fortie was the first player in the school's history to be so honored. As the Newspaper Enterprise Agency's first team all-American selection, the Phantom inspired coach LaVell Edwards to say later, "Eldon was living proof that weight doesn't matter in football." Before his graduation in 1963 Fortie received radio KEYY's award as the Most Valuable Football Player and the Crippled Children's Booster Award for the "athlete who has been most inspirational to the handicapped children."

Eldon decided to play Canadian football for the Edmonton Eskimos, because he didn't want to play football on Sundays, as he would have to do had he signed with the National or American Football League teams. His low weight was actually a factor in professional ball, so after one season he moved full-time into the field of business. He is currently director of a sales department for O.C. Tanner Jewelry.

In 1976 Eldon was elected to the BYU Athletic Hall of Fame. On that occasion one of his most exciting adventures at BYU was retold: "Eldon was the central figure in one of the most electrifying incidents in the history of BYU sports. He sustained a shoulder injury the previous week. The doctor refused to let him dress for the game. Eldon pleaded—the doctor relented, but made Eldon promise he wouldn't play. Grantland Rice could not have written the script more appropriately. The afternoon was cold and bleak. The opponent— the University of Wyoming. The score, 7-0, Wyoming. Late in the first half Eldon convinced the coach that he should be allowed to play. The electricity in the stadium that afternoon as Eldon trotted onto the field has never been duplicated. With Fortie alternating on the carries (his arm strapped to his side for protection), the Cougars moved 48 yards in seven plays. The ball was resting on the five, and the Cougars knew there was only one person to carry it over, the fans knew it, so did Wyoming. Fortie took the ball and headed off-tackle. The Cowboy defenders were ready, and no fewer than five players took a shot at him. But Fortie, as if exerting some kind of supernatural power, wormed his way free and kept plowing toward the end zone, and he went in standing up. Final score—BYU, 14—Wyoming, 7. A memorable victory." Fortie responded, "BYU provided me with a once in a lifetime opportunity, and everything I have I owe to the school and the Church."

In 1978 this great athlete coached an eleven- and twelve-year-old boys' team to the National AAU Finals in Miami. In 1980 he was elected to the Utah Sports Hall of Fame.

Like most Mormon athletes, Eldon has much respect for his body and spirit. He understands their close relationship and that one influences the success of the other. Believing that the body is the temple of the spirit, he has always attempted to keep his body in good physical condition to promote that relationship. He did agility drills, weight lifting, and daily workouts as an active athlete, and presently he plays basketball, tennis, softball, volleyball, and rides a bike.

Reminiscing on his success in athletics, he comments,

"My own success was related to an attitude to do the very best I can in whatever I attempt. Being a Mormon has given me the heritage of a hard-working people, the doctrine of keeping my body fit at all times so it is easier to get in shape, and the self-discipline to draw out the most that my athletic abilities possess. It also offered the facilities of BYU, which made it possible to get an education while participating in athletics." To aspiring athletes he advises, "Play as many sports as you can while you're young. Have fun. If you decide to specialize, then practice. Keep yourself in condition the year around and get good grades in school. Play against the best competition you can as much as possible. Mental attitude is one of the more important areas to work on. Always remember that there are many coaching philosophies and that a good athlete is 'coachable' and is responsive to what the coach is trying to get out of him. Do the very best you can in whatever you do and *don't quit!*"

Eldon has had many opportunities to serve in the Church. Among his callings he has been a priests quorum advisor, ward Aaronic Priesthood president, and stake and region athletic director. He has also served as a high councilor and in a bishopric. He declares, "Mormons have always been known as an industrious, hard-working people with high standards. When people in the business world know that you are an active Mormon, and have high standards, it seems like their expectations of you go up, which makes you try harder to meet those expectations. I have been given several opportunities and jobs because of my high standards and moral ethics." In action and words, he has always challenged the young men of the Church to live their religion and to use the gospel as a basis for their decisions. His own story exemplifies that philosophy.

Eldon Fortie, the Phantom, setter of numerous BYU, WAC, and national football records, BYU's first bonafide first team All-American in football, has finessed his way through holes and barriers to find the daylight and establish himself as one of the legendary figures in Mormon sports history.

NEIL ROBERTS

Phenomenal All-Around Athlete and Champion Coach

Cedar City High School(Utah), 1960-63:

Four-sport letterman (football, basketball, baseball, track)

All-state football, 1961-63

All-state basketball, 1961-63

State champion, three events in track (high jump, javelin, medley relay), 1962

State champion, four events in track (high jump, javelin, broad jump, medley relay), 1963

State broad-jump record of 23 feet 6¾ inches

BYU Invitational all-around track champion (nine events), 1962-63

New record (7,144 points) and first place or tie for first place, all events, 1962

New record (7,343 points), first place, all events, 1963

All-American, three sports (football, basketball, track), 1963

Sports Illustrated High School
Athlete of the Year, 1963

Brigham Young University 1963-67:
Four years college basketball

Member undefeated freshman team,
1964

Member and starting forward WAC
championship team, 1965

Member and starting forward, NIT
championship team, 1966

All-American (honorable mention),
1967

All-Conference All-Academic Team
and team captain, 1967

High school coach 1969-77:

Burley High School (Idaho), 1969

Payson High School (Utah)—Eighth
place, state tournament, 1971

Skyline High School (Salt Lake City),
1971-77:

Athletic director and chairman of
physical education department

Eighty-five percent winning record

Two first place state championship
teams, 1976-77

High School Coach of the Year,
1976-77

Dixie College, 1968-69, 1978-present
BYU Hall of Fame, 1980
National junior college third place,
1979, sixth place, 1982

On April 1, 1963, *Sports Illustrated* recorded, "The greatest prep athlete in the U.S. most likely is Neil Roberts of Cedar City High School, Cedar City, Utah." In the mid-'60s, veteran Tribune sportswriter Bill Coltrin said, "I'll stick my neck out and keep it out when I pick the best high school athlete I've seen in the last 25 years in Utah. That athlete is Neil Roberts."

Roberts believed that concentration on a sport was the single most important "mind-occupier" in preparing for athletic events. He worked out three hours per day running, shooting baskets, and lifting weights. In junior high school he took second place in the 440-yard run at the Brigham Young University Invitational (1960) and captured fourth place in the junior-high low hurdles at Dixie College.

At Cedar City High School he was one of the most dynamic athletes in history, being named the 1963 *Sports Illustrated* High School Athlete of the Year. He made all-state in basketball during his sophomore, junior, and senior years as center or forward, and all-state football as a quarterback during both his junior and senior years. Although he was an outstanding baseball player for the Redmen and had excelled in both football and basketball, such achievements were probably secondary to his track accomplishments. Both as a junior and senior in 1962 and 1963, he participated in the BYU Invitational all-around competition, a sort of "nine-event decathlon," and broke the record both years as he took first place in all events or tied for first. Those nine events included the 100-yard dash, 180-yard low hurdles, 440-yard run, shot put, discus, javelin, high jump, pole vault, and broad jump. As a junior he smashed the record by more than 500 points, scoring 7,144—the only athlete in the history of the all-around competition who scored first or tied for first in all events. Astonishingly enough, he did the same thing as a senior, breaking his own record and scoring 7,343 points in miserably cold weather. At 6 feet 4 inches, 195 pounds, he was a great performer. Bill Coltrin said, "He could high jump about 6 feet 5 inches, broad jump 23 feet 6 inches, hurdle as well as anyone in the state, throw the javelin nearly 200 feet and he once ran the 440 in less than 50 seconds flat.... Every track coach in the country wanted him—especially UCLA where guys like Rafer Johnson and C. K. Yang, both world decathlon champs wanted to help him along."

As a junior in prep competition he was the state champion in three events: high jump, javelin, and as a member of the medley relay team. That year he took second place in the broad jump. Then as a senior he captured first place in all four events while establishing a new state broad jump record of 23 feet 6¾ inches, which stood as a record through 1979. He broke several regional track records, and by the end of his senior year in 1963 had been named a high school all-American in football, basketball, and track. It is no wonder that his jersey, number 31, was retired at Cedar City High School after all of his astonishing accomplishments. A special portion of an honor assembly was devoted to this great athlete and student as he graduated with honors, having been named the Outstanding Male Student and Mr. Touchdown during his senior year. He was also the president of the Boys Organization, president of the Key Club, and president and organizer of the Lettermen's Club. He also graduated from seminary with honors.

Sportswriter Coltrin knew that Roberts wanted to play basketball in college, but he had always hoped that he would major in the decathlon and become the world's champion. Though he was sought after as a college football player, he had his sights set on the hardwoods. He did win some track events as a collegian—third place in the WAC high jump in 1964 and first place in the javelin during several meets in 1965, but basketball was "his baby." He was a member of the freshman basketball team, which was undefeated in 1964. As a sophomore he was the starting forward on the WAC Championship Team and toured with the Cougar team to South America. As a junior he was again starting forward of the team that became the NIT champions in 1966, but in addition was named to the WAC All-Conference Academic Team with the second-highest grade point average. As a cager he was noted for his great speed in the fast-break and averaged better than 52 percent of his shots as both a sophomore and junior. Although he played part of his sports career with an injured knee, in the last league game of his junior season he was put out of commission and unable to play in the NIT. Surgery pretty well took its toll on his track career also. As a senior, however, he was a member of the Co-Champion Cougar basketball team, was named all-conference and the 1967 All-Academic Team Captain, and made *Look* magazine's All-American Team. He earned his bachelor's degree in 1968 with a physical education major and biological science minor, achieving a 3.5 GPA. The year of his graduation he was a teaching assistant in basketball under Stan Watts and was named Physical Education Man of the Year. In 1969 he earned his master's degree with a 3.85 GPA.

After college Neil sparked as a coach. He coached basketball at Burley, Idaho, in 1969 and was the coordinator for physical education for the Cassia County School District that year. In 1971 he was the basketball coach at Payson High School, his team finishing eighth in the Utah State Tournament. From 1971 to 1977 he coached the Skyline High School cagers and served as athletic director and chairman of the physical education department. During these six years, his teams finished eighth once, second once, and won two state championships in 1976 and 1977. His teams had an 85 percent winning record. His back-to-back championships earned him Coach of the Year honors both years. Danny Vranes, later a University of Utah basketball giant, was one of his brightest stars during those championship bouts. Roberts was the Great Southwest Coach of the Year in 1977, and Vranes was named Player of the Year in the Great Southwest Awards. Roberts was President of the Utah High School Coaches Association, coaches representative to the UHSAA, coached in McDonalds All-American Games (Washington, D.C.), and was the Medalist Sports Education Dinner Speaker in 1977. He was Utah coach for the Arizona All-Star Games during 1976 and 1977.

After his successful prep coaching, Roberts was called to be the head basketball coach at Dixie College (St. George, Utah), where he previously coached in 1968 and 1969. His first year, 1978, his team had a 22–6 record, finishing second in Region I. Then, in 1979, Dixie College was the ICAC conference winner, Region I winner, and defeated CSI in the biregional playoffs. In the National Junior College Basketball Championships, Dixie perked. The Rebels proved that they were better than 568 of the 570 junior college teams in the

nation, as they took third place in the tournament. Roberts was named Region I Coach of the Year and NJCAA Western Coach of the Year. He has continued his success during the past two years, and during the 1981-82 season his team had a 10-0 record in conference play and a 28-4 mark before entering the national tournament, placing sixth among junior colleges. As a junior college coach, he has sent fourteen players to major colleges.

Although this great all-around athlete never fulfilled Coltrin's dream of becoming the world decathlon champion, what he accomplished both as an athlete and coach would have brought great satisfaction to the heart of the late journalist. His exciting athletic career has been an outstanding pattern for any athlete to follow. In 1980 he was installed as a member of the BYU Hall of Fame as a member of the NIT Championship Team of 1966.

Neil's philosophy of athletics and coaching is one to be emulated. He says, "Early development is essential to an aspiring athlete. A young athlete must set his goals early and commit himself to the necessary training programs, so that he can refine his skills as quickly as possible. Good coaching and proper techniques should be sought as soon as possible. This will insure correct learning. Superiority of athletics requires that an athlete begin at an early age. To become the best and surpass the competition, he must begin as soon as possible and work hard." His own example highlights that sage advice: "The Lord gave me a body with some special characteristics and capabilities. I felt compelled to develop my skills and talents in the most proficient way possible. I entered competition at an early age and enjoyed the experiences I had. Each success motivated me to work harder."

Acutely aware of his own God-given blessings, Neil feels that spirituality enters into athletic achievements. He says, "I feel that the relationship between the body and spirit is definite, but that each functions separately. I have had two knee operations and one back operation since the time I was actively involved in athletic competition; therefore, my physical health has become somewhat depleted, even though I have continued to condition my body. My spiritual strength has grown continuously. It is constantly advancing, though this requires continuous conditioning also."

He comments on Mormonism and athletics, "The Church has always stressed good health through the Word of Wisdom and the athletic programs it offers. Skill development at an early age in these programs of volleyball, softball, and basketball offered me encouragement. I chose to attend BYU because I am a Mormon and had many choice experiences and much success there. I had surgery on my knee during my junior year and played my senior year after four doctors said that this would not be possible. Being a Mormon made this possible because the Lord answered my prayers and a special blessing was given to me."

Neil's spiritual philosophy has been important to him as a coach. He states, "I have always believed in pregame prayer. It has not mattered what religion, race, or standing the members of my team possessed; we have always participated in prayer, each member taking a turn. I feel this helps my players to get the game in the proper perspective and project an image of gentlemen.

"While at the NJCAA National Tournament this year, our sponsor, Mr. Bob Boyd, was thoroughly impressed with this tradition. He commented about it on the radio and talked of the direct opposite action he had seen in other dressing rooms where the coach was found yelling at his team, trying to get them up and ready for the game. Because our team behaved like gentlemen on and off the court, we were invited back to a preseason tournament this fall. Prayer is not a sign of softness, just humility and gratitude for the opportunity to compete."

Coach Roberts still golfs, lifts weights, and plays racquetball to condition himself physically. To condition himself spiritually, he has served in the Church as a home teacher, priests quorum advisor, assistant Scoutmaster, YMMIA counselor and secretary, Sunday School and elders quorum teacher, and in other capacities.

Neil Roberts, phenomenal all-around high school athlete, the "greatest prep athlete in the U.S.," champion collegiate cager and champion high-school and junior-college coach, is one of the greatest all-around Mormon athletes.

DOLORES LIER

Swiss National Skating Champion

Holder of fifty Swiss skating records

"The Fastest Zurich Skate," 1969-70, 1971-72

Wilfried Janssen Memorial Skating Champion, 1971

Swiss speed-skating champion, 1973, 1976

Junior Speed Skating World Championships:

Eighth place, 1974
Tenth place, 1975
Twelfth place, 1976
Eighth place, 1977
Fourth place (3,000 meters), 1977

Twenty-eighth place, world skating championships, 1978

World record (5,000 meters— 8 minutes 22 seconds), 1978

Church sports—volleyball:

European zone champions, 1973, 1974, 1978

Swiss champion speed skater Dolores Lier has set over fifty records in beautiful, picturesque Switzerland. For the past decade she has accomplished some great achievements and has been called a pioneer in this area of female Swiss sports.

Initially Dolores was a figure skating queen—carving out figures, running, jumping, and designing patterns to her heart's content. After proper discipline and instruction she made the transition to a speed skating queen. Because of the low interest in Swiss speed skating, it was possible for a pioneering effort to be made in this area, and Dolores helped greatly.

In the 1969-70 season she captured the title of Fastest Zurich Skate and then began serious training. Under the guidance of Franz Krienbuehl, she captured the same title in the 1971-72 season. In 1971, in her first full-fledged competition, she won the Wilfried Janssen Memorial in Zurich and then went on to establish some significant records. She even triumphed over the boys of her same age during her growing period. With much vigor and under the guidance of international experts, Dolores greatly improved her technique, times, and reputation. In 1972 she broke the prewar records. By the end of the winter skating period in 1973, she had already smashed nineteen records and won the first ladies' Swiss master title on record. In 1974 and 1975 she took second place in the Swiss speed skating championships. She again became the Swiss champion in 1976, and then repeated in second place in 1977 and 1978. In European competition, she took twenty-ninth place in the European championships in 1974, and in the junior world skating championships she captured eighth place in 1974, tenth place in 1975, twelfth place in 1976, and eighth place in 1977. In the 3,000-meter speed skating, she took fourth place in 1977. In the world championships in 1978 she placed twenty-eighth, but had a world-record time in the 5,000-meter race, although this was unofficial because the race is not run often for women. In establishing her fifty Swiss records, she has had the following best times: 500-meter: 45 seconds; 1,000-meter: 1:29.56; 1500-meter: 2:16.50; 3,000-meter: 4:52.10; 5,000-meter: 8:22.10.

Dolores has participated in Church athletics and was a member of the European Zone championship volleyball team in 1973, 1974, and 1978. Her team took second place in 1975.

This champion Swiss maiden concedes that the move-

ments of speed skating are "very elegant and require tremendous strength and muscles." She has had to discipline herself to a rigorous training schedule requiring three and a half hours of speed skating daily plus one or two hours off the ice running, climbing mountains, lifting weights, and doing other exercises. During the summer she trains two hours a day, six days a week, in "dry" training: rollerskating, bicycle riding, running, mountain climbing, lifting weights, playing volleyball, and participating in other sports. During the seven "summer" months, she has to train mainly in the evenings because of her work. During the five "winter" months she spends most of her time in Europe and Scandinavia training and competing. Because of the immense costs of traveling and skating, she is extremely appreciative of her father, Arnaldo, who has given her much help. Her sister, Conchita, is also a figure skater.

Dolores believes that a healthy spirit is possible only in a healthy body. She says, "No one should be fanatical enough to seek for success at any price, which is applicable both to the body and the spirit. I could never picture my own life without either the gospel or sports." Her counsel to young athletes has a ring of European wisdom: "If one has trained sufficiently, he should never have any fear of his competitors. He must believe in himself. I personally try before each race to concentrate on loosening up and achieving mental self-confidence. In winter sports it is especially important to keep the body warm and to keep the muscles in motion. Prayer is certainly helpful."

She attributes her athletic success to a number of factors. She believes it is necessary to live according to the rules of the sport and to have a good training schedule. She avoids harmful substances (alcohol, tobacco, and drugs) and is aware of proper nourishment.

Dolores believes in the power of prayer. She says, "I have had the feeling that man is never alone. I pray before each competition to have peace and the necessary strength that I need. It is truly a wonderful feeling to know that there is always someone to help overcome weaknesses and nervousness. Many times during competitive racing I have said a quick prayer—'Dear Father in Heaven, I pay my tithing, keep the commandments, and always try to attend Church on Sunday. I study daily and always try to communicate to other people the importance of thy gospel. Please help me now. My legs are aching so much that I feel I could die. Please help me to run a good race. I have always tried to do thy will, so may I now ask these blessings, please? Amen.' It may sound like a selfish request, but when I work so hard and breathe so heavily during a race, the prayer comes almost spontaneously as a plea for the last hope. Most of the time after the prayer my legs feel lighter and my desires have been fulfilled."

Dolores has been active in the Church as a chorister and a teacher in the Junior Sunday school.

Dolores's employer is also a member of the Church, so they often talk together about their work in the Church. She also helps take care of vacationing Swiss children.

Being a Mormon in competition has often brought Dolores derision from her fellow competitors, because she lives differently than they do. Most of the time her competition has taken place on Saturdays and Sundays. In the small cities and villages she was unable to attend Church. Now that she owns her own car, she has been able to travel into the larger cities to attend sacrament meeting and other Church services. She says, "It is very important for a member of the Church to stay close to those in the Church, especially if one is away from his home for long periods of time. Inactivity comes very easily. It is easy to pray only once a day and then only once a week. Then one reads the scriptures only occasionally, and the influence of others rapidly leads to a falling away. One may know that the gospel is true, but it is easy to neglect various teachings and then to forget them.

"At one time in my life I experienced that exact course. While away from my family it was necessary for me to travel back home on Saturday evenings in order to attend Church. It took three and a half hours both going and coming. At that time I was a chorister and had to hurry, hurry between meetings to coordinate with the organist. I never had time to converse with other young members of the Church. I never had time to dance or take part in Church activities. I lost much contact with normal Church activity and that was a great failing.

"In the winter I was totally inactive because I lived in a small village and was unable to attend any meetings. All of my friends were of various nationalities and were not Mormon, or had no religious desires. Most were married but did not take their vows seriously, living immoral lives. Of even more importance, I found that I was not disturbed by this and yet I called them my friends. I feel very lucky today that I can say that I was spared from serious sins. I had to really fight with myself until I again obtained a testimony of the truthfulness of the gospel. At present I never miss seminary or youth activities. I now realize where I may find my true friends.

"I believe if I had to do it all over again, I would probably not be an ice-skating competitor. The danger of falling totally away from the Church is very real for an athlete. It may seem wonderful to have honor, glory, and medals, but I am now old enough to know that there are many more worthwhile goals and eternal values to achieve in this life. I still plan on participating in the Winter Olympics in Lake Placid (New York) in 1980, but then I am going to retire. I shall then concentrate wholeheartedly on the assignment of being a true woman in life."

This remarkable champion is convinced that it is important to maintain mental alertness. She studies the gospel daily and has an interesting sideline of writing stories and fairy tales and making sketches to coincide with her creations.

Swiss speed-skating champion Dolores Lier, a pioneer in women's speed skating in Switzerland, has worked hard to establish multiple records, thereby achieving fame and honor, but has seen her athletic competition in its true perspective, secondary to the eternal principles and values of the gospel.

REX BERRY

Pro Football Player

Captain of every team of which he
has been a member

All-state, football and basketball,
1942

Second place all-around, Brigham
Young University Invitational, 1942

All-conference, Carbon Junior
College (Price, Utah) football, 1947

All-conference at BYU as halfback,
1950

San Francisco 49ers, 1951-56

All-Pro Defensive Team, 1953

All-49er defensive cornerback, 1960

Utah Sports Hall of Fame, 1974

BYU Hall of Fame, 1976

Rex Berry was an outstanding football star at Brigham
Young University and with the professional San Francisco
49ers, but the athletic title he achieved at Carbon High
School, the Carbon Comet, pretty well describes his athletic
prowess. At Carbon High he starred in football, basketball,
and track. He was all-state football and basketball in 1942
and in track placed second in the BYU Invitational all-around.
He spent four years in the Navy during World War II and then
returned to Carbon Junior College, where he was all-
conference in 1947. He enrolled at BYU and participated in
football, baseball, and track. He was an all-conference
football player as halfback in 1950. In the 1951 National
League football draft he was picked thirteenth by the 49ers

and became known as one of the top defensive backs in the league. He played six years of pro football, achieving the honor of being a member of the All-Opponent Team of the Western Conference of the National Football League in 1953, and during the same year being named to the All-Pro Defensive Team. In 1960 he was elected to the All-49er Team as defensive cornerback. He was one of the professional greats and rated as one of the smartest defensive men in pro football. The defensive coach of the 49ers, Mark Duncan, once said, "If I stay around Berry long enough, he'll make a coach out of me!" After quitting pro football in 1956, he became a talent scout for the 49ers.

He was a team captain of every team he played on, including the pros, where he was defensive captain. In fact, he was only the third full-time captain in San Francisco history. In 1973 he was voted into the Utah Sports Hall of Fame and in 1976 was named a member of the BYU Hall of Fame.

Rex continued his title of captain by later becoming a district manager with U.S. Steel. He has been active in the Church as his ward and stake priests advisor, a Sunday School president, a member of the stake Sunday School presidency, a high councilor, and other positions. One of his sons, Doug, became a football all-American in the NAIA, performing for Southern Utah State as a wide receiver. He was the leading NAIA receiver in the nation.

During his active years in athletics, Rex prepared himself physically by concentrating on his opponent, one on one, for each coming week. One of his greatest challenges was the great receiver Elroy "Crazy Legs" Hirsh of the Los Angeles Rams. Rex handled his challenges well, as shown by the fact that he became known as one of the smartest defensive players in pro football.

Rex respects the body as the tabernacle of his spirit and declares emphatically, "This I have been taught, this I believe! It is every person's responsibility to take care of his body, not to overindulge in food or drink, and not to take into the body anything harmful. One must keep physically and mentally alert by actively pursuing a program to accomplish that."

Viewing athletics philosophically, he says, "A person has to be born with a certain physical makeup to succeed in athletics. All those who are born with physical ability do not necessarily succeed. To reach a pinnacle of success, an individual needs a combination of physical and mental excel-

169

lence. He must set goals and strive with all his capabilities to reach those goals, to recognize his weaknesses and direct his efforts to overcome them."

He credits his own success as an athlete to his desire to succeed and his fear of failure, taught by his parents early in his life. He says, "If you think you can do it, and want to do it, then try it, but only with your best efforts."

Rex believes that being actively associated with the Church played a significant role in his athletic achievements. He says, "Being a member of the LDS Church has taught me that I have been given certain talents by the Lord, and that those talents should be developed and used to fulfill goals and desires. The early teaching of the principles of the Word of Wisdom helped me remain physically strong and achieve my physical goals." Regarding his pro football years, he says, "Being a member of a major league team was the highlight of my athletic career. I was the only member of the LDS Church on that team, and in fact, many of the team members had never seen and talked to a Mormon. I was different, and that difference in personal philosophy and actions caused much comment by my team members. The comments didn't bother me. I did my job, and probably worked harder than most. I did not force my personal philosophy, religion, or habits on anyone, but I lived them and went out of my way to be friendly and helpful, where I could, to all the team members. As a result of how I lived and acted, which of course was related to my LDS background, my team members elected me their captain. They wanted me—the different guy—to represent them. I'm sure they saw in me qualities of living and activity they knew and felt were the right way."

Rex Berry was known by many as "Reliable Rex." He represented the Church and the Lord well through his athletic achievements.

RICHARD GEORGE

National Javelin
Champion and Olympian

Millard High School (Millard, Utah),
1968-71:

Three sport letterman (football,
basketball, track), 1968-71

All-state, track and field (javelin),
1969-71

All-state, football, 1969-70

All-state, basketball, 1970-71

All-American, football, basketball,
track, 1970-71

Javelin state champion, 1969-71

World record, fifteen-year-old age
group, javelin, 224 feet, 1969

State records, javelin,
1969 (224 feet),
1970 (241 feet),
1971 (246 feet 11 inches)

Brigham Young University:

Freshman football 1971

Track and field letterman (javelin),
1972, 1975-77

National AAU champion
(272 feet 11 inches), 1975

Bronze medalist, World Games
(Helsinki), 1975

Second place, NCAA Finals, 1976

Second place, Olympic trials
(Eugene, Oregon), 1976

Montreal Olympian, 1976

Collegiate all-American, 1975-77

BYU javelin record holder
(275 feet 1 inch), 1976

Longest throw (official 275 feet 1
inch—National AAU 1976; 286 feet
unofficial, Montreal Olympics
warmups, 1976)

Richard George, the kid from Kanosh, Utah (population: about 319), has distinguished himself as a world-class javelin thrower. In high school, his throwing of the spear would have easily won most college meets, and in college he became a national champion and Olympian.

Not lacking in size, Richard's outstanding accomplishments at Millard High set him apart as one of Utah's fine athletes. His football and basketball feats were significant, but his wafting of the javelin won the greatest acclaim. As a sophomore in high school, he set a state record in the javelin of 224 feet, which was also a world record for the fifteen-year-old age group. That same year he won first place in the discus at the state meet. As a junior and senior he continued to better his sophomore record by heaving the javelin 241 feet in 1970 and 246 feet 11 inches in 1971, both of which were state records. Besides earning all-state honors three years in track and field, he garnered all-state recognition in football during his junior and senior years, and was an all-state basketball player as a senior. His excellence as an athlete was outstanding enough to earn him all-American honors in all three sports as a high-school star in 1971. He was also the winner of the Tom McAn Trophy that year.

As George entered Brigham Young University, he was a quarterback on the freshman football team and once threw a pass that traveled about 60 yards—he was off balance when he threw. His strong arm led Coach Clarence Robison to say, "He has a natural arm. Many javelin throwers have to develop the arm, but for George it just came natural, and that is a big help to him."

This 6-foot 4-inch, 210-pound athlete, who started throwing the javelin in the ninth grade and became second-best in the nation as a prepster, had a nagging elbow injury throughout his freshman year, but still placed second in the Western Athletic Conference (253 feet). At the end of his first year in college he fulfilled a mission to Alabama and Florida for two years and then returned to continue his javelin career. Upon his reentry into spear throwing, Clarence Robison, who according to Richard George, knows as much about the javelin as anyone in America, said this about his athlete: "I think he's the finest javelin thrower in America."

Although Richard placed only fifth in the NCAA competition in the spring of 1975, after returning from his mission, he became the national AAU champion later that year with a toss of 272 feet 11 inches, proving that Clarence Robison was right. In a post-AAU European tour he competed against some of the best throwers in the javelin world. He made respectable marks of 265 feet in Stockholm and 268 feet in Helsinki, but then threw an embarrassing 214 feet in Kiev, Russia, because he had to throw on a new artificial runway. His last meet of the tour he threw 272 feet 7 inches in Prague, Czechoslovakia. His throw in Helsinki at the World Games was good enough for the bronze medal.

As a junior in 1976 George took second place in the NCAA finals as runner-up with a toss of 270 feet 6 inches. His throw of 275 feet 1 inch at the AAU meet in Los Angeles registered as the best in the nation, and this defending WAC champion traveled to Eugene, Oregon, for the Olympic trials. He took second at the trials with a throw of 268 feet 9 inches and in July of 1976 became a dweller in Olympic Village as a member of the United States Olympic Team in Montreal. Of that occasion Richard commented, "The idea of being with the world's greatest athletes will always be a thrill for me."

While there he roomed with fellow Mormon athlete and national steeplechase champion Henry Marsh; with Dave Roberts—a pole vaulter—and Bruce Jenner, the decathlon

champion and record holder. The kid from Kanosh had come a long way. His Olympic experience was disappointing in performance, however. He actually made the best throw of his career in practice (287 feet), but was 2.2 feet short in the final qualifications. A series of events hampered his performance (an official stepping in front of the lane, a broken javelin by a Russian performer delaying George's performance, and a double gun resounding throughout the stadium for the start of a race). Richard lost his stride and never regained it in all three throws. This outstanding javelin thrower who beat everyone in the warmups with an eighty-five meter toss, nervous and lacking in his timing, was unable to make the seventy-nine meter (259 foot) mark for qualifications. Despite his disappointment he found the Olympics to be a tremendous experience.

In 1977 Richard graduated from Brigham Young University with a degree in economics, and his collegiate career ended. He had been a three-time WAC champion and three-time all-American in the collegiate ranks, and had participated in international competition.

Track coach Clarence Robison, an Olympian himself, once made this comment about the two Olympians, Henry Marsh and Richard George, who both completed missions just before their Olympic challenge: "The real champion in this life is the man that takes care of all responsibilities, but places the emphasis on those that give the greatest and most lasting influence in their lives and the lives of others. Being a champion in the gospel of Jesus Christ is the greatest championship of all, and what a pleasure it is to have Henry and Richard aspire to athletic greatness following their dedication and service to their Church." Perhaps that statement best exemplifies Richard's attitude throughout his competing years. For example, he has said, "The Church is the foundation of everything I do....I would not have felt good competing in the Olympic Games in the place of a mission, knowing my responsibility is first to the Church."

Richard says, "In competing at BYU I always felt that I was not only representing my school, but also the Church. As a result, I tried to exhibit Mormonism before, during, and after competition, and would try to be an example to other athletes I encountered. Also, being a Mormon has helped me maintain a total balance in my life, due to the emphasis the Church places on developing the whole person, and therefore giving me a different perspective than someone whose whole reason for existence is sports."

While in competition, Richard spent twenty-five hours a week in practice, enabling him to stay in top physical shape. His workout routine consisted of running, weight lifting, throwing the javelin, and several agility exercises. He found that mental conditioning could be maintained by earning a respectable grade point average. Presently a graduate student at Harvard Business School, Richard jogs and plays some ward basketball. He is deeply aware that the body and spirit are "integrally related." He says, "My experience has been that when I neglect either one, I am overall less success-ful. I find that when I am in great physical shape, my mental and spiritual senses are much more keen."

To budding athletic champions Richard offers some sound advice: "Take care of your priesthood responsibilities first and athletics will follow. Probably the most pertinent advice to recommend would be to maintain a balance in your lives. I have seen many examples of individuals becoming so dominated with one aspect of their lives that they fail to develop into a complete individual. I suppose this is often evidenced by a person's disproportionate emphasis in sports at the expense of school or Church. My advice would be to strive for excellence in each area of endeavor."

In assessing his own success as an athlete, Richard com-ments, "The single most important thing has been parental support. The fact that my parents allowed time for me to practice basketball, football, baseball, and other sports in my youth, when there were many more immediate demands on the farm, enabled me to develop my skills to the fullest. In addition, their attendance at *every* event confirmed to me their support of my activities. I could never have been so successful without the wise and supportive parents I was blessed to have." Further, he acknowledges, "I feel that not being totally dominated by an athletic event has been of significant benefit to me—not that it has made me more suc-cessful athletically. Many people outside the Church are tremendously successful athletically, and there are equally as many who are successful and violate many moral, as well as spiritual and physical, codes of health; but I maintain that these individuals are extremely gifted physically, and could be even more successful if they lived lives in conformity with gospel standards. Having that balance has improved my feel-ings about myself and has reduced the risk of losing every-thing—should athletic abilities be taken away. Most impor-tantly, in the eternal scheme of things, a balance is vital!"

Richard George, world-record age-group javelin thrower, three-sport all-American in high school, national-champion javelin thrower, collegiate all-American and Olympian, balances his life well in athletics, school, and Church, performing as a champion in each area.

DON FULLMER

American Middleweight Boxing Champion

Intermountain AAU boxing
champion, 1955-57

WBA American middleweight
champion, 1965

Professional boxer, 1957-73:
Eighty-six fights
(65 wins—16 losses—5 draws)

Fought nine world champions

Fought for the middleweight crown
of the world, December 14, 1968

Ranked number-one middleweight
contender for a year

Don Fullmer, a true champion in and out of the ring, has set an inspiring example as an athlete and Mormon. He was a fighter since age five. At that time, his father ("Tuff") started him and his brothers boxing at Church benefits. He fought as an amateur for thirteen years and then became a professional. Besides boxing, he has enjoyed hunting and fishing and been very interested in quarter horses. In high school, he played football, wrestled, and threw the javelin. He also participated in Church basketball.

During his professional boxing career, which lasted sixteen years, from 1957 to 1973, he had eighty-six fights. He won sixty-five and had sixteen losses and five draws. He won the intermountain AAU boxing title in 1955, 1956, and 1957. He won the American middleweight championship in 1965. He fought for the world middleweight title December 14, 1968. In all, he fought nine world champions, and was ranked the number-one middleweight contender for a year.

One of the highlights of his career was his ten-round

decision in 1965 over the welterweight king turned middle-weight, Emile Griffith. This gave Fullmer the World Boxing Association's American Middleweight Crown and ninth place in *Ring World's* middleweight rankings. Griffith really wanted the middleweight championship (having won the welterweight championship three times), and had all the prefight publicity; Don Fullmer was kept in the background. Fullmer was a stalker. The unheralded middleweight decisioned the welterweight champ for the championship title. The same year he defeated Joey Archer, who was one of the ranking middleweights. Fullmer's manager later declared, "Beating Archer in New York is like beating Jack Gardner (the great Utah basketball coach) at home with a ten point spot." Archer had just won fifteen straight fights at home before Fullmer's upset win.

In Europe Don Fullmer had the opportunity to fight the renowned Nino Benvenuti in Rome. Benvenuti had been undefeated in fifty-seven professional fights, and had never fought out of Italy. Fullmer lost the bout, but gained much respect from the Italian people and press. More than 885 different newspaper articles were written about the American challenger, and the Church he represented was mentioned in more than three hundred articles. His manager, Angelo Curly, his father, William, and his brother, Jay, were very helpful in bringing the name of the Church before the people. They distributed pamphlets about the Church to give the reporters a better idea of the magnitude of the religion growing so rapidly in Italy. At that time the country praised Don Fullmer as "an apostle of peace" and a hard-working religious man.

Another interesting bout in Europe did much to publicize the Mormon Church. Don had the opportunity to fight Tom Bogs, the European middleweight champion. Before the fight, however, the two boxers went to church together before they met in the ring, probably the first such event in the history of boxing. The LDS Copenhagen meetinghouse was filled with young members of the Church and the Danish press, as the two fighters were speaking and interviewed. The European champion was puzzled by the prayer offered in their behalf. In essence the prayer was, "We pray for a fair and fine fight. We pray for Brother Fullmer and Brother Bogs. We pray that Thou wilt protect both of them so no harm or accident may befall them. Keep Thy protecting hand over both of them, and let the best man win. Amen."

Bogs was completely dumbfounded; he could not imagine anyone praying for him in such a manner. During the course of the evening Don Fullmer said, "Next Thursday I'm going to meet Brother Tom in a fight, and it will be a milestone in my life if I can gain victory over him. It will give me another chance to meet the world champion, Benvenuti. I believe in victory because I believe in the gospel. Without it I wouldn't be the person that I am, and this also holds good in the ring.

"I wish to thank you people in Denmark for the fine reception, and I hope Brother Bogs treats me just as fine next Thursday. It will not be the same way of course as he has here, but you ought to know, Brother Bogs, that there is no hate in my heart. We both fight to win, and the best one will win. Amen."

The European champion was very pale as he spoke from the pulpit: "I almost feel like a Mormon, for like Don Fullmer and all of you here, I don't drink beer either. I am a milk baby just like Don. I say Don because I feel like he is my friend. And I am proud of standing before you on the stand."

As he left the meetinghouse, the champion of Europe remarked that he regretted coming to such a meeting, because he normally has to be really mad at boxers he meets in the ring. He confessed that he was not mad at Don Fullmer. He said, "He is so pleasant that it borders on the incredible. He stands there and speaks about love to me and much more. He talks about my girls and his sons, about our families, about our trades both inside and outside the ring.

"It is no secret that I feel completely lost, and this is absolutely the last time I will talk with an opponent before the fight. It is ridiculous even if it is wonderful to meet such a congenial man. I wish he had not been a boxer."

Bogs's fears were well-founded; Don Fullmer won that bout.

Later in his career Don Fullmer became a light-heavyweight boxer. The West Jordan fighter won a split decision over former heavyweight champion Jimmy Ellis in Louisville in 1964, and a split decision over the number-one ranked light-heavyweight contender, Andy Kendall, in Frankfort, Kentucky, which sprang him into championship contention again. He was ranked number four as a light-heavyweight going into his bout with Kendall (by *Boxing Illustrated*).

Don completed his fighting career in 1973. He not only boxed, but worked as a brick mason. He is presently employed as a fire fighter for Salt Lake County. He has remained active in the Church throughout his life, and has served in positions of responsibility in his elders quorum and the YMMIA.

Don keeps physically fit by running, exercising, and watching his diet. He advocates the laws of health physically and spiritually. He says, "They go hand in hand; a good, clean body helps to keep a clean spirit. If we are spiritually in tune, then we are going to keep our bodies in tune with the spirit. Therefore, we are going to have strong, healthy bodies. When my spirit is in tune with my Father in Heaven, then I am going to keep my body clean and strong."

He counsels aspiring athletes, "Keep the Word of Wisdom! The Word of Wisdom is for all mankind, not just the Mormons. Set goals in life and then put forth every effort to see that everything possible is done to meet those goals. If you want something bad enough, then there is a price to pay—and we have to be willing to pay that price. To excel in athletics means a clean mind and body, as well as a lot of hard work. Be willing to take advice and learn!"

He is grateful for his success, and attributes it to a good, clean life and the support of a wonderful wife and family. He has been close to the Fullmer clan, a tightly-knit family who live close to each other on the same street. Don is the brother of former middleweight champion of the world Gene Fullmer. He is thankful for a good mother and father who taught him the value of hard work and honesty in all things.

Proud of his Mormon background, Don declares, "It helped me to get where I am today. The Church not only taught me to live a clean life and to keep my body clean, but it taught me that if I keep the Lord's commandments, he is bound. I felt that meant bound to bless me in the things I was engaged in—as long as they were wholesome and clean.

"The Church also teaches us to have love at home and a close family. That also gave me something to fight for. I knew, also, that when I was away to train for a fight, that my wife and companion was true and faithful to me; therefore, I never had to worry about other things.

"The Church has also taught me to be honest not only to my fellowman, but to myself. In order to do that, I had to put forth 100 percent, or I knew I wasn't honest with myself."

In the boxing world Don was surrounded by temptation. When he first went to New York City to fight, he was thrown into many situations where he might have dropped his guard. Many men tried to get him to cast aside his standards. Meeting them head on, he says, "That gave me the opportunity to tell them of my moral beliefs. After taking that first stand of letting them know how I stood on morals, they never again tried to get me to go against my beliefs.

"Once in England a lady from Salt Lake saw me eating in a hotel coffee shop. She noticed I had turned down a cup of coffee that a waitress tried many times to get me to take. The woman had seen my picture in the paper and knew I was Don

Fullmer and a Mormon. She came up to me and said, 'Brother Fullmer, you don't know me, but I do you, and know you are LDS and know of your Word of Wisdom. My, was I glad to see you turn down that cup of coffee.' I said, 'Lady, so am I. Because if I hadn't, the word would have beat me home!'"

A motto Don has espoused and practiced is, "If you don't want someone to know what you are doing, don't do it."

Don Fullmer, a great champion in the ring, has kept his guard up out of the ring as well, defending truth and righteousness.

BRAD HANSEN and the Wrestling Hansen Brothers

BRAD HANSEN
All-American and
Record Performer

Teton High School (Teton, Idaho):

District and Idaho state champion, 1970-72

Third place National Wrestling Federation, 1972

Brigham Young University, four-year wrestling letterman:

Wrestled both 167- and 177-pound weight divisions

Freshman record 21–6–1, third in WAC

Sophomore record, 37 wins–3 losses

Junior record, 37 wins–3 losses

Senior record, 30 win–2 losses

Fifth place, NCAA finals, 1978

All-American 167-pound division, 1977-78, 1978-79

Mountain Intercollegiate Wrestling Association champion, 1975-79 (the

first wrestler in the seventeen-year
history of the tournament to win four
individual titles)

WAC record for career tournament
victories after his senior year (65)

WAC champion, 1976-79

WAC Outstanding Wrestler, 1979

Oklahoma State Invitational
champion, 1978

Chosen for Annual East-West All-
Star Match, 1979 (unable to compete
because of fractured elbow)

Ranked number one and number
two in the nation in the 167-pound
division for all of the 1978-79 season

Fourth place, NCAA finals, 1979

Winningest collegiate wrestler in
Utah history (career mark 125–14–1)
and twenty-six straight WAC
victories, 1978-79

BYU Competitor Award for Men,
1979

MIKE HANSEN

(College record, 73–12)

Idaho state high-school wrestling
champion

WAC wrestling champion at Brigham Young University

All-American at BYU

177-pound weight division

LARON HANSEN

(College record, 83–13)

Idaho state high-school wrestling champion

WAC wrestling champion

All-American at BYU

134-pound weight division

MARK HANSEN

(College record, 52–15)

Idaho state high-school wrestling champion

WAC wrestling champion

158-pound weight division

DAVID HANSEN

(College record, 58–29–1)

Idaho state high school wrestling champion

WAC wrestling champion

150-pound weight division

RONNIE HANSEN

Teton High School wrestler—district champion

BYU heavyweight division

Brad Hansen has distinguished himself in the world of athletics by becoming one of the best collegiate wrestlers in Utah's history. He was preceded at Brigham Young University by his four wrestling brothers, the Fearsome Foursome, Mike Laron, Mark, and David, who have become a legend at BYU. The sixth brother, Ronnie, now serving a mission, was a district champion at Teton High School and wrestled his freshman year for the Cougars.

All of these brothers are good Mormon farm boys raised in a beautiful farming community in northeastern Idaho, Tetonia, in the backyard of the glorious Grand Tetons. They learned to work hard from the very beginning. They hefted thousands of bales of hay and several thousand sacks of potatoes each year to build strong, sinewy bodies, capable of physical challenge. This extraordinary family, led by humble and hardworking parents, cultivated championship attitudes—never to quit or give up until the work was accomplished. That marvelous philosophy obviously carried over into their athletic careers. All six boys and two sisters shared with their parents in work and play, developing a close family relationship. All the family members wrestled each match mentally as though they too were on the mat each time one of the brothers competed.

At Teton High School Brad Hansen followed in the footsteps of his older brothers. Although he enjoyed many sports, his specialty has been wrestling. He lettered four years in wrestling, capturing the division title as a sophomore and both the division and state championships as a junior. He repeated this championship performance in division and state matches as a senior. He went on to win third place in the National Wrestling Federation Matches in 1972. His brothers, Mike, Laron, Mark, and David, were previous Idaho state high-school wrestling champions. After high school Brad followed in the footsteps of his brothers by attending Brigham Young University. Although each of the boys inter-

187

rupted his athletic career by fulfilling a mission for the Church, this seemed to have no pronounced effect on their athletic accomplishments. As a freshman Brad posted a 21–6–3 record and finished third in WAC competition. As a sophomore he won thirty-seven matches against only three losses and captured the WAC Crown. As a junior he had thirty-seven wins and three losses, was the WAC champion, and became an all-American in the 167-pound weight division, taking fifth place in the NCAA finals. As a senior he won twenty-six matches in WAC competition against no losses and took fourth in the NCAA matches. His career

record made him the winningest wrestler in Utah collegiate history, with a mark of 125–14–1, superseding the previous record of Utah's Bob Erickson of 117–13–3. During the first half of the 1978-79 season in the 167-pound division, Brad was ranked number one—the first such ranking for a Utah collegiate wrestler. During the second half of the year he was ranked first and second, but was plagued by nagging injuries. Although he was selected as one of the representative wrestlers for the West team at the thirteenth annual East-West All-Star Classic to determine the top wrestler in each weight classification, he was unable to participate because of a fractured elbow, so he had to withdraw. Two of his brothers, Laron and Mark, also participated in the All-Star match in previous years. Laron won his match in 1973, and Mark lost in 1974. Along the course of Brad's remarkable achievements, he won the Mountain Intercollegiate Association title four consecutive times to become the first wrestler in the seventeen-year history of the tournament to accomplish that feat. He also smashed the WAC record for career tournament victories at the end of his junior year with a 52–11–0 record. He won tournament titles at the Arizona Invitational (1976-77), the New Mexico Invitational (1977), the Beehive Tournament (1977-78), and the Oklahoma State Invitational (1978). During his senior year he not only wrestled in the 167-pound weight division, but also in the 177-pound weight division, and lost no matches. This dynamic athlete wrestled much of his senior year with a fractured elbow, but did not surrender to this injury, except upon the urging of his coaches. At the conclusion of his college wrestling performance in 1979, he was given the BYU Competitor Award.

All of Brad's brothers—Mike, Laron, Mark, and David—preceded him at BYU. Each was an excellent wrestler. All four were WAC champions at least once, and Laron and Mike were also named all-American. In the 1973-74 wrestling season, the Fearsome Foursome wrestled on the same team. They had a combined record of 108 wins (over half of them by pins), 19 losses, and 2 ties. Their victories helped lead their school to the conference championship and to fourth place in the NCAA tournament—the best ever for BYU. At that time a major university wrestling coach said, "I'm having Hansen nightmares." He should have; during their college careers, the four brothers had a winning average of 79 percent (Mike 73–12, Laron 83–13, Mark 52–13, and David 58–29–1).

The Hansen philosophy of work has been a remarkable force in their lives. All of the trophies accumulated in the Hansen home are mementos of this dynamic philosophy. All of the brothers feel that their accomplishments in wrestling are the results of hard, physical work. They were also in constant competition to see who could stack the most hay and who could stack it the highest. Their wrestling prowess was passed on from the eldest to the youngest brother. They passed on the tricks of the trade to each other, giving pointers on certain holds. They depended on each other for advice. They learned to see each assignment through to the end. They also developed an insatiable desire to win at whatever they did. David said, "Before you're going to be a champion you've got to run. You've got to work out every day. You've got to work your hardest. This is how I believe that the Lord gives you what you want—he lets you work for it."

Mark said, "When I go out on that mat I represent all of my friends. I represent the greatest family in the world, and I represent the Lord. People look at me and what I accomplish and associate it with my religion. This has placed a big challenge upon me. I know the Lord has blessed me."

Mike said, "I think athletes have to be close to their Father in Heaven, especially in my case. When you go out on the mat, it's just you and what you've accomplished, and I think you need the Lord's help. Without his help, and without a constant prayer in your heart for a little more strength and maybe even a greater desire to push a little harder, I don't think you are able to accomplish really great heights."

Laron, thankful for his ability to work hard, says, "Our dad is a great guy. I could talk all day about his good qualities. He taught us to get up early, get organized, and then to go out and get the day's job done."

A wrestler from an opposing team once asked Laron the question, "What makes you guys in such great condition? You can't work out that much harder than we do. You just can't!" Laron answers that question, "Coaches have told us that we have natural endurance. I think this so-called natural endurance has come from living clean lives and obeying the Word of Wisdom." This Fearsome Foursome have expressed the principles that bring success: Mike said, "Set your goal now as to what you want to be, and then go after it." Laron said, "Avoid discouragement. It is the tool of the devil." Mark said, "I always think of President Harold B. Lee's words, 'Live the commandments.'" David said, "Don't stop until after the final bell has rung." It is no wonder that the Hansen brothers have been such great competitors.

Lee Benson, *Deseret News* sports editor, recently described the Hansen secret: "It's not muscles that win matches, Brad Hansen, or any of his brothers, will tell you. Wrestling's a sport, not a body-building contest. It requires more than anything else, dedicated practice. 'Dad made sure we knew how to work,' says Brad of his farm rearing. 'I guess that's our greatest attribute...you know, we're not real skilled.'"

The fifth of his brothers to attend BYU, Brad says that they always tried to do whatever the coach asked them to. He says, "When we work out we try to give it our all. We've had some great coaches and they've taught us some great things." Thankful for his talents, he says, "My body is a temple of God. It should be looked after and taken care of. I believe that the spirit can have a controlling influence on the physical body. Over the years I have seen many wrestlers achieve because they had the desire to really do their best. Mark, my brother, is one of the best examples of a spiritual wrestler. He isn't exceptionally talented, but he believed that he could win and he believed that wrestling at BYU was not just for himself, but for the school, the family, and the Church. It seemed like Mark was invariably behind by five points, but he never gave up. His spirit wouldn't let his body say, 'I can't do it.' Generally he would come back in the third period, when the other guy was tired. Mark would physically beat his opponent, who would just sort of give up. Mark would either out-scare him or pin him."

Brad's philosophy of success in athletics needs to be passed on to all aspiring champions. He says, "Believe in your coach and never give up until the match is over. Learn to fight and give it all you have, every time, every practice and every match. If a young man can learn that 85 percent of competitors beat themselves, and that they are their own first challenge, then they can set their goal to win and be a champion. Mentally they must never say, 'I can't. He is so strong, he is so good. He has all that talent.' The man can win if he just sets it in his mind that he can, and works to that end. If a person wants to be a state champion, he must say, 'I am going to be a state champion' the morning before the tournament. He has to prepare. He has to climb the mountain before he can ever get to the peak. Some examples of this I have seen in my own attitude. I guess that my family is quite unusual, because my brothers and my parents never told us that it was hard to be a state champion or make the team—that it couldn't be done. So we never did take stock of someone saying, 'So-and-so is super tough.' At one time I was at a freestyle tournament (two weeks previously I had just won the state championship). I wrestled in the next highest weight division and was wrestling against two other state champions for that weight division. It is what I had planned. One of these contestants was built like Hercules. His upper body was awesome. Some of the guys I knew kept trying to tell me how good he was. Well, I found out he thought I was a fish. That didn't matter, because I had already made up my mind when I found out he was in the tournament that I was going to beat him. We wrestled and I took him down and beat him soundly. It was an easy match. Then I went into the dressing room and I heard him talking to the other state champion. He said, 'That Hansen is really something else. He looks like a fish. He hasn't got any arms on him, but he comes at you and it's just like stink on a skunk. Don't underestimate him because he is pretty good.' Well, I beat the other state champion, also."

Brad relates another story about how important it is to practice before competition: "When I was a sophomore in high school before the state championship tournament, I got beat in the quarter finals. I made a mistake in the match before the consolation round. I locked my hands, which gave my opponent one point, and that is how I got put out of the tournament. That night I resolved that the following year I was going to be state champion. Every practice and every match, that was my goal. In the district and state meets I pinned everyone and won the state championship. In my senior year there was an opponent that I never pinned, but I beat him 21 to 2. I don't want anyone to get the impression that physically I was just born with talent. That's just not the case. No one ever told me that I couldn't win, nor did I ever think that I couldn't." Perhaps many wrestlers have had hopes that they might be fortunate enough to end up as the opponent of that skinny wrestler, Brad Hansen, but after their matches they undoubtedly changed their minds.

Brad credits his own success as a wrestler to his family. He says, "I have been blessed with a great family. Their love and confidence in me have been a real boon. Dad and Mom have been a real example to us. They taught us to work hard and thereby their example and persuasion motivated us to work like they did. Dad and Mom have always been looking after our needs. They have sacrificed greatly to bring us up. They have never held back when their kids needed things such as money, support, and love. Then they taught us to be men, even if we lose."

The Hansen brothers are convinced that their Church

membership has been a real plus in their accomplishments. Brad says, "Being a Mormon is an honor. We have tried to live up to the principles, duties, and commandments. We have always lived the Word of Wisdom and have been blessed with strength to run and not be weary, and wrestle and not faint. I believe that the Lord answers prayers, and that we have to be obedient to the commandments that are associated with that blessing. During the last period of a match, the Lord has blessed us with strength to endure—the strength to be a champion."

Brad comments about one of his most challenging goals the first year he became a WAC champion, "I have worked for that goal many years. I believe that without the brotherhood of our family and their confidence and belief in me, it would have been extremely hard to live up to my own expectations. I believe that he has blessed us all with strong minds. During that WAC championship match, I was down 6 to 2 and came back and tied the score 6 up. Just before I tied him, I knew that I had to come back and beat him. I had to have the strength to beat him, and I realized that I had to try harder and give it everything I had. I tied him, and then we went into an overtime. There I beat him 6 to 0. I couldn't believe I was a WAC champion. I had wanted it so long, but it was hard to believe."

Brad recently returned from a mission in the Philippines and is an assistant wrestling coach at BYU.

The Brothers Hansen, legends at BYU, have set remarkable examples as Mormon champions.

DICK MOTTA

NBA Coach of the Year and NBA Champion Coach

Grace Junior High (Idaho) basketball coach 9 won–1 lost, 1953-54

Idaho state high-school champions (24 won–2 lost), 1958-59

Weber Junior College, 1960-62:

First place ICAC both years

Weber State College head basketball coach, 1962-68:

120 won–33 lost, 1962-68

Big Sky Conference champions 1965, 1966, 1968

Big Sky Coach of the Year, 1964-65

Non-professional coaching record, 237 won–64 lost for 78.7 winning percentage

Professional basketball coach, 1968-present

NBA Coach of the Year, 1971

In fourteen years of professional basketball coaching, his teams went to ten NBA playoffs, including two NBA finals

NBA champions, 1978

Coach, NBA East All-Stars, 1979
One of only five coaches in NBA history to register 500 career victories
In fourteen years coaching in NBA 584 won–564 lost for 50.8 winning percentage

One of the more fascinating stories about Mormon athletes is that of John Richard (Dick) Motta, whose life story began in Union (Salt Lake County), Utah, the son of an immigrant Italian father, Ambrose. His story is certainly not one of fame, but in the athletic world he ranks among the giants. When this five-foot-ten-inch leader of athletics talks, his seven-foot athletes listen and look up to him.

As a kid Dick had the fighting heart of a champion and played first team basketball for his junior high school from 1943 to 1946. Then at Jordan High School he played sophomore and junior varsity basketball as well as sophomore baseball from 1946 to 1948. The heart of this champion was set on playing senior basketball for the Beetdiggers. However, his world collapsed when he was cut in the tryouts for his senior team. He felt that he could no longer trust anyone.

From adversity new beginnings arise. Little did this young man realize that his course would lead to a remarkable destination. That Motta wouldn't have been an outstanding basketball player—in spite of his size—is unthinkable, had he been given the opportunity as a prepster. Even at Utah State Agricultural College some of his athletic skills were plainly evident. He made the freshman baseball team, and then by defeating one of the team wrestlers at 147 pounds, earned the right to wrestle for the Aggies the following three years. His fighting spirit led him to a third-place standing in the conference as a grappler before he received his bachelor's degree in physical education in 1953. His own words best describe his success: "I think my size has helped make me a battler. Little people always have to work harder."

Although Dick majored in physical education and was learning the rudiments of coaching, one of his first experiences as an organizer came during his senior year in college when he was asked to be the head manager of all intramural sports at his university. It proved to be an important experience.

Upon graduation he accepted a position in Grace, Idaho, as assistant football and basketball coach in the high school and as head coach of all sports in the junior high school. His junior high school basketball team chalked up a 9 won–1 lost record that year to take first place in the league. One of his budding athletes at that time, Phil Johnson (who followed him at high school, at Weber College, and as an assistant basketball coach both at Weber College and in the NBA), made this remark about the way the athletes felt toward their coach: "None of us could wait to get out of school and onto the practice field or into the gym. We sensed that he felt the same way." That was the beginning of Dick's coaching career.

After his first year of coaching he fulfilled a military obligation in the Air Force with his new bride from Grace, and had the opportunity to do some coaching while stationed in Shreveport, Louisiana. He resumed his coaching duties at Grace High School in 1956 for the following three years.

That was an exciting period in his life. There he really began trusting people again through the efforts of the school superintendent, Homer Williams, the one employer and friend who gained his deepest respect. He actually ended up coaching basketball strictly because he was not inclined to coach football in the cold, outdoor weather. As the basketball season started, his first hurdle developed. He learned that his five top players had broken team rules (drinking alcohol), which necessitated his cutting them all off the team. The town was furious. He couldn't even get his hair cut by the local barber, but had to go to a neighboring town. At his own home games half the student body cheered against their own team. In a town of only seven hundred, failure was almost certain. With only a hundred and eighty students in the four high-school grades, there weren't many athletes with which to field a team. With his starters gone, his team was composed chiefly of sophomores. His first year they had a 15 won–9 lost record.

The second year he had mostly juniors, and the team and town spirit began to pick up. The school began to support this indomitable coach. They posted a 24 won–2 lost record, becoming the conference champions.

197

The following year, 1959, Dick took his team all the way. He had the same won-lost record, but his little school won the Idaho State Basketball Championship. His fabulous ability as a coach began to blossom.

After his successful season he applied for a high-school coaching job at Twin Falls, Idaho, and for the head job at Weber Junior College in Ogden, Utah. Unfortunately he was turned down, and so he decided to complete his education for his master's degree. After two quarters at Colorado State University, where he also assisted as coach in football and basketball, he was chosen as the new Clearfield High School basketball coach. Before the term began, he was offered the head basketball coaching job at Weber Junior College. He accepted and also completed work on his master's degree at Utah State University.

At Weber he became a winning coach. In an eight-year period from 1960 to 1968, his teams won 164 games and lost 50 for a 77 percent winning record. The first two years as a junior college competing in the ICAC, his teams took first place in the league and won eighth and twelfth place in the National Junior College Athletic Association. In 1963 Motta brought Weber, now a four-year school, from a junior college power to the limelight in major college basketball. During the next six years, his teams won three Big Sky Conference championships. He was named Coach of the Year in the Big Sky Conference in 1965, and in 1968 the Wildcats went to their first NCAA playoffs. To that point in his basketball coaching career he had a total of 237 wins and 64 losses for a phenomenal 78.7 percent winning record.

Whoever thought that this upstart coach would take a small high school in the Gem State to the state championship and then make a two-year junior college in transition to a four-year college a major collegiate basketball power? Dick Motta certainly didn't, and later said, "I've never had a job in my life in which failure wasn't predicted for me."

Next, Motta was challenged to become a head coach for the Chicago Bulls in the NBA. This exciting coach, who lost only three games in the Wildcat Gym since it was dedicated in 1962, who won forty-six straight home games between February 1964 and February 1967, was asked to coach for the pros. This gentleman-coach who put his basketball players up at his own expense in his own home when Weber didn't offer scholarships, who had earned what he worked for the hard way, was headed for the real basketball wars. Right off the bat Dick let people know he would not be a "rubber-stamp coach." Dick Klein, who had recruited him, introduced him to the Chicago press with perhaps the truest words to describe his coaching ability: "We've checked him out very thoroughly. From the junior high to high school and college levels of basketball his teams have won over eighty percent of their games. When you have a toothache, you go to the dentist. When you're sick, you go to the doctor. When you have a losing team you go to a winner. We have a losing team and we have gone to a winner. Dick Motta."

From that electrifying beginning with the pros, Motta's enthusiasm spilt over to build up the spirit of the Bulls. His mightily disciplined two-hour training sessions paid off—his players responded. In his first-ever NBA regular season game against the New York Knickerbockers in Madison Square Garden, his team won. One of the reporters at that game said, "We expected to see some little hick, but even your clothes are in style." Another intimated that it was the most important game in his career, but the new NBA coach admitted frankly that the most important game in his career to that point was when his Grace High School basketball team won the state tourney.

Although failure was sometimes predicted for this young upstart college coach in the pro ranks, Motta's accomplishments were phenomenal during his next fourteen years as an NBA coach. He rose to become one of the highest-paid NBA coaches with one of the best records in NBA coaching history. He coached the Chicago Bulls for eight years, the Washington Bullets for four years, and is now with the Dallas Mavericks. He never saw a live NBA game before he coached one in 1968. In ten of his fourteen seasons, he took his teams to the NBA playoffs, and during two seasons took them to the finals. In his third season he was named NBA Coach of the Year for his remarkable accomplishments in turning the Bulls around from a losing to a winning team (51 won–31 lost). He was declared the messiah of Chicago basketball and imbued his team with the "all-for-one-and-one-for-all" spirit of the musketeers. He had the last laugh on those who said he wouldn't be able to make the transition from a college basketball coach to a professional one. His rigorous training program reaped wonders. He never tolerated sloppy execution, and developed to a more intense degree his uncanny ability to communicate with his players. In his fourteen years of pro coaching his teams won 584 games versus 564 losses for a 50.8 winning percentage. In the 1979 season he became only the third coach in the NBA history to register 500 career victories, joining Red Auerbach and Red Holzman in that elite group. His 1978 team won the NBA championship. His 1979 team won the playoffs, but lost in the finals to Seattle. He also coached the annual NBA East All-Stars against the West team during the 1979 season.

Motta is known for his intensity both in victory and defeat and for his volatile nature. John A. Forster, *Church News* reporter, described his personality: "His competitive spirit and will to win seem insatiable, his drive for perfection in the grueling world of professional basketball and his quips and comments to the press and fans have aroused anger and delight from coast to coast."

His philosophy of coaching is deep and inspiring. Following are some "Mottaisms":

"I have a team meeting about half an hour before each game where we informally talk over assignments and strategy. Then we have a moment of silent prayer, because, whether or not they believe in anything, there are those of us who do. I pray that the players will play to their potential, that the fans will be entertained, that there won't be any serious injuries, and that the team that should win will win."

"You touch a whip to a jackass and he balks. Touch it to a thoroughbred and he responds."

"I'm not a good loser, and I don't intend to be a loser in the NBA."

"I expect to be criticized. But I make all of my basketball decisions after good, hard thought and in the best interest of the team. I like to be the one who controls my own destiny."

"I get to deal with physical geniuses. When people ask me how I communicate with the players, I tell them the first thing I do is have the players sit down so I can look them in the eye!"

"I win basketball games with great people—not great players."

"I will not try to coach a person who feels he is more important than the entire group."

"A key to the Bullets' success is that we have great harmony, great camaraderie on the team."

"I don't mind being beaten, but I hate to lose."

"I only have two rules: be on time and hustle. And don't con me."

"There's always a place in this world for the little guy—in sports as much as any place else."

This astounding individual practices what he preaches. In 1979 he had surgery on his knee, requiring him to miss two games—the only ones he ever missed in twenty-six years of high-school, college, and pro coaching. His battle cry as his team climbed the championship trail in 1978 was, "The opera isn't over until the fat lady sings." That theme has become prevalent in his championship efforts and play. His philosophy and secret of success seem to be totally related to his ability to "communicate" with his players and his own personal philosophy of striving for total teamwork.

In 1978 Motta was honored by the Salt Lake Area Chamber of Commerce after his team won the championship "congratulating him on his fine achievements and excellent reflection it makes on Utah athletics and Utah coaching in particular." In 1979 he was presented a Distinguished Certificate of Achievement from Maryland Governor Harry Hughes and a small sculpture of "another extraordinary man and athlete"—the Prophet Joseph Smith, who was known for his physical as well as spiritual strength.

In spite of a tremendous workload as an NBA coach, Coach Motta tries to keep things in perspective: "I try to remind myself this is just an ordinary job. Sports are exciting, but the building block of our society is the home." He praises his wife as a real "rock" and spends time with his family at Bear Lake, Idaho, in the off season to allow a rest from the demands of pro basketball.

Dick Motta, an outstanding Mormon athlete who didn't make his senior-high varsity basketball team but placed third in conference wrestling in college, has accomplished a phenomenal record in advancing from a junior-high to a high-school coach to a college coach with a formidable record. He is one of the finest NBA coaches in the history of basketball.

CECIL BAKER
(1895-1980)

Track and Basketball
Star and Super Coach

Murdock Academy (Beaver, Utah)
track star

Utah State Agricultural College
basketball and track star, 1921-25:

Broad jumper, high jumper,
220-yard sprinter, and member of
the mile relay team

Conference record mile relay team,
1924

All-conference center, basketball,
1923-25

Member, National Junior AAU
Championship Basketball Team,
1925

Granite High School basketball and
track coach, 1927-50:

Track and field state champions,
1943-44

Entered state basketball tournament
twenty-two of twenty-three years

Played in twenty-one of twenty-two
consecutive state basketball
tournaments

Played for the state championship fourteen times

Won six state championships 1929, 1933, 1934, 1936, 1938, 1947

75.7 percent winning teams (played 358 Games: 271 won–87 lost)

Utah State Agricultural College basketball coach, 1950-61:

Nationally ranked, 1959-61

Winner of two sportsmanship trophies

Skyline Conference Coach of the Year, 1958-59

Third Place, National Invitational Tournament, 1960

H. Cecil ("Cec") Baker, the "gentleman of basketball," has been a legend in Utah high school and Intermountain West basketball circles. His accomplishments both as an athlete and a coach are truly inspiring.

Cec Baker, the second of thirteen children, grew up in Minersville, Utah, near the turn of the century. As a teenager he drove a freight wagon between Newhouse, Frisco, and Milford. Gordon B. Hinckley described his early life in this way: "He became acquainted with hard country and rough men. He learned to keep quiet, mind his own business, and go about his work. He has retained the traits cultivated in those days, including a dislike for the profanity he heard and the drinking and the debauchery he witnessed in the mining camps."

Cec started his long sports career at the old Murdock Academy in Beaver. There he first earned his reputation as a track star. His personal athletic career was not a continuum, for after his high school days he filled a mission to the eastern states. Even after his return from the mission field in 1919, he

204

did not begin his college education right away. He played the piano in a dance orchestra, traveling to the mining camps and cowtowns to perform. He eventually borrowed some money and went to Utah State Agricultural College. Between 1922 and 1925 he earned his degree, and at the same time was a member of the basketball and track teams each year. In track he was a broad jumper, high jumper, 220-yard sprinter, and a member of the mile-relay team. He was an excellent high jumper and one of the fastest 220-yard men in the old Rocky Mountain Conference. In 1924 he was a member of the conference record mile relay team. He was an all-conference center in basketball in 1923, 1924, and 1925. His team won the National Junior AAU championships in 1925. He was also captain of both the basketball and track teams in 1924-1925. He graduated from the Aggie School at the age of twenty-eight and then began his remarkable coaching career at Pinaca, Nevada, a Mormon-scattered cattle town west of Cedar City. His Lincoln County High School team placed second and fourth in Nevada state tournaments during the two years he was there, from 1925 to 1927. In 1928 he started his fabulous coaching career at Granite High School in Salt Lake City, where he coached the next twenty-three years as basketball and track coach.

He became one of the most respected coaches in the state during those years. His reputation and teams were phenomenal. He won two state track and field titles in 1943 and 1944, and his basketball teams were perpetually power teams to be reckoned with each year. His basketball quints were known for their "fight." As the coach of the Fighting Farmers, he instilled within his teams the ability to remain cool and calm and to have a desire to win. Often his teams barely made it to the tourney and then walked off with the highest honors and surprised many of the top contenders. During his twenty-three years as basketball coach, his teams entered the state high school tournaments twenty-two of twenty-three years and played in twenty-one of twenty-two consecutive state tournaments. They played for the state championship an unprecedented fourteen times. His quints won six state championships in 1929, 1933, 1934, 1936, 1938, and 1947. Only once did they fail to win at least one game in a state meet. In addition to their six championships, they finished second twice, third three times, fourth twice, and fifth twice. In 1929 they played in a national tournament

in Chicago, where they were defeated in their second game. In 1943 there was no state tournament due to World War II, but his team won the AAUW tournament over all entries from Utah and Idaho. His 1937 team also beat the "Olympic Champions." In his twenty-three years of coaching the Farmers, his teams played in ninety-four out of a possible ninety-six tourney games. Of 358 games played, 271 were won and 87 lost for an amazing 75.7 percent winning record.

As a consequence of his amazing high school coaching career, Baker was chosen in 1950 to take the helm as head basketball coach at Utah State Agricultural College, which position he held for the next eleven years. During that period of competition, he never had a winning conference team, but coached some of the finest teams in the nation. He had the ability to bring out the best of an athlete's talents. During that time his teams were ranked nationally in 1959, 1960, and 1961. Their rankings were as high as fourth and seventh in the nation. Following the example of their gentleman coach, his teams won two sportsmanship trophies. They won first place in the Holiday Festival in New York and also won first place in the Oklahoma Festival in the All-College Tournament in 1959. Coach Baker was voted the Skyline Coach of the Year during the 1958-59 season. His team won third place in the National Invitational Tournament in 1960. In 1960 he was further honored by being the recipient of the Dale Rex Memorial Award for his outstanding contributions to Utah athletics.

After a long and honorable coaching career, this respected Utah State mentor retired from the coaching ranks in 1961. He and his wife, Edna, a member of the Utah State Board of Education, were cited for their contributions to Utah State University in the areas of athletics and academics and for their service in the Church and community. A newspaper editorial complimented him upon his retirement in the following manner: "And win he did, not only by the score-book but in the manner by which his players reflected his keen knowledge of the game, his ability to develop the individual skills of his boys, his insight into human nature.... 'Cec' Baker has demonstrated in his coaching career an even greater ability. He has inculcated deeply into his players the principles of true sportsmanship. Regardless of the breaks of the game, Baker's boys have been taught to rise above the whims of fate.... Coach Baker himself has set a worthy example in self-control in the crucial moments in many a fiercely-contested game, calmly struggling with his emotions on the bench among his reserve players, while rival coaches have often-times ranted and raved on the side-lines or have charged out onto the playing court." This superb gentleman of the hardwood knew his business and went about it quietly, allowing no swearing or shouting, and inspired his teams accordingly.

After his retirement as a coach he continued to serve the Aggies as an instructor in the physical education department. This devoted personality served well not only as a notable sports figure, but in many Church callings during his active life. He has been a high councilor, bishop, and a member of a stake presidency.

Throughout his life Cec enjoyed competition. As a boy he was active in many sports. He rode horses and competed whenever he could get another person to try to beat him. He says, "[Competition] has been essential to my physical and mental well-being to excel athletically. I have not had an exercise routine, but have played handball, tennis, basketball, and have been on track teams. As a coach I have often competed with the players, especially as a golf teacher and in P.E. classes. When I retired, golf became my major sports activity—until hip surgery made that impossible. Gardening—vegetable and flower—and limited walking at present help keep me physically fit."

His philosophy of athletics and coaching depends on spirituality. He says, "The important thing in my life that led to success was my desire to excel for parents and myself. I liked to compete. I had good examples to follow. I liked the company of good active fellows when I was growing up. I had learned to work and wanted to match my ability with other men. As a coach I received great satisfaction in influencing the lives of boys. I like to see an awkward boy develop into a graceful, self-confident man who could play with, work with, and serve others. Athletics has done this for many boys I have had the great privilege of coaching. Together we learned the heartbreak of defeat and found our weaknesses, and the good feeling of victory and learned our strengths. So desire, good examples to follow, and willingness to work and strive where I could helped in my athletic career.

"Being a Mormon had its hourly effect on me as a player-athlete and as a teacher and a coach. The principles of the gospel were a constant guide in my career. I adhered to the Word of Wisdom, which helped me excel without fatigue. The principles of honesty, brotherly love, and charity helped me in my dealing with players, coaches, and officials. Some of the first outstanding black players at Utah State University were on my basketball teams, and though they were not treated well by some of the conference players and coaches, I treated them as I feel a good Mormon should treat others—with respect and gratitude for them and their efforts to play under trying circumstances."

Having coached hundreds of excellent athletes, Cec understands well what must be done to achieve excellence. He says, "Aspiring athletes must learn that their bodies and minds must work together to excel. A goal should be set and fundamentals mastered, and willingness to spend time and effort to achieve the goal is imperative. Training rules should be followed. Sacrifice of other things is necessary. Good attitudes toward work, leaders or coaches, and fellow participants or teammates are absolutely necessary to achieve as an individual or as a member of a team. Success means hard work, giving 100 percent, self-denial and dedication, and a deep respect for the task ahead." He says of physical excellence, "I have great respect for the tabernacle which houses my spirit. They seem to work well together when I keep them in good condition. The spirit is affronted or damaged when the body is soiled or misused. Both are God-given and are inseparable until death. Both should be developed with loving care. My body is aging but my spirit remains rather youthful."

In summarizing his long, event-filled sports career, Baker says, "My personal philosophy of trying to do unto others as I would be treated or have my children treated has been a pattern by which I have tried to live. I was conscious of my example of good sportsmanship to my ballplayers in how I reacted to what I thought were bad calls by officials. Intimidating officials and calling players for mistakes can arouse a whole student body to unsportsmanlike responses. In good conduct I could not bring myself to yell, swear, drink milk publicly, prance on the sidelines, or cuss the officials. To me these are plays used to get reactions favoring one team or distressing another. Though the best team does not always win, and officials make mistakes, each player should have the opportunity to do his best. In forty-two years of coaching I had one technical called on me, none on my players. In two national competitions where sportsmanship trophies were given, our team received the trophy. These were compliments of which I was proud. Often the hotel managers commented on the quality of men on our teams. During the summer of 1977 one of my players brought his two teenage sons to meet the 'old coach' and has often written of the influence and example my coaching meant in his life. This has happened numerous times. Men who are coaches, physical therapists, and businessmen have written and told me that their opportunity to play for me set their goals for a better life. These are rich rewards for anxious hours during forty-two years of associating with some of the best boys and men in Utah and around the nation."

"Cec" Baker, a veritable legend in Utah high school and collegiate sports, "gentleman" of the hardwoods, spiritual and athletic leader of championship teams, great Mormon athlete and coach, has greatly influenced the destiny of many athletes and teams.

HOMER "PUG" WARNER
(1896-1956)

All-Around Athlete and M-Men Basketball Originator

Three-sport letterman, Ogden High School (football, basketball, baseball)

Three-sport letterman, University of Utah (football, basketball, baseball)

Member, National AAU championship basketball team, 1916

Captain, football, basketball, baseball teams at University of Utah as senior, 1918

All-conference end, senior, 1918

Director of physical education at Deseret Gym, 1921-24

Established M-Men basketball program, 1921

Helped establish the "biggest basketball league in the world"

Helped cultivate the Church athletic program

Football and basketball commissioner, Mountain States Conference, 1939-48

M-Men, high school, college officiator, three decades

Honored by the Homer Warner Award given by the MIA each year to the outstanding contributor to LDS athletics

Utah Sports Hall of Fame, 1970

Homer C. "Pug" Warner was one of the great all-around athletes, sports figures, and contributors to sports, and especially to LDS sports. He was not only a great competitor, but was honest and full of encouragement.

Homer Warner lettered in baseball, football, and basketball at Ogden High School in 1914. He then attended the University of Utah and was a member of the first national championship basketball team, which won the Amateur Athletic Union championship in Chicago in 1916. During his senior year in college he was captain of the football, basketball, and baseball teams and was an all-conference end during that year.

After serving in the heavy artillery branch of the armed services in World War I and completing his tour of duty as a second lieutenant, he returned to Utah and coached at Davis High School for two years (1919-20). His team won the state championship tournament in basketball in 1920, after which he became athletic director at the Deseret Gym from 1921 to 1924. One of his duties was conducting the "boys' department" at the Deseret Gym, while assisting Vadal Peterson at the old LDS University. At the Deseret Gym, Homer started one of the greatest athletic programs in the world—the Church sports program. Since there was hardly enough room for both the adult classes and the boys in the program (approximately 150), he conceived the idea of "farming out" the program to four of the most popular LDS stakes in Salt Lake City. The result of this effort was the creation of one of the most remarkable recreation programs in the world and the "biggest basketball league in the world." The M-Men basketball tourney grew from 150 in 1921 to 22,000 in 1956 at the time of his death. He gave this program all of his boundless energy and enthusiasm. The program

became a world-wide tournament and was called the "All-Church Tournament." An outstanding leader of young people, Homer helped establish the first set of rules for M-Men competition, helped new teams get started, and was instrumental in organizing and running the first M-Men tournament.

Pug Warner not only devoted untiring and ceaseless efforts to organizing the Church sports program, but also officiated at high schools, M-Men, and college games. He served as football and basketball commissioner for the Mountain States Intercollegiate Athletic Conference from 1939 until 1948. This later became the Skyline Conference, which was subsequently commissioned by Dick Romney, his successor.

Homer served on the General Board of the MIA from 1929 to 1948. During this time he and his associates were able to organize the M-Men basketball tournament and the splendid LDS Church athletic program, bringing young men into activity in softball, volleyball, tennis, and golf, in both senior and junior divisions. The magnitude of the Church program was overwhelming. Homer envisioned sportsmanship, high ideals, good companionship, and faithfulness in Church activity, all of which he exemplified throughout his life as a sportsman. This was the greatest monument that he offered to the world of athletics. To honor him, the "Homer Warner Award" was established by the General Board of the MIA in 1960 to be given to the outstanding contributor to Church athletics for "outstanding athletic ability, sportsmanship, spirituality, leadership, reliability, personality, attendance at meetings, participation in MIA general program, home activities, school activities (or work), friendliness and help-fulness."

In addition to his great achievements in the sports world, Homer Warner was a partner, vice-president, and general manager of Bennett Motor Company. He was past president of the Utah State Automobile Dealers' Association and also of the Salt Lake City Chamber of Commerce. In 1942 he served as Salt Lake City War Bond Drive chairman.

In 1970 Homer Warner was named to the Utah Sports Hall of Fame.

This great all-around athlete and contributor to sports, this organizer of the world's largest basketball tournament, this giant who foresaw the significance of sports for the youth of the Church, exemplified all of the characteristics of the Homer Warner Award in his personal life.

MICKEY OSWALD
(1899-1977)

Outstanding All-Around Athlete and Super Coach

East High School (Salt Lake City), 1915-19:

Earned thirteen of possible sixteen letters, 1915-19

Four-sport letterman (football, basketball, baseball, track)

All-state, baseball, 1917

All-state, football, 1917

Leopard football captain, 1918

Leopard baseball captain, 1918-19

Utah state champion, 220-yard hurdles (28 seconds), 1919

Fred C. Richmond Medal as the best all-around athlete in the Salt Lake City high schools mentally, morally, and physically, 1918-19

University of Utah, 1919-22, 1924-26:

Four-sport letterman (football, basketball, baseball, track)

One of four men in Redskin history who won a letter in four major sports in one year, 1920-21, 1921-22

Coach and teacher, East High
School, 1926-65:

Full-time coach, 1926-49

Coached football, basketball,
baseball, track, tennis, swimming,
and skiing

President and charter member, Salt
Lake Basketball Officials Association

Helped organize first Utah high
school all-star football game, 1947

President, Utah High School Coaches
Association, 1948

Prominent LDS sports figure:

Ward, stake, region and zone athletic
director and chairman of region and
zone athletic committees

Member of the Priesthood Softball
Committee, 1960

Manager, George Morris Park

Member, All-Church Basketball
Tournament Committee, 1962-63

Recipient of the Homer "Pug"
Warner Award, 1970

Distinguished High School Coach
Award, 1972

East High Hall of Fame, 1981

One of the best-known athletes ever produced at the
University of Utah, W. McKinley (Mickey) Oswald was not only

an outstanding athlete but a coach of thousands of athletes at East High School, where he taught for thirty-nine years.

Born in the twilight of the nineteenth century, one of seven children, and named after a president of the United States (William McKinley), Mickey started his athletic career in the vacant lot west of his home. He played his first organized sports on a soccer team at Stewart Training School on the University of Utah campus. Habitually he and his chums went to Cummings Field after school to watch the University of Utah football team practice. The Redskin players would often hide some of the boys under their warmup blankets and take them through the gate, saving them the cost of a ticket. Entering East High School in the ninth grade, he was too bashful to try out for any of the teams initially, but through the urging of friends he tried out for baseball in the spring. Although at first he sometimes purposely forgot his mitt, he won a letter in baseball his freshman year and then participated in every branch of athletics in each of his following years to earn a total of thirteen of sixteen letters in football, basketball, baseball, and track. He was a member of three state championship teams and one division championship team. He made the all-state baseball team in 1917 and was an all-state halfback on the football team the same year in the fall. He captained both the football and the baseball teams his senior year. His 1917 grid team not only won the state championship, but defeated the Utah State frosh 60 to 0 and the University of Utah frosh 50 to 0. Seven of the eleven regulars on the East State Championship Team received all-state honors. Mickey starred for his basketball team and was a member of the baseball team all four years. He served as baseball team captain during both his junior and senior years. On the cinderpath his heels were the best in the state, winning first place in the low hurdles (28 seconds flat). He was also a member of the champion relay team.

This all-around star received the Fred C. Richmond Medal during his senior year, awarded to the best all-around athlete in the Salt Lake high schools mentally, morally, and physically. Mickey always considered the award a great honor and wore it on his watch chain throughout his life. This stellar athlete became one of the great prepsters in Utah high-school history. Coaxed and coached by C. Oren Wilson, Tommy Fitzpatrick, Loren Briggs, Piggy Ward, and the great Ott

Romney, he had an excellent start both as an athlete and a coach.

Mickey was deeply appreciative of his father, a sheep-herder, who always left camp early enough in the morning to attend Mickey's games. He remembered that his dad would never sit down at a game, but would stand and pace back and forth between the top row of seats in his big Stetson hat.

In the fall of 1919 Mickey enrolled at the University of Utah, where he played freshman football and basketball. As a greeny he also won letters in varsity baseball and track. During both his sophomore and junior years he participated in football, basketball, baseball, and track, winning a letter in all four sports each year. He was one of only four men at the University of Utah who ever won a letter in four sports in the same year.

At the end of his junior year he accepted a call to the British Mission, where he served under President David O. KcKay. After an exciting and eventful mission, he returned home and again played football and basketball during the fall and winter quarters of the 1924-25 school year. During the spring quarter he went to the desert to help his dad bring in the sheep. In the fall of 1925 he again enrolled at the 'U' and was hired as freshman football coach under Ike Armstrong and Ben Lingenfelter. His football team captured the state freshman title, and he turned out a creditable freshman basketball team. He also assisted in track that year and earned his bachelor's degree in business, minoring in physical education.

Then came an opening for a new coach at his former Hilltop School. He was chosen for the position at East High School from over one hundred applicants. Little did he know that he was to become the "dean" of East High School coaching. His first year he coached the Leopards to a state championship tie in football. He stayed to coach and teach the Leopards for a full thirty-nine years. He was head coach in football for twenty-three years, but also coached basketball, baseball, tennis, track, swimming, and skiing. You name it, he coached it. East High turned out some exceptional state championship teams in each sport during his tenure. His football teams piled up an impressive record, winning 70 percent of their games. They played a total of 156 games (110 won–30 lost–16 tied). He coached and helped produce such greats as Herman Franks (outstanding baseball player

and coach in the major leagues), Marv Jonas, Dave Freed, Dick Warner, Pete Carlston, Oscar McConkie, Fred McKenzie, and Cal Clark. In 1947 he helped organize the first Utah High School All-Star Football Game. He was president and a charter member of the Salt Lake Basketball Officials Association, and was elected president of the Utah High School Coaches Association in 1948. In 1949 he retired after a fabulous prep coaching career. He was honored with a plaque that read, "In grateful appreciation for 24 years of devoted service in the development of good sportsmanship and character building while serving as athletic director and coach at East High School."

After his "retirement" he served as a teacher and part-time coach from 1949 through 1965. He coached the East High swimming team for several years and was sponsor and coach of the Leopard ski teams that won the Knudsen Cup in 1958 and 1961. In accomplishing that honor, his skiers had to win the skiing title of Utah high-school supremacy six years in a row.

In 1965 Mickey stepped down after thirty-nine years as a teacher, coach, and athletic director. He said he taught approximately ten thousand boys during that time.

As a coach, Mickey declared, "In athletics the man with the 'do or die' spirit is the man who comes to the front." That philosophy pervaded his entire career both as an athlete and a coach. It has been said that "East has made a name for itself . . . partly due to there being a large number of talented young men who year in and year out turned out for football at the Leopard school—but most of the success has been traceable to this same Mickey Oswald. They don't make 'em any better in the coaching fraternity. They don't produce coaches who ask less and give more than Mickey Oswald. They don't manufacture men like Oswald simply because the mold wouldn't be able to produce such perfect specimens once in a blue moon."

Besides his high-school coaching, Mickey coached American Legion baseball and in 1930 took one of his teams to a tournament in Sacramento, California. He also coached Little League baseball.

Oswald's contributions to Church athletics are well known. He served as a ward, stake, region, and zone athletic director and as chairman of the region and zone athletic committees. He also served as secretary to the MIA Athletic Committee, gave enthusiastic support to all of the Church activity programs, and had a special enthusiasm for the all-Church basketball tournaments. He was a member of the All-Church Basketball Tournament Committee from 1962 to 1963 and was a member of the Priesthood Softball Committee in 1960. He also managed the George Q. Morris Park. This honorary master M-Man, because of his outstanding contributions to the Church athletic program, received the Homer Warner Award from the YMMIA in 1970 for his service to young men.

Mickey enjoyed life to the fullest. Among his many interests, he found time to raise prize chrysanthemums and pigeons. He was president of the Wasatch Men's Garden Club and the Beehive State Chrysanthemum Society. He won the Queen of the Show Award in four state shows for his chrysanthemums.

In addition to his many athletic contributions to the Church, Mickey was a high councilor in the Bonneville Stake and with his wife served in the Tongan Mission in Fiji. While fulfilling a second mission, he contemplated whether or not missionary work differs much from athletics. He said, "Only the game is different here. All the boys who have labored here have only one goal, and that is to preach the gospel of Jesus Christ, so something great can be brought into the lives of the people. These young elders are just as devoted to their work here as the young men on the teams of East were in their respective sports."

In 1972 Mickey was given the Distinguished High School Coach Award from the Utah Old Timer Athletes Association. In 1973 he was honored by the University of Utah as a member of the Emeritus Club Board of Control, and in 1976 received the Emeritus Club "Merit of Honor Award." He died in 1977 after complications following open-heart surgery. He was again honored in 1981 when a permanent monument was established at East High for the great coach—the Mickey Oswald Fieldhouse.

Throughout his life this gallant athlete taught his players and students by participating with them and thus keeping physically fit. He was always studying and devising football strategy and preparing health lessons. He had a great desire to win and liked all kinds of competitive athletics. He was a competitor in everything he did. He was constantly encouraged by his religion to keep mentally and physically fit, believing in the Word of Wisdom and living in moderation. He was often heard to say, "The most important thing is desire." No matter what he did, he put his whole heart and soul into it. He played to win. He taught his athletes to play fair and to observe the rules.

Mickey's wife, praising her husband's memory, says, "His greatest achievement was the influence he had on the young men he coached and taught at East High School. His life was always an example of the things he believed in: honesty, moral integrity, physical and mental fitness, hard work, and loyalty to family, friends, and Church." She has been particularly impressed because whenever they would meet young men, former students at East High School, they would always say, "I remember what you taught me, Coach. I'll never forget the things you taught me. I'd like to thank you for the things I learned." She further states, "They all seemed to have great admiration and love for him—and he had a host of friends. Mickey Oswald was a famous name, and I was proud to be his wife."

This great athlete-coach, Mickey Oswald, devoted most of his professional life and spare time to working with young men and furthering the cause of athletics in Utah and in the Church.

CLARENCE "ROBBIE" ROBISON

Track Star and Master Coach

Utah state prep champion, 880, 1942

Four-year track letterman, BYU

Conference champion, 880 and 1 mile, 1947-49

Conference record, 1 and 2 miles, 1948

Third place, Olympic trials, and member, U.S. Olympic Team in London (5,000 meters), 1948

BYU and Intermountain AAU cross-country champion, 1946-48

Member, U.S. track team that toured Europe (1,500 meters), 1949

Head track coach, BYU, 1949-82 (BYU ranked among the top ten in the nation twenty of thirty-three years and was conference champion fourteen times)

Coach of sixteen Olympians, twenty-one NCAA champions, ninety-one all-Americans, and one world record-holder

Skyline Conference Coach of the Year five times

President NCAA Track and Field Coaches Association, 1968

NCAA Rules Committee, eight years

BYU Athletic Hall of Fame, 1976

Utah Sports Hall of Fame, 1981

One might say that Brigham Young University and Clarence F. Robison, great distance track athlete and BYU track coach, are synonymous.

"Robbie" Robison was a track and basketball star in high school. At Millard High, Stan Watts was his basketball coach. He was the state high-school champion in the half-mile (2:01) in 1942. Upon attending BYU he became one of Utah's greatest distance runners. In four years of conference track competition he was defeated only once. He set conference records in the mile and two-mile events and held those records for many years. He competed in three running events—the 880, the mile, and the two mile—often running all three events in the same day. He pretty well ruled the conference from 1947 to 1949. Over thirty years ago his best times were 1:56.6 in the 880, 4:11.8 in the mile, and 9:17 in the two mile. His running career was sandwiched around a three-year tour of duty as a naval officer in the Pacific during World War II.

In 1948 Clarence Robison was third in the Olympic trials. As a member of the U.S. Olympic Team, he competed in London in the 5,000 meters, a distance he had run competitively only twice. Robison was BYU and AAU cross-country champion for three consecutive years. In 1949 he was a member of the U.S. track team that toured Europe, running the 1,500-meter race. He won twelve of sixteen major races that summer in Europe. He graduated in physical education and mathematics from BYU in 1949 and later received his master's degree from the University of Michigan in 1955.

Robbie Robison nourished his spirit as well as his body during his years of competition. During the European tours he had the opportunity to room with the great Olympic pole vaulter, Bob Richards. At that time Richards was studying for

the ministry. The two had many discussions on religion during the hours between their meets. In later years Richards spoke at BYU and was introduced by Coach Robison. Richards recalled that Robison had for years tried to talk him into being baptized into the LDS Church. "And now when I arrived in Utah and Robbie met me," he said, "the first thing he said was 'Well, Bob, are you ready to join?'" Richards's concluding remarks were, "No one ever quits the Mormon Church." What a great example Robison had set for that Olympic champion and minister.

Coach Robison has been head track coach at BYU for over thirty years. One of his rules has been that "every BYU runner should go all out all the time." His basic philosophy of coaching can be summed up in his statement, "I've always felt that being a track coach gave me a great opportunity to build young men who are not only great athletes, but great citizens, great Christians. One of my goals is to build the whole man, not just his muscles." It has always been his contention that spirituality and athletics blended easily and naturally. He says, "Unless I try as hard to help develop a boy's entire personality, to help him to be a fine human being, I feel that I'm not a good coach."

Another one of his outstanding comments is, "It doesn't hurt nearly as much when you're in front." He believes with all his heart in this philosophy, and that it works in life as well as in track.

During his outstanding years of coaching, Robbie has built a track empire rivaled by few colleges or universities in the nation. His teams were among the top ten in the United States fourteen times.

Credited to his record are fourteen conference championships (runner-up most other times), two WAC indoor titles, cochampions of the NCAA in 1970, and Cougar track tours a half dozen times. During this period of time he has coached ninety-one all-Americans, twenty-one NCAA champions, sixteen Olympians, and one world record-holder. He has also been associate professor of health education.

He has been Coach of the Year in the Skyline Conference five times, received the Adrian H. Pembroke Award for his contribution to college track, and been the recipient of the Dale Rex Memorial Award for his contributions to athletics in Utah. He was also president of the NCAA Track and Field Coaches' Association in 1968 and served on the NCAA Rules Committee for eight years. In 1976 Robbie was elected to the BYU Athletic Hall of Fame. In 1981 he was elected to the Utah Sports Hall of Fame.

Active in numerous Church positions, he has been a bishop, a member of the General Board of the YMMIA for nine and a half years, a Regional Representative of the Quorum of the Twelve for six and a half years, and a branch president in the Language Training Mission for three years.

Robison has been a member of the Provo City Recreational Board and served on the Provo Board of Education for over seven years (also serving as chairman). In 1976 he was selected as Citizen of the Year by the Utah County Council of Governments. He has also been the public address announcer for Cougar basketball for twenty-six years.

A father of nine children, this great track athlete also did much running at home. Fortunately, his wife has been BYU's greatest track and field fan.

Robbie keeps horses, enjoys hunting and fishing, and plays racquetball to keep himself physically fit. Understanding the sanctity of the body, he declares, "We are spiritually charged with the responsibility of caring for our physical bodies. I personally believe it is a sin if we allow our bodies to be torn down with idleness or dissipation."

He attributes his successes to the love of competition, and with soberness declares, "Many times I ran beyond my own abilities as an answer to prayers."

His greatest distance run has been the run of life, which challenge he is accepting well. Clarence Robison is not only winning a personal victory, but helping others to become champions as athletes and in life.

GEORGE "DOC" NELSON
(1890-1970)

Light Heavyweight Wrestling Champion of the World and Fabled Wrestling Coach and Athletic Trainer

Wrestled and boxed approximately twelve hundred contests, 1911-34

Wrestled "Big Jim," the 480-pound bear, 1913

Intermountain states heavyweight wrestling champion

Light heavyweight wrestling champion of the world, 1923

Athletic trainer, all sports, Utah State University, 1921-58

Started first college wrestling team in Utah, 1922

Utah State University wrestling coach, 1922-58

National Athletic Trainers' Twenty-five-Year Award, 1954

"George Nelson Fieldhouse" at USU, 1956

Helms Hall of Fame for Athletic Trainers, 1962

Utah Sports Hall of Fame, 1973

George "Doc" Nelson, originally christened Jorgen Nilsen at his birthplace in Larvik, Norway, the grand old man and wrestling pioneer of Utah State University, outstanding wrestler and boxer, emerges as one of the most colorful sports personalities in Utah history. His life story is so spectacular and exciting that a condensation of his accomplishments is challenging.

One of nine children, Nelson was born in 1890 in the beautiful country of Norway. He was active in all kinds of sports, but preferred gymnastics, soccer, football, track, skating, skiing, swimming, rowing, and sailing. Since he was a full-fledged butcher by the time he was thirteen, he participated in sports activities after work, sometimes practicing soccer until midnight—made possible by the midnight sun.

In 1906, at the age of fifteen, George left his beloved Norway, traveled a difficult but exciting voyage around Cape Horn, and arrived at Diamond Point near the village of Honolulu. He ultimately landed at Tacoma, Washington, where his adventure in the New World began. After working in a sawmill and on a construction crew, he eventually arrived in Salt Lake City, where he was employed as a fireman.

He started his athletic career as a member of the Norwegian Athletic Club in Seattle, Washington, and perpetuated this course by becoming a wrestler in the Intermountain Area. He was called the Fighting Fireman on mat cards. He wrestled his way through Utah and the intermountain region. Because of his many wrestling wins, he soon attained the title of intermountain states heavyweight champion. The newspapers heralded his prowess: "Known throughout the country, Doc tested the great and near greats of the era who though oft times were much larger, were never smarter or better competitors than himself." "Always the cleanest of competitors, George Nelson was idolized by fans. They knew they were in for a treat of clean, rugged and 'unfixed' entertainment."

Doc once accepted the challenge of wrestling Big Jim, a 480-pound wrestling bear that had been throwing champion wrestlers on the national circuit. No one had been able to throw the bear using a legal hold in four years. After an initial struggle with the "furry fury," Nelson "caught the giant in a half crossbar, put his weight on the hold, and threw the big Alpine bear on his back." He met and won the challenge. He wrestled the bear for six performances, the house being filled each time with excited spectators. The bear's trainer said he was the only one ever to get the bear off his feet.

Doc wrestled and boxed approximately twelve hundred matches between 1911 and 1934. He wrestled such greats as Ira Dern, Jim Londos, Dock Roller, Dean Detton, and Ed "Strangler" Lewis. He was billed by the *Los Angeles Daily Times* as "one of the truly great mat men of his time." The *Times* also said that he possessed a deadly headlock, considered second only to "Strangler" Lewis. The Fighting Fireman fought Ad Santell for the light heavyweight championship of the world in 1923. Winning that match, he held the title until his retirement. He also fought such headliners as Joe Stecher and Tom Drake. In 1919, when Doc went to San Francisco for wrestling engagements, Ed "Strangler" Lewis, the world heavyweight champion, called Nelson and asked him to train with him at his home. He did, for six weeks. Later the Strangler said that George Nelson would have been the heavyweight champion of the world had he chosen to follow wrestling as a career. Although wrestling was his field, Doc was a fair boxer. He boxed Primo Carnera in Logan in 1928 and had an exhibition match in Logan in 1932 with the great Jack Dempsey. He made his last professional ring appearance in 1934 at the age of forty-three.

In spite of his accomplishments as an athlete, Nelson's real honors came as an athletic trainer and coach. He initially spent six years as director of physical education and coach at the Oneida Academy in Preston, Idaho, from 1915 to 1920. He began attending the LDS Church in Preston and was baptized in 1914. There he became acquainted with Harold B. Lee, who was the basketball manager and one of his best friends. Ezra Taft Benson was also there at the same time. President Lee later told Barbara Jeppsen, a daughter, how much the two supported each other; in fact, Harold B. Lee

and a few others would stand out in front of the hall where Doc wrestled and play their musical instruments to help gather spectators.

In 1921 Dick Romney, athletic director and coach at Utah State Agricultural College, wrote to George Nelson, asking him to come to that institution as a trainer for all sports. Nelson accepted the position and became the college's athletic trainer and wrestling and boxing coach. He coached and trained thousands of athletes who knew him simply as Doc. He served from 1921 to 1958, a period of thirty-seven years. In 1922 he formed the first collegiate wrestling team in Utah. His wrestling teams always did well, and in over thirty years won a state, western division, or conference championship each year. At one time they won seven straight western division championships.

In June 1954, he was honored, with eleven other athletic

231

trainers, at the National Athletic Trainers Convention for twenty-five or more years of service in the training profession. In 1956 great tribute was paid to this rugged Norwegian when the Utah State University fieldhouse was named for him. A *Deseret News* editorial stated, "'Doc' is a man that believes that sportsmanship involves playing just as hard, though fairly, as a man can play, and for one main reason—to win. The many strong men whose muscles and characters have taken shape under his rough, skillful hands have grown up in the same tradition."

His daughter Barbara pays great tribute to her father in telling the influence he had on many athletes: "Probably one of dad's greatest contributions was that of counseling. When his athletes would come to him for an ankle wrap or a back rub, they often really came for a little counsel. The comment has been made by several that his advice for helping them set goals for what they really wanted to accomplish, urging them to keep their bodies clean, and especially urging them to live clean, moral lives, was of great influence. He was never afraid of hard work and advised good hard work for keeping fit—for everyone, including his girls. He also counseled them to choose their friends carefully, because they can help or hinder."

Doc always believed in keeping his own body clean and in good physical condition in order for it to be a fit place for his spirit to reside. He was much displeased to see any of the men he worked with not taking proper care of their bodies, and he would tell them so. He believed that self-discipline and a sense of self-worth were important features of his own athletic achievements, and that active Mormons had influenced his career. He also believed that active Mormons influence the athletic careers and lives of others, and that the teachings of the Word of Wisdom and the value of work play a great role in this regard.

After Nelson retired from USU as trainer and coach after thirty-seven years of service, he was a part-time instructor in wrestling and boxing for the physical education department until he was almost seventy-five years old. All his life he believed in good physical conditioning and lived the principle of hard work and hard training. He used to run from the Salt Lake City Fire Department fire station number one (now the Federal Building downtown) up to Ensign Peak, then to Beck's hot springs and back to the station. That was a morning routine. He watched his diet to keep at his best wrestling weight and ate well-balanced meals. Until he was seventy-five years old, he walked to and from Utah State University and his home regardless of the weather—a distance of three or more miles, partly uphill. He worked out with his boxing and wrestling classes while teaching, and it was common knowledge that none of his boys could pin him, even at the age of seventy. At age seventy-three his health was impaired by Parkinson's disease, and this progressed until the time of his death at age eighty in 1970. He remained active in his vegetable garden and walked as much as possible until the time of his death.

In 1962 George Nelson was recognized as one of the great athletic trainers in the United States, at which time he was honored as a charter member of the Helms Athletic Trainers Hall of Fame. He was one of twenty-six who had been singled out whose careers had been completed after a period of twenty-five years or more of service. In 1967 he was honored at the USU coaching school banquet with a special award for long service and his "intangible" benefits to Utah State as a "second father" to hundreds of young athletes. In 1973 he was named to the Utah Sports Hall of Fame.

Doc enjoyed handball and was one of the first to start skiing in Cache Valley. He taught all of his six children to ski and to appreciate the beauty of the snow-covered mountain slopes.

He was a family man and appreciated the Church. His first wife, Emma, died in the 1919 flu epidemic, but he was blessed with a wonderful second wife, Anna, who loved the young men who were his pride and cared for some of them when they needed nursing or a good meal. He served as one of the first scout commissioners in the Oneida Stake in Idaho and was an explorer leader in Logan. He was a high priest in the Church at the time of his death.

This great man was a monument of strength to all who knew him. A newspaper once said, "Few men have become more of a living legend than George, and few men are better-loved than the noble Norseman."

Jorgen Nilsen, George "Doc" Nelson, rugged noble Norseman, the Fighting Fireman, venerable and ageless Aggie, was a living legend as an athletic trainer and grappler, a true champion in and out of the ring, a great Mormon athlete.

EUGENE "TIMPANOGOS" ROBERTS
(1880-1953)

All-Around Athlete, Coach of Olympians, Master Sports Innovator and Promoter

Brigham Young Academy,
1898-1904:

Captain of the track team

Captain of the "Outlaw Eleven"

President of the athletic association

BYU director of physical education
and athletics, 1910-28

BYU Coach, 1910-28

Founder, BYU Invitational Track
Meet and Relay Carnival, 1911

Founder, Annual Timpanogos hike
and summer caravans to scenic
features, 1912

Author of the Legend of Timpanogos

Gave BYU teams the name of
Cougars, early 1900s

Originated first official BYU
homecoming, 1920

Professor of health, physical education, and education, University of Southern California, 1928-46

Trojan high jump coach, USC, 1930-42

Grand national president of Phi Sigma Epsilon (national recreation honor society)

Helms Athletic Foundation Medal for noteworthy contributions to basketball

BYU Alumni Association Distinguished Service Award, 1949

BYU Athletic Hall of Fame, charter member, 1975

Eugene Lusk (Gene) Roberts, "Father of BYU Athletics," "Timpanogos," was one of the greatest organizers, athletic directors, coaches, educators, and innovators ever to come from Brigham Young University and the state of Utah. His accomplishments are so remarkable that it is difficult to believe that one person could have as much talent, creativity, ingenuity, enthusiasm, and ability as he did.

Gene Roberts was the tenth of eleven children and had a fascinating childhood. As a young man he was a great lover of the outdoors, and especially enjoyed hiking. He enjoyed the companionship of his talented father, who related pioneer and Indian stories as long as time permitted. His interests were varied and helped to create a solid background for his marvelous future. In the foothills he herded cattle, but found the challenge of climbing the higher points on the mountains surrounding Utah Valley to be more stimulating and attractive. He sold newspapers, bellhopped at the Roberts Hotel, worked in the Eureka Mines, built pole lines, worked on the railroads and in the old Provo post office, and was occassionally a hotel clerk. He enjoyed watching well-known athletes, was a jockey for amateur races, and even gave instructions to a boot black who became famous as a world champion, Jack Dempsey. Before college, he was captain of a football team and a basketball group, boxed preliminaries for prize fights, trained three fighters, and entered every event in a track meet.

He entered the Brigham Young Academy in 1898, where he distinguished himself in many activities. He was captain of the track team that won the first Utah intercollegiate track and field championship, was substitute quarterback on the last great football team before that sport was discontinued at the academy, and later captained and quarterbacked the "Outlaw 11" of BYA, which became known as the "Provo Team." He was also a campus journalist and became managing editor of the college paper, the *White and Blue.* He was president of the class of 1904 and of the athletic association at the academy.

After missionary service to Germany and Switzerland, Gene Roberts achieved much at BYU during his term as director of physical education and athletics from 1910 through 1928.

When he first started his coaching career, many thought that he might not last out the school year. Later, he wrote, "Imagine what the students thought, especially those athletically inclined, when they got their first glimpse of poor little me. I was 5 feet 9 inches tall, skinny, thin-faced, sallow-complexioned, wearing glasses and weighing 127 pounds." He went on to announce that he was not there to produce star athletes or Olympic heroes: "We are mostly concerned with the physical and social welfare of every student, not a favored few." Immediately he introduced a comprehensive program of physical education to reach all students. In spite of his comments about star athletes, his record of turning out brilliant teams and individual stars defied his original utterance. He built one of the most well-rounded programs in the country. He was a pioneer in promoting physical education, athletics, and recreation on both state and national levels.

During his years at BYU he coached several state and conference championship basketball teams, one of which took second place in the National AAU Championships in Chicago in 1917. He produced some of the best track stars in the world. Dr. Edwin R. Kimball praised him in this way: "He studied each of his men so that he would know exactly what to do or say to stimulate them to produce their best. Every person was different; one may need a pat on the back or a word of encouragement, another may need a man-to-man talk with a personal evaluation and still another could profit from a 'tongue lashing.' Roberts always seemed to know what was needed. I've never known anyone with his ability to 'get his men up' for the big game. His teams often won when the odds were overwhelming and victory seemed impossible. Coach Roberts was a perfectionist whose teams were brilliantly coached in fundamentals, rules, team play and strategy." With such an approach he coached such renowned track and field athletes as gold medal Olympian Alma Richards and Clint Larson, who won the high jump at the Paris Inter-Allied Games after the first World War (which took the place of the Olympics). He also tutored Owen Rowe, nationally prominent low hurdler, and Dale Schofield, champion hurdler and runner.

In 1921 he reintroduced football to BYU, the first time it had been played in twenty years, and coached the first two or three BYU grid teams representing the Church during that era. He coached some outstanding basketball teams and was noted as an authority on basketball in the West. He was an advisory member of the National Basketball Rules Committee prior to 1928 and a regular member the following year.

During his eighteen years at BYU, Roberts initiated many outstanding events. In 1911 he started the BYU Invitational Track Meet and Relay Carnival, which has, except for two years during World War II, been an annual affair. It has become one of the largest events of its kind in the nation. First he mailed invitations to nearby schools and was encouraged by their hearty response. Later, athletes from junior high schools, high schools, and junior colleges converged on Provo to take part in the annual event. Contestants from Idaho, Wyoming, Arizona, Colorado, and Nevada (as well as from Utah) participated, sometimes exceeding three thousand. He patterned the program after the Penn Relays, with the idea of making the events general enough to make it a track carnival.

This famous Provoan was also a poet, cartoonist, editor, and writer. He was a regular sports columnist for the *Deseret News* and other newspapers, and during a quarter of a century wrote stories, fables, and sermons, as well as satires under pseudonyms. One of the pseudonyms was Harry

Davidson Kemp. This Kemp was supposed to be an eastern journalist of note who was camping among the Utah mountains for his health. Many of Kemp's articles were directed toward civic improvement and appreciation of Utah scenery and culture. This helped to bring about extensive street paving and beautification programs in Provo. Even the editor of the *Provo Daily Herald* only later learned that this critic was none other than Eugene L. Roberts, even though Kemp's articles were front-page features.

One of the events dearest to the life of "Timpanogos" Roberts was the Timpanogos Hike. The tradition started in 1912 when the professor led a small group of hikers to the Timpanogos summit. He proposed the hike as an annual pilgrimage, and it has continued since its initiation through two wars and mountain storms. It is the largest community climb of its kind in the nation. As the founder said, "It was never intended as just a canyon outing. It's more like a sacred ceremony encouraging lofty appreciation of God's out-of-doors." He was the first to write down the famed Timpanogos legend, "Utahna and the Red Eagle."

Thousands of hikers and nature lovers have conquered the twelve-thousand-foot summit of Timpanogos. As the honorable David S. King of the Utah House of Representatives once said, they "played on its tiny glacier, drank the icy, sun-pure water from its many waterfalls, and breathed the enchanting aroma from its myriad bloom of delicately colored flowers."

The Timpanogos legend has been summarized by Cal Pratt in the "Brigham Young Alumnist": The great god Timpanogos was to be appeased "by sending the most beautiful maiden in the tribe to cast herself from its peak into the jaws of the great glacier. She was stopped by a young brave from another tribe, whom she mistook for the mountain god himself. They lived happily for many years in the famous Timpanogos Cave, until one day she discovered he was not really the mountain god, whereupon she knew that she had been deceived and feared she had angered the real god of Timpanogos. Thus, she carried out her sacrificial plan by leaping from the topmost peak of the mount. Her name was Utahna; and her lover, Red Eagle, when he discovered her body, carried it back to the cave and died of sorrow over her. To climax the story the great god, Timpanogos, did a wondrous thing. Up from the bodies of his children, he commanded their bleeding hearts to rise and merge into one. And over the lifeless bodies rose a great red heart and fastened itself to the cave ceiling, where it hangs to this day over the sacred burial chamber of Red Eagle and Utahna. So goes the story, a romantic setting to the Central Utah Mountain whose name actually means 'sleeping woman,' and whose peak yearly hosts thousands of its admirers."

Early in the 1900s while writing a column for the *Deseret News*, Roberts gave the BYU team the name of Cougars. He looked upon the cougar as being a thoroughly western and even Utah product noted for its agility, cunning, and strength.

Roberts was responsible for all of the introductory physical education classes at BYU except for freshman gymnastics. While President of the BYU Alumni Association in 1920, he introduced the first official homecoming as a three-day celebration. He initiated the summer-school caravans to scenic features and the annual winter carnival. He also introduced the Thanksgiving cross-country run.

After eighteen years of phenomenal accomplishments at BYU, Gene Roberts continued his prominent life at the University of Southern California from 1929 through 1946. He served as director of teacher-training for the men's division of physical education and as assistant professor and later associate professor in the division of health, physical education, and education. He delivered papers and addresses and gave technical instruction upon scores of subjects related to his rich experience. He was also a radio broadcaster on several stations. He was a member of many national societies, including the National All-University Scholarship Honor Society, the National Education Honor Society, and National Philosophy Honor Society, the National Physical Education Honor Society, and USC Honor Society (Skull and Dagger), the Varsity Club (USC Honor Society) and the National Recreation Honor Society—of which he was the grand national president for two years. He was also a vice-president of the Sons of the Utah Pioneers.

While at Southern California, Gene was asked to assist in the coaching of the Trojan high jumpers. He did this from 1930 to 1942 until World War II. His jumpers won first and second place in the 1932 Olympics in Los Angeles and were high-point winners in most of the track meets they entered. He coached four Olympic high jumpers at BYU and Southern California.

In 1949 Roberts was awarded the BYU Alumni Association Distinguished Service Award and in 1975 was elected as a charter member of the BYU Athletic Hall of Fame. He had previously been awarded the coveted Helms Athletic Foundation Medal for "noteworthy contributions to basketball."

A prolific writer, Gene prepared a history of the Mormon Battalion that no one has ever surpassed. At the time of his death he was preparing a history of physical education at BYU.

Sportswriter Les Goates once said, "In thirty years of sports I never knew a man who was so vitriolic in his denunciation of sleazy and unfair conduct in sports. On several occasions the 'maestro,' as the boys often called him, made remarks that cut the four-flusher virtually to ribbons. Gene was big enough and fair enough to help the obscure athlete, equally as well as the star, and never failed of commendation for the big and worthwhile men in the game."

A eulogy delivered by the great Dr. Harvey L. Fletcher depicted the way Gene dealt with people throughout his life: "He hated insincerity and hypocrisy greater than anything else in the world, and he would strike at it with all the vehemence he had—sometimes to the great embarrassment of him and his family because of the repercussions it sometimes created. Likewise, when he would see the genuine, someone who had really accomplished, one who in very deed could see the truth, one with sincerity and honesty, then he would praise it with the powerful weapons he had at his command."

His philosophy was summarized in this editorial from the *Provo Herald* at the time of his death: "The ideal that fashioned his own life and personality dominated his work as a builder of bodies and athletic teams. The body beautiful was to him not the body with the bulging muscles of special strengths. It was the body made strong through the symmetrical and harmonious development of all its parts. It was a body disciplined by the mind to serve mental and spiritual ends. Coach Roberts had teams and teams. The best ones he said were beautiful when they played as a unit, when the excellence of the individual was lost in the excellence of the group. They were beautiful when what mattered was not the star but the team.

"He wanted his boys to be 'fellow students,' participating not only in sports, but also in the whole social and academic life of the school. They should find ample compensation for athletic skills in the privilege they had of representing school and student body. Athletic programs were only a means to comprehensive educational ends."

Gene Roberts played the game of life well. He loved the canyons, the stars, and the sound of mountain waters. Perhaps his closeness to nature helped him dedicate his life

241

to the service of God and his fellowman. He believed that every person should be healthy and happy as far as possible. He worked to that end both in athletics and as a member of the Church. He was Provo's first scoutmaster and did much to promote scouting. He was also extremely active in the MIA both in Provo and later in California. He served on the Utah Stake MIA Board and later when he settled in California was a member of the Los Angeles Stake high council.

Over the door in the George Albert Smith Fieldhouse at BYU is a picture of "Timpanogos" Roberts facing the majestic Timpanogos which he loved so much. Could there be anything more appropriate for this great athlete and servant of God?

Eugene L. "Timpanogos" Roberts, builder of athletes and men, brilliant innovator and creator of athletic and recreational events, marvelous author and poet, outstanding director and contributor to sports and recreation on a local and national level, has fashioned one of the most remarkable records in the athletic and recreational world, attaining heights as lofty as the great mountain he loved so well.

LaVELL EDWARDS

Outstanding Football Player and National Coach of the Year

Utah State University:

All-conference football, 1950-51

Aggies' captain, 1950-51

BYU coach, 1962-82; head football coach, 1972-present:

Winningest football coach in Cougar history

74.4 percent winning record: (88 wins–32 losses–1 tie)

WAC Coach of the Year, 1974, 1979, 1980

District eight Coach of the Year, 1974, 1977, 1979, 1980

Utah Sportsman of the Year, 1974

Seven WAC championships, 1974, 1976 (tie), 1977 (tie), 1978, 1979, 1980, 1981

Six post-season bowl games (Fiesta 1974, Tangerine 1976, Holiday 1978, 1979, 1980, 1981)

Coach, North Staff Blue-Gray Game, 1978

Churchmen's Coach of the Year, 1979
Bobby Dodd National Coach of the Year, 1979
National UPI Coach of the Week (Texas A&M), 1979
Coach (West Squad) East-West Shrine Game, 1980, Hula and Japan Bowls, 1981

The "winningest football coach in the history of BYU," LaVell Edwards has earned his place as a great Mormon athlete and coach not only because of his remarkable statistical record (which speaks for itself), but because of his true greatness and impeccability as a gentleman of the gridiron and a moral leader in sports.

In ten years as head coach at BYU he has had a 74.4 percent winning record (88 wins–32 losses–1 tie). Credited to him are seven WAC championships since 1972. He has also guided the Cougars into post-season bowl action in 1974 (Fiesta Bowl), 1976 (Tangerine Bowl), and the 1978, 1979, 1980, 1981 Holiday Bowl. He was the Utah Sportsman of the Year after the 1974 season and also the recipient of the coveted Dale Rex Memorial Award, presented annually to the person who has substantially contributed to Utah sports. Athletic director Glen Tuckett has appropriately dubbed him "the Moses of BYU football," responsible for "leading us out of bondage into the promised land."

In his first season as head coach in 1972, he was the "winningest first year coach," compiling a record of 7–4, the most wins ever for a first-year coach at BYU. He was the eleventh BYU football coach and worked under Hal Mitchell and Tommy Hudspeth as an extraordinary defensive coach. He was thrilled at the opportunity to become a football coach at BYU. As a youngster in Orem he followed BYU football regularly, and his ambition was to be a coach. His dream was fulfilled to its fullest when he came to the BYU coaching staff. Prior to collegiate coaching he was at Granite High School, where he served as head coach in football, wrestling, and golf for eight years, and also in tennis and basketball during the 1954 and 1955 seasons. He was president of the Utah High School Coaches Association from 1959 to 1960.

In addition to his impressive record at BYU, he has been named WAC Coach of the Year three times (1974, 1979, 1980) by the American Football Coaches Association. He has been Kodak district eight Coach of the Year four times (1974, 1977, 1979, 1980). In 1974 he was given the Sportsman of the Year Award while guiding his gridders to a comeback season that netted his team the Western Athletic Conference title. This award is given by the Chamber of Commerce to the man who has done the most for Utah sports during the year. He was also named to the coaching staff of the West Squad for the fifteenth annual All-American All-Star Game in Lubbock, Texas, in 1975. He coached on the north staff of the Blue-Gray Game in 1978, and was called upon to be the head coach of the East-West Shrine Game (West Squad) in 1980. Although none of his teams ever finished lower than fourth in the WAC, his 1979 grid team was one of the best. They started off a super season by defeating fourteenth nationally ranked Texas A&M, propelling the Cougars into the top twenty nationally ranked teams. Going into the season as the "Dean of WAC Coaches" and as a member of the board of trustees for the American College Football Coaches Association, and ranking twenty-first among the nation's winningest coaches, his earlier victory earned him UPI National Coach of the Week. His gridders, lead by consensus all-American quarterback Mark Wilson, had an undefeated season (11 wins–0 losses) and at the end of season play were ranked in the top ten (ninth and tenth) in the AP and UPI polls. Statistically the Cougars were first in total offense, first in passing offense, first in scoring offense, and first in kickoff returns in the national rankings—and eleventh in scoring defense. Despite the brilliant season, BYU lost to Indiana in the Holiday Bowl 38–37—a heartbreaking ending, climaxing a great season. It was aptly described by Marion Dunn, *Provo Herald* sports editor, who wrote, "With two minutes to play in the game, BYU stopped Indiana and took possession of the ball on their own 17. With a two-minute offense that the Dallas Cowboys would like to have, quarterback Mark Wilson drove the Cougars to the Indiana 10 with eleven seconds to play.

"Never mind that the field goal attempt from there misfired.

"Never mind that the Cougars lost the game by a single point.

"The people who saw that game should remember it for a long, long time. It had everything a fan could ask for. It had sensational offense, it had stubborn defense, it had human mistakes in which the outcome swung. It wasn't decided until the final ten seconds when the Cougars' last try came up just short."

Edwards then led the West Squad to victory in the East-West Shrine Game, accompanied by Marc Wilson. He garnered further honors by being named the Churchmen's Coach of the Year for 1979 and the Bobby Dodd National Coach of the Year, recognizing "a style that emphasizes something more than winning the game, a belief that the game of football should be kept in perspective with college life in general." That award, presented by the American Sportsmanship Council, pretty well sums up the life and philosophy of LaVell Edwards.

In 1980, after a brilliant season under BYU's best quarterback ever, Jim McMahon, the cards finally turned. The twelfth-ranked Cougars had a 12–1 record. In the Holiday Bowl the "Cardiac Cougars" pulled off a "miracle," and in the process Coach Edwards looked like he was in the process of having a "coronary." It was a fairytale, come-from-behind win over Southern Methodist University. With SMU leading 45-25 and only 3 minutes and 50 seconds on the clock, the Cougars had a series of spectacular plays (two quick touchdowns, recovery of an on-side kick, and a block of an SMU punt). BYU pulled to within six points with thirteen seconds left. Tight end Clay Brown caught a miraculous forty-one-yard bomb from the brilliant all-American McMahon. With the score tied 45-45 and no time remaining, Kurt Gunther kicked the extra point for the "miracle" win, 46-45. The 'Y' never gave up, and the Edwards epitaph became: "Hard work precedes the 'miracle'."

The 1981 season was again one of Edwards's best. Consensus all-American Jim McMahon led the Cougars to a final national ranking of eleventh. It was the most prolific passing team in the history of college football. McMahon set fifty-five NCAA records in his career at BYU as the "Cardiac Cougars" again led the nation in total offense and garnered another

Holiday Bowl victory 38-36 over Washington State. Edwards coached two post-season victories (Hula Bowl and Japan Bowl).

Besides his impressive record as a football coach, LaVell Edwards was one of Utah State's all-time football greats. A native of Orem, Utah, he was a three-year regular at Lincoln (now Orem) High, where he was a two-time all-state football center in 1946 and 1947. He also lettered for two years in basketball and track. At Utah State, he was offensive center and defensive linebacker. He lettered for three years and was

247

captain of the team. He was also all-Conference for two years. His teammates called him Ironman because he played every minute of every game on both offense and defense. Sportswriter Hack Miller said, "He was the hardest hitter, pound for pound, in Aggie history. He had the hardest heart of anyone on the grid; the softest heart off it. In fact, the man was so meek one wondered why he played the game at all." After graduation from USU in 1952, where he obtained his bachelor's degree, he served in the Army for two years. He served at Fort Meade, Maryland, and Fort Lee, Virginia, and in Japan. During his stint in the Army, he was able to play and coach service ball.

Coach Edwards has the gift for working with other people. He has excellent rapport with the players and coaches, including opposing coaches. He gets along well with everyone. His grit and determination earned him his master's degree from the University of Utah in physical education and educational administration while he was coaching at Granite High School, and then he received his doctorate in education at BYU in 1978. He is one of the few head football coaches in the nation to achieve that honor.

Coach Edwards has remained active in the Church during his many years as an athlete and a coach. He has served as a bishop, high councilor, quorum advisor, and in other positions. He has been a popular speaker for athletic, civic, and church groups.

Perhaps Coach Edwards's philosophy has been one of his greatest attributes during his athletic career. He was raised in a family of fourteen children (a cousin and his own family of thirteen children). He attributes his success to his parents and the Church. He says, "Whatever I do, I approach it the same way, whether it be acting as a football coach or serving as a bishop....I'm a firm believer in hard work to reach desired goals. But I also believe football should be fun: a sport the players, as well as the fans, should enjoy. It doesn't have to be regimentation or drudgery. The outgrowth of football should be strong, positive values that will benefit a player for the remainder of his life."

He has truly felt a responsibility for the spiritual welfare of the players as well as for their ability to play a good game. He says, "The most important thing in playing football is for each team member to find himself and understand his relationship to his Heavenly Father. After that, they can all come together as a team; then everything falls into place as far as winning games and championships." Before and after every game Coach Edwards leads the team in prayer: "We pray for the protection of both teams, give thanks for the opportunity we have to play and for the closeness and unity we feel, and ask the Lord for help to play to the best of our ability and to accept the outcome of the game whatever it may be." His great attitude may be summed up by another statement he made: "The Church is part of my life, part of me. Everything I do, whether coaching, going to school or raising my family, the Church is related to it. I'm a product of the Church and of close family unity. It's all one and the same—always a part of me."

His close relationship to his players has been an important part of his winning teams. The players know that they can come and talk to him anytime about personal problems and whatever is on their minds. He says, "I do a lot of counseling with players and I feel as responsible for their spiritual welfare as I do for their sports and educational welfare." He has gained much happiness in helping young men find themselves during periods of turmoil and uncertainty. It is interesting that he has had a hand in many of the baptisms among his players, although he stresses that many other people were involved in their conversions as well. He feels that there is much more to teach the players than just winning games. "When all is said and done," he says, "when the playing is through and the cheering is over with, the most important thing for the players is that they have a good feeling about themselves. They should have more to show for their football experiences than just a scrapbook."

LaVell also says, "When BYU succeeds, the whole Church will succeed. There are some people who read no more in the news than the sports page, and if they see BYU's success in sports it will draw their attention to the college, its people and the Church." He truly feels that this is a way that he and other coaches at BYU can help build the kingdom of God.

One of Coach Edwards's great athletes, all-American quarterback Gifford Nielsen, echoes the feelings of many others: "I can't stress too much the team's spirit and unity, and that comes right from Coach LaVell Edwards. He would do anything within the rules to help his players.

"With us, Coach Edwards has a father image, but he puts a lot of responsibility on the individual athlete. I feel this may give us a maturity which some players lack, because they were not delegated responsibility."

Coach Edwards also believes that his athletes are taught lessons on the playing field that will help them in life. He says, "Commitment, courage, facing up to adversity. It's not all fun and games.

"To put the game in proper perspective, learning to live with defeat is a great lesson. A lot of people don't know how to live with defeat." Even though he knows that coaches are hired to win games, he states that only 50 percent of the coaches can win weekly. He believes that football is one of the great unifying forces of the student body and that schools who have dropped the program have felt the lack of unity on campus. One thing he appreciates is the proper attitude he has been able to maintain while coaching. He states, "It's really a pressure-packed profession. There is often a tendency for things to get out of perspective in college athletics—too much elation in winning and too much disappointment in losing. The Church helps me keep things like this in proper perspective. My testimony is a leveling influence in my life."

Coach LaVell "Ironman" Edwards is an inspiring example of an athlete for all with whom he associates—a champion coach and a spiritual giant.

MIKE REID

All-American and PGA Golfer

Age ten and under national
Philippine junior champion, 1962

Colorado State junior champion,
1971

Semifinalist, National Junior
Championship, 1971

All-WAC four years at Brigham
Young University

All-American three years at BYU

WAC champion, 1975

Edwin Stein Award, 1976

Low-Amateur U.S. Open, 1976

Semifinalist, Western Amateur, 1976

Pacific Coast champion, 1976

Professional golfer, 1977-present

Mike Reid, professional golfer and former Brigham Young University great, nicknamed Radar by his peers because of his accuracy off the tee, was born in Maryland. A son of an Air Force colonel, Mike has lived all over the United States and in the Philippine Islands. In 1962 he won the ten-and-under division in the Philippine National Junior Competition. In 1971 he won the Colorado State Junior Competition and was a semifinalist in the National Junior Competition. He was district champion in San Antonio, Texas, in 1972. He was the WAC champion in 1975 and low amateur in the U.S. Open in 1976. He was also semifinalist in the Western Amateur

Tournament in 1976 and Pacific Coast champion the same year. His first year on the PGA tour (1977), he earned $26,000. In 1980 he won over $206,000 and placed ninth on the money list. Although he didn't win a tournament, he was considered one of the most accurate players on the tour with the best fairway woods. Although he placed second and third in many tournaments in 1980 and 1981, he has yet to win outright. In 1981 he won $93,000 and continues his quest on the tour.

As a freshman Reid was honorable mention all-American. He was an astonishing first-team all-American during his sophomore and junior years. As a senior he was named second-team all-American while capturing fifth place in the NCAA. He was all-WAC for all of his college years. In 1976 he won the coveted Edwin Stein Award as the outstanding senior BYU athlete.

He astounded the golf world by being the first round leader of the U.S. Open as an amateur in 1976. He was the first amateur to lead a round of the U.S. Open in over five years. Modestly he admitted that he just had a good first round; however, he did go on to be the low amateur golfer in the U.S. Open.

Mike's philosophy is tough to beat. He says, "I always try to have fun. I like to play.... If it can't be fun, I don't want to play. I've worked to keep golf in perspective—to realize it is just a game.... I think it has a lot to do with where you set your goals. Some golfers set their goals so high they can't ever realize them." He does not live and die with every shot on the course during a match. He believes, with Walter Hagan, that one should "take time to smell the flowers along the way."

As a high-school performer Mike didn't feel that he had the talent that a lot of other kids had, so he compensated by hard work. He golfed all day and hit dozens of bad shots; however, because he played so much, he developed an excellent short game and unshakable confidence.

On the PGA tour since 1977, Mike has had some good rounds and acted as his own secretary, trip coordinator, and financial counselor. He almost won his first tournament victory at the Pensacola Open in 1978 when he came in second after a sudden death one-hole playoff, in spite of his heroic efforts.

Reid believes in hard exercise five or six days a week. He

jogs ten to twenty minutes on each of these days and does one-legged knee-bends, sit-ups and push-ups. He says, "I believe the body and spirit are inseparable while here on earth and that in order to be happy they should complement each other—the spirit ever-disciplining, ever-training the body to accomplish goals. Doctrine and Covenants 101:37 ["Care not for the body, neither the life of the body; but care for the soul, and for the life of the soul."] leaves no doubt in my mind of the correct perspective. While the body should be cared for, maintained, and improved, the spirit is in need of constant nourishment and is improved with age, not necessarily slowed down as is the body with age."

Mike's advice on how to excel in athletics is profound. He says, "I can answer that in *eight letters*: PRACTICE! You can't learn it out of books or by talking about it. You've got to dig it out of the ground. Secondly, always have a goal in mind. This is what makes practice worthwhile. Thirdly, never lose sight of your personal priorities. If you are a Mormon, then it is family, Church, and personal development. I feel that you can't excel in one aspect of life without good order in the other aspects. For instance, the burden of unfinished homework or an unkept lawn which you are responsible for will weigh down your efforts to progress in sports. There is time for all if you *want* it bad enough. In this way, your time will always be well-spent and productive. This is the key— *productive time*, however little it may seem."

Having excelled in athletics both before becoming a member of the Church and after his baptism in 1974, Mike assesses the change in his own personal life as follows: "Since joining the Church I would have to claim the gospel's stabilizing effect as the most important part of my athletic success, plus the new perspective on life and golf's place in my life." He credits his brother Bill, the pro at a golf course in Wenatchee, Washington, for helping the physics of his golf game, and John Geertsen, Sr., as one of his fine golf teachers in California. He is also highly appreciative of his father for starting him out and teaching him the fundamentals of golf.

"Being a Mormon," he says, "has affected my golf career all for the good. It helps me keep in proper perspective the idea that what I do athletically isn't nearly as important as how I react to it. It helps me to remember that this is the Lord's world and we are here to help carry out his program. It gives me an improved insight into my talent and the responsibility which it carries. Being a Mormon gives me strength because of this guidance and direction that is so helpful. The Lord's promises that he made to man are true, if we live obediently. The faith and confidence this knowledge gives is, and can be, a well of strength each day." He further says, "I think the very fact that I am what I am is a tremendous testimony to me that the Lord will bless those who seek to cultivate a talent for good causes, to reap good benefits and strive always to do the Lord's work. I don't claim to be a paragon of perfect sainthood, but I know the gospel has given me hope, and my prayers have helped me to overcome self-doubt that could have stopped me."

Active on the professional golf tour, Mike still finds time to do his home teaching and to lead a family home evening group.

Mike Reid, former BYU great and all-American, PGA

golfer, the "Radar" of golfing, has excelled in his field and is embarking on his stiff competitive career with ordinary golf clubs supplemented by implicit faith in the gospel of Jesus Christ.

LES GOATES
(1894-1975)

Champion Sportswriter

University of Utah 1914-17:

Chronicle staff reporter

Teachers training college

Deseret News 1919-64:

Initiator of all-state prep basketball teams in Utah, 1919

Founder of first all-state prep basketball honor team in the United States, 1919

Deseret News reporter, sports editor, columnist, editorial writer, and makeup editor, 1919-64

Deseret News sports editor, 1920-49

For twenty-nine years, author of "Les Go," the longest continuous column of any western newspaper

Helped organize the Utah-Idaho baseball league and pioneer league

For twenty-nine years helped organize, promote, and publicize the M-Men basketball program and select all-star teams for the *Deseret News* and *Improvement Era*

Nationally known as a sports authority on such champions as Jack

Dempsey, Bobby Jones, Bill Tilden, and Babe Ruth

Magazine and LDS *Church News* editor, columnist, and make-up editor, 1943-64

George Washington Honor Medal (1955 Freedom Awards), 1956

Sigma Delta Chi (national journalism fraternity) citation for forty years in journalism, 1959

Outstanding Member of the Sons of the Utah Pioneers Award for service as editor of the *Pioneer*

Banquet of Champions Award from Utah State University for contributions to athletics, 1964

In 1894 in Lehi, Utah, a little country town not far from Salt Lake City, a little seven-week-old newborn, weighing only three pounds, was not expected to live because of prematurity and a serious physical deformity. This baby was kept in a small basket filled with medicated cotton for its bed. The doctors and most of the family had no expectations for his survival, but his mother kept up faith. Courageously she took him to fast and testimony meeting to have his name and blessing given. A "patriarchal-looking gentleman who was bent over and scarred from the mobbings he had suffered in the old country because he was 'running away with the Mormons,'" the baby's maternal grandfather, pronounced the name and blessing upon the baby. During that fast and testimony meeting, a woman of rare spirituality, Mary Elizabeth Woofinden, bore her testimony and then spoke in a strange language, smooth and melodic, which sounded like sweet music. She occasionally made a gesture toward the mother and small babe. When she concluded, patriarch James Kirkham arose and interpreted the testimony, saying

257

that she had spoken in the language of Adam and had conveyed a message and a promise to this mother who had fasted and prayed so long for this little one. He said that "on account of the exceedingly great faith of this mother, her prayers had ascended to the high heaven, and that her child, who was appointed to come into the world only long enough to receive an earthly body, would now be privileged to live, to grow to manhood and rear a family in Zion and would perform a work of which this mother would be well pleased." After arriving home that day, the baby was found to be perfectly normal; all signs of physical deformity had disappeared. So began the life of a great man and a great sportswriter, Lesley (Les) Goates. He said, "Thus my life began—as it will end—with a miracle, the miracle of death and the newer and better life."

This infant grew into one of the best sportswriters of the 1900s. A comment made by other great sportswriters, Damon Runyan and Grantland Rice on one of their visits to Utah, showed his status: "You know, that fellow Les Goates is one of the greatest writers in the United States. He deserves the best."

The promise that he would fill a work with which his mother would be well pleased was fulfilled. His achievements as a journalist are countless and his writing some of the most beautiful in the English language. It has been estimated that over forty-four years he wrote over 2,500 columns and editorials and 250 verses. During that entire time he was a champion of Utah athletics.

In his later life he penned an article about immortality that undoubtedly showed a lifelong conviction: "The best answer that I can give to the question of immortality was provided by my dad many years ago in the Old Field near Lehi at 2 o'clock one mid-summer night. We stood out in the tall grain listening to the thirsty soil drink in the water we had brought to it. A full moon wheeled its broad disc over majestic Mount Timpanogos and made a sparkling mirror of picturesque Utah Lake. The trees along the long field lanes silhouetted against the eastern horizon in dark contrast to the fleecy, gaily illuminated clouds. A million stars blinked in softening splendor. From the big willow tree a night bird calls to its mate.

"My dad, who seldom spoke more than a dozen words at a time, took a deep breath, wiped the perspiration off his brow

and said, 'You know a night like this makes you feel like you wanted to live forever.'

"'My Sunday School teacher says that is exactly what we do,' I recalled. My dad said, 'A night and a place like this could not just happen, and it could not just come to an end.'

"So, Mr. Skeptic, I cannot prove that life goes on after death, but the moon over the fields, the sunset on the lake, a sweet little babe in its mother's arms, a lovely young girl lying cold and still in her casket—all whisper to me, this gospel truth: 'These things could not just happen and could not just come to an end!'"

As a skinny kid at Lehi High School, Les participated in basketball, baseball, and track. Upon his graduation in 1913 he set his goals on higher education and enrolled under a scholarship in the University of Utah Teachers Training College in 1914. During his two years there, between 1914 and 1917, he trained in music and journalism. He then accepted a job as principal of the Hinckley, Millard County, Elementary School. From there he served in the army at Camp Lewis, Washington, on the psychological examining board and as camp newspaper editor.

In 1919 Les embarked on his great journalistic career. He was appointed sports editor, which was his great desire. He said, "As sports editor of the *Deseret News* in 1919, I came up with the idea of an all-state Utah state high-school honor basketball team, after the manner of Walter Camp picking the first all-American college football team from the players of the Ivy League—Yale, Harvard, Princeton and Dartmouth, mostly. In fact, I got the idea from the immortal Mr. Camp in an interview I had with him at the Hotel Utah one day. This turned out to be the first all-state prep honor team in the United States, as far as I could learn, with Indiana following a year or so later. After choosing the 1919 all-state five at the state tournament, I went back ten years and 'posthumously' selected the honor team from each year from newspaper reports, interviews with the coaches and players, and the several who deemed themselves experts on the game. This research took me back to the year 1908 and the Lehi versus Granite Playoffs (the first state tournament, between Lehi—Southern Division—and Granite—Northern—which Lehi won both the years and earned for themselves the honored name of 'The Pioneers.')" So began the all-state prep teams in Utah and the United States.

From that beginning Les served with the *Deseret News* as reporter, columnist, editorial writer, sports editor, and make-up editor. He was the *Deseret News* sports editor from 1919 to 1949 during the "golden age of sports," a period of twenty-nine years. His wonderful column, "Les Go," continued during his term as sports editor and was the longest continuous column of any western newspaper. He became a magazine and LDS *Church News* editor in 1943. Although he was a columnist and make-up editor following his years as regular news sports editor until he retired in 1964, he was always known as a champion of Utah athletics for a full period of forty-four years. He was known as the "dean of mountain-west sportswriters."

Early in his career Les was a prime factor in organizing, promoting, and publicizing the M-Men basketball program and continued in that capacity as a newspaper man. He selected all-star teams for the *Deseret News* and the *Improvement Era.* For his long and meritorious service in that regard he was given the Honorary Master M-Man Award in 1956. He served in the Liberty Ward and the Liberty Stake YMMIA presidency and was an M-Men class leader.

In 1956 he received the 1955 Freedom Award of the Freedom Foundation at Valley Forge, a George Washington Honor Medal Award for an article he had written, "Our Capitalistic Nation vs. Biggest Monopoly-Capitalist." In that article, Les said, "The U.S.S.R. is the biggest monopoly-capitalist of all time. It owns all the land and all the tools of production. It owns all the goods and all the services of all the people. It is a slaveholder, without parallel in all history."

This sports champion received the Sigma Delta Chi (national journalism fraternity) Citation in 1959 for forty years in journalism. He also received an award as Outstanding Member of the Sons of the Utah Pioneers for service as editor of the *Pioneer.* He received the Hot Stove League Award in 1964 for thirty years as a baseball writer and official scorer in the Pacific Coast League. Also in 1964 he received the Banquet of Champions Award from Utah State University for his contributions to athletics.

Even with his many activities in the sports world, Les never lost sight of other values. He gave much service in music and to his Church. He was a stake Sunday School music director and superintendent, a ward choir director, and bishop of the East Millcreek Ward. He was also a stake high councilor and Salt Lake Temple ordinance worker. For fifty years he was a singer and director of choirs, including twenty years as director of the Symphony Singers, seven years as director of the Associated Women's Choruses of Utah, and twenty-seven years as ward choir director.

Les joined the Pi Kappa Alpha social fraternity in 1914. He served four years as Utah alumni president and seven years as regional president and was made a member of the Golden Chapter in 1964, having been an active member for fifty years.

A coach once said, "Les Goates has produced more all-

Americans than Ike Armstrong." Many athletes who might otherwise have gone unsung were heralded by this great sportswriter. He not only reported accurately, but hired many athletes and helped finance their way through college, since there were no athletic scholarships. He set them up as reporters and score collectors in part-time jobs. These athletes included such notables as Jack Howells, Marwin Jonas, Frank Christensen, Jack Johnson, Jimmy Hodgson, Howard Pearson, Walter Deland, Conrad Harrison, D. Chipman, Mark Corbett, and Ivan and Elmo Smith.

When Les retired from the *Deseret News*, president Harold B. Lee said, "Les has run a vigorous race that one only realizes as he reads the paper and is amazed at his versatility. Here is a man who has done all that he could and has little to regret." Many of Utah's finest athletes present at that time said in effect, "If it hadn't been for Les Goates I don't think the athletic world would have known I was around. He helped me to become what I was in the athletic world." This colorful sports booster responded, "It's so good of you to remember the 'old goat' on the occasion of his retirement." Maxine Martz, staff writer for the *Deseret News*, described Les in these terms: "Sportswriter...friend...a man who saw and recognized greatness and magnified it...rare ability as a writer...always a gentleman...always fair to the underdog...a man of courage."

In 1974 he was honored on his eightieth birthday at a party. He was "King for a Night," befitting this royal writer.

The following year, as sports editor Hack Miller so aptly stated, he was "called home by the great umpire." Hack said at that time, "He would rather feel the warmth in a man's handshake than all the cold and tinny awards this planet could offer." This man of poise and soft voice was said to be the "greatest contributor in *Deseret News* history." His life was a full one—full of humor, poetry, and warm experiences. Perhaps his own words are appropriate to describe his passing: "There are priceless, heart warming 'enchanted moments' in the once-in-a-lifetime experience of a veteran newsman as he clears out the battered old desk and calls it a career. These you would like to retain, to keep you humble and grateful, but all good things must come to an end, so all you can do is put them away in your Book of Remembrance."

Les Goates has rightly taken his place among the great athletes and in the Eternal Hall of Fame.

MARV HESS

Outstanding All-Around Athlete and Hall of Fame Coach

Four-sport letterman, Davis High School (football, track, basketball, tennis):

All-state, football, 1944
Lineman of the Year in Utah, 1944
All-state, basketball, 1944

University of Utah letterman (football, basketball, track):

Member NIT Championship Basketball Team, 1947

Second place in conference high jump, three years

All-conference, football, 1949

Redskins head wrestling coach, 1954-80

Chairman, NCAA Nomination Committee for Wrestling, 1960

Chairman, NCAA Wrestling Rules Committee, 1968

President, National Wrestling Coaches Association, 1967-68

Member, Olympic Wrestling Committee

Helms Hall of Fame for Amateur Wrestlers (coach), 1970

Executive vice-president, National Wrestling Coaches Association, 1972-80

Marvin Hess, former outstanding athlete and well-known University of Utah coach, started making records at an early age. At the age of eleven in 1937 he was the winner of the *Deseret News* Junior Pentathlon Championship. As a Dart from Davis High, he was a four-sport letterman for two consecutive years in football, basketball, track, and tennis. He was a member of the Darts' number-one doubles team in tennis. In 1944, as a senior, he won second place in the Utah State high-jump competition and was an all-state performer in both football and basketball. He was also Utah State High School Lineman of the Year in 1944.

Serving a tour of duty in the marines, he participated in football and basketball in 1945 and 1946. He was offered a scholarship to the University of Southern California in football, but decided to attend the University of Utah in order to remain at home. In 1947 he was a member of the University of Utah NIT Championship Basketball Team. He was also outstanding in track and won second place in the conference high jump in 1948. In fact, he took second place in the conference high jump three years in a row. In 1949 he was an all-conference end in football.

In 1950 he started at the University of Utah as an assistant coach in football and track. In 1954 he became the head wrestling coach and in 1958 took over as head coach. He also played Recreation League basketball from 1948 through 1955, and was selected to the all-AAU first team in the state of Utah for a number of years. In 1965 he resigned as head track coach in order to more fully take care of his responsibilities as wrestling coach and assistant professor of physical education. That must have been somewhat painful to Marv, since he coached such track greats as Blaine Lindgren, the great national and Olympic hurdler, who credited Marv with his success.

During his twenty-eight years of coaching at the University of Utah, he has coached some outstanding athletes in

both wrestling and track. In 1976 he was the first wrestling coach to break the two-hundred-win mark. His teams have entered numerous WAC and conference championship competitions (238–166–17).

Noted for his excellence in his field, he has served in many national positions. In 1960 he was named chairman of the NCAA Nomination Committee. He was president of the

National Wrestling Coaches Association in 1966, and was chairman of the NCAA Wrestling Rules Committee in 1968. He was a member of the Olympic Wrestling Rules Committee in 1968. He was a member of the Olympic Committee and was instrumental in organizing the U.S. Wrestling Federation. In 1970 he was named to the Helms Hall of Fame for Amateur Wrestlers as a coach. In 1972 he was named the executive vice-president of the National Wrestling Coaches Association.

Always a fierce competitor as an athlete, the same spirit carried over into his coaching career. He didn't wrestle during his prime athletic days, but has said, "I really think that of all sports, wrestling would have been the one I excelled in the most. I always enjoyed the physical aspects of sports. I always loved to get in with the action." Marv learned wrestling by watching, studying, and practice. He is considered one of the top authorities on the art. He was asked by the staff of Encyclopaedia Britannica to author an article on wrestling for that publication.

Marv has had an interesting philosophy of sports over the years. He is a strong believer in the "sandlot sports" and not the highly organized little leagues. He says that the Word of Wisdom has had a strong influence in his life as an athlete and that his athletic successes have been achieved because of his great desire to excel. He has been closely associated with the young people in the Church, serving as a deacons and priests advisor.

Marv believes in keeping his body in good physical condition and participates in racquetball, tennis, swimming, and some basketball. Perhaps his activities as a coach have also kept him in good condition, since it has been said of him, "He twists with every takedown, jumps with every counter, and reacts to every decision as though it were his hand left hanging in defeat, or raised in victory. If Hess were a nibbler of nails his fingers would have been stubs years back. If blood pressure over 200 won titles, Hess would be a king." Ray Grass, *Deseret News* sportswriter, reported, "It can be said of Marv Hess that he has fought 10,000 matches, pinned a thousand foes and shot for more takedowns than one cares to count." Marv himself said, "I have to be in twice the physical condition you are [his wrestlers], because while you each fight one match, I wrestle all ten."

In addition to all of his other responsibilities, Marv has

been the swim director for the Salt Lake Swimming and Tennis Club.

Marv Hess, remarkable athlete, outstanding coach, the only Utahn named to the Helms Amateur Wrestling Hall of Fame, has served well as a Mormon and Utahn.

ANDERS ARRHENIUS

Swedish National Shot-Put Champion and All-American

Swedish national junior shot-put champion, 1967

Shot Put, BYU 1971-75

Second place, WAC, five times

BYU record, 1975
(65 feet 1¼ inches)

NCAA shot put:

Fifth place, fourth place, fourth place, third place

All-American

Swedish National Track Team, 1968-78

Swedish national senior champion, 1971, 1977, 1978

Anders Arrhenius is a big man physically and spiritually. At six feet six inches and 270 pounds, he is not easily overlooked. A shot-put champion from Bromma, Sweden, he had seen the performance of Jay Silvester, former Mormon discus world-record holder. Knowing several other athletes who had attended Brigham Young University from his native Sweden, Anders decided to attend BYU in 1971. While there he had the opportunity to receive part of his training from Silvester.

In Sweden he had worked as a shoe salesman and was a member of the Swedish National Track Team. Having a new country, a new language, and the Mormon philosophy placed upon his shoulders was quite a change for this fine athlete. The giant Swede, however, soon mastered the language and felt at home traveling in competition and dwelling among the Mormons on the BYU campus. He observed, "As an athlete I have had the opportunity to travel around to other schools for meets. From my observations I would have to say that BYU is the best school all-around." While attending BYU Anders took second place five times in the Western Athletic Conference; in NCAA competition he achieved fifth place once, fourth place twice, and third place once; he achieved all-American status and is cited as one of the best five all-time BYU shot putters. In 1975 he achieved a BYU record with 65 feet 1¼ inches. Also in 1975, Anders joined the Church.

As a member of the Swedish National Track Team, Anders was the Swedish junior champion in 1967 and the Swedish senior champion in 1971, 1977, and 1978. He has been in the European championships in Helsinki, Finland (1971), and in Prague, Czechoslovakia (1978). His personal best throw was 65 feet 4 inches in 1978.

Anders not only had a rigid training schedule during the past ten years in competition, concentrating continuously on how to do things better and more correctly, but still practices daily two or three hours lifting weights, running, throwing the shot, or playing basketball and racquetball. He gives the following advice to those who want to achieve in athletics: "Stay close to the Lord, for if you live right, he will help you. Don't get involved with all the bad things surrounding athletics: drinking, drugs, and trying to be something you are not. When you practice and compete, give it 100 percent; then you know that you've done your best. The body should be disciplined so that the spirit will be in command and not give in to temptations, like overeating, physical lust for sex, laziness, and oversleeping. The body is a temple and should be treated as such. The spiritual growth is the most important thing."

As a competitor, this Swedish champion admits, "I am very stubborn and never give up. I always try to improve, and this requires much dedication, suffering, and pain." He also recognizes that his success is related to the wonderful support given him by his mother and family.

Anders says, "The Church has changed my life a lot. People have told me they have seen the change in me since I became a member. I was afraid I should lose many of my

friends in athletics, but I can honestly say I have more friends than before. I have had many good experiences with other athletes talking about religion and the purpose of life. I have also learned to have another view of athletics. I do it for fun now, and my whole life doesn't revolve around track anymore. I know now there are other things more important in life."

The athletic career of this great athlete has not been easy. He describes some of the problems that have beset him during the last decade as follows: "I've had bad luck with injuries a couple of times. In 1972 I made the Olympic team, but I developed an inflamed wrist a month before the games. In 1974 I was in top physical condition, but I ripped my right pectoral muscle while weight lifting. In 1976 I was going to make the Olympic team again, but I had problems with a fallen arch in my right foot, and was unable to do anything for eight months. I watched the Olympics on television and was very frustrated to see those athletes competing, when I knew I could compete with them. I prayed and prayed and promised the Lord that I would do my part to live righteously and stay close to him. I needed his guidance and help to succeed. I prayed that he would give me at least two more years of competing.

"I have now had my two best years in track, became the Swedish senior champion both years, and have had the opportunity to travel all over Europe competing. I have had no injuries at all, and the best thing is, I have a temple marriage and a master's degree in physical education, too. I know it's because I have tried to stay close to our Father in Heaven, and that I became a member of the Church."

Presently Arrhenius is a physical education instructor at the Mission Training Center in Provo and a part-time track coach at Provo High School. He is also serving as athletic director in his ward.

Anders Arrhenius, former BYU great and national champion of the shot put in Sweden, is unquestionably a giant in athletics and in spirituality.

BILLY CASPER

Golf Superstar

PGA golfer, 1955-present

Fifty-one PGA tour victories (sixth winningest player in golf history)

Eighth all-time career money winner on PGA tour (through 1981)

Golf's second millionaire

PGA leading money winner, 1966, 1968

First golfer to earn over $200,000 on PGA tour in one year, 1968

Member of the victorious Ryder Cup Team eight times

Vardon Trophy winner five times (lowest stroke average of the year) 1960, 1963, 1965, 1966, 1968

PGA Player of the Year, 1966, 1970

Sport magazine's Golfer of the Year, 1966, 1968

U.S. Open champion, 1959, 1966

BYU Exemplary Manhood Award, 1967

Masters' champion, 1970

Lowest stroke average, 1960-70 (70.437)

World Golf Hall of Fame, 1978
Beehive Hall of Fame, 1981

Billy Casper, the Magnificent Mormon, is one of the greatest golf professionals who has ever lived. He has been both a great athlete and a spiritual giant. He believes in dedicating his life to helping his fellowman, in sharing his talents and blessings with others throughout the world.

Billy was born in San Diego, California, and started playing golf as a young boy of four. He played in a pasture on three makeshift holes laid out for him by his father, and from that humble beginning has developed into one of the greatest golfers in the world. As a youngster he was a caddy and junior member of the San Diego Country Club. He played on the San Diego American Legion baseball team and really intended to play professional baseball. Later, however, he set his goals on golf. He played basketball, baseball, and golf in high school, and was captain of his golf team. He won many high school titles, and in 1950 was the Southern California interscholastic champion. He went on to win the San Diego County Amateur Crown in 1953 and the Open Crown in 1954. His expertise earned him a golf scholarship to Notre Dame, but he stayed only one semester because he did not like the Indiana winter. He subsequently joined the United States Navy and spent four years serving his country, part of which was devoted to teaching and playing golf, laying out driving ranges, and operating golf courses for the Navy in the San Diego area.

In 1955 Billy started his professional golf career, being sponsored by a San Diego businessman. One who helped Casper launch his fabulous career was former Sandy, Utah, resident Don Collett, now president of the World Golf Hall of Fame. On the PGA tour Billy started winning many tournaments. In 1958 he reached the big money, winning four tournaments, and was runner-up in the PGA championship—also finishing number two on the money-winning list. In 1959 he won five tournaments, including the U.S. Open. In that tournament his great skill as a putter was established. He used only 114 putts for seventy-two holes, a new National Open record. Golfers the world over began emulating his style on the greens. In that United States Open victory he overcame a seven-stroke deficit on the final round to tie one of the all-time great golfers, Arnold Palmer, and then defeat him in one of the most difficult ways—winning in an eighteen-hole playoff by four strokes.

Casper really peaked during the next decade, garnering the lowest stroke average of 70.437 for a full ten years (in 900 rounds of play). He won the Byron Nelson Award twice, the National Academy of Sports Award twice, many tour victories, was named to the All-American Golf Team many times by *Golf* magazine, was named to the Ryder Cup Team many times, and was one of the leading money winners on the PGA tour. He was proclaimed Golf Putter of the Year in 1963, named *Sports* magazine's Golfer of the Year (1966, 1968), given Brigham Young University's Exemplary Manhood Award (1967), and garnered Golf Writers' Golden T Award in 1969. He was PGA Player of the Year in 1966 and 1970, and won the Vardon Trophy an unprecedented five times for the lowest stroke average of the year (1960, 1963, 1965, 1966, 1968). (Even Arnold Palmer, who was golfer for the decade, won the Vardon Trophy only four times.) Casper was the PGA leading money-winner in 1966 and 1968, the first golfer to earn over $200,000 on the PGA tour in one year (1968), and was the second golfer in history to win a million dollars (the first was Arnold Palmer). He won the U.S. Open the second time in 1966 and went on to become the Masters' champion in 1970.

In the 1970s Billy won more tournaments to become the sixth-winningest player in golf history, with fifty-one PGA tour victories. In his third decade on the PGA tour (1955-81), he was ranked as the eighth all-time career money-winner with earnings of almost 1.7 million dollars. In 1978 he was named to the World Golf Hall of Fame and is regarded by many golf historians as one of the top five players of all time. His fifty-one tour victories rank him just behind Sam Sneed, Jack Nicklaus, Ben Hogan, Arnold Palmer, and Byron Nelson. Billy Casper was the thirty-fifth player to be enshrined since the Hall's opening in 1974. This caps a beautiful twenty-six year career, thus far, in Casper's golf story.

Billy Casper found that golfing was his niche and that his abilities were not misdirected. He won many tournaments and did well financially. In spite of his success, he always felt that something was not quite right. He described his dilemma in his personal story, "Alone in the Crowd" (*Guideposts*,

August 1967): "I felt nothingness, emptiness, yet I was playing successful golf." Paying tribute to his wife, he injected, "And I felt particularly guilty because of my wife. How could I tell Shirley about emptiness when she had brought such richness to me? Shirley and I came together from different backgrounds, and, all things considered, I am amazed that she consented to marry me. She was brought up in a fairly normal, well-rounded way, with strong family ties and a firm faith in God. On the other hand, my upbringing was lopsided. My parents were separated when I was twelve. I had little family life and, in fact, was making my own way from the time I was 16. I knew there was a God, but I knew nothing about going to church and felt no commitment to anything but sports. To me, golf was the most important thing in my life.... So what I offered Shirley in marriage was me, my love, and the world of golf. But what Shirley got in me was a moody sort of one-track fellow with a bundle of allergies and a problem with overweight. If the sportswriters called me an angry man, I knew I wasn't. People often mistook my quietness, my concentration, my moodiness for something else. There were times that I would look at Shirley and want to tell her about this strange void within me. I never did. The amazing thing is, Shirley knew. She didn't tell me, but all our married life she was praying for me to discover myself."

His devoted wife always went to church and took the children, but did not pressure Billy into attending. He loved and respected her, and each Sunday watched her and the children go off to Sunday School. One morning one of his daughters, Linda, commented, "Sundays are days for mommies and children to go to church and for daddies to play golf." Billy realized that he was separating himself from his family by not attending church. From then on he went to church with them if he wasn't involved in a Sunday tournament. Both Billy and his wife found that they were not completely satisfied with their spiritual lives and were searching for something different.

As early as 1959 Billy had played golf at the Utah Open in Salt Lake City, and he and his wife had been entertained during that visit in the homes of Salt Lake City people. They were impressed with the close-knit families and their way of life. During that visit, he met Hack Miller, sportswriter for the *Deseret News.* Hack informed Billy that he was a Mormon and that if he ever wanted to know anything about the Mormon religion he could give him a call. This great Mormon sportswriter kindled the fire in Billy Casper and was highly instrumental in helping this wonderful family enter the Church.

On New Year's Day, 1966, the Caspers were baptized by Hack Miller. Billy found that the emptiness in his life disappeared.

When Billy sincerely began his study of the gospel, he faced a great test of will-power and determination. Struggling with allergies and obesity, Billy found the solution to his problems—the gospel of Jesus Christ. He said, "I'm dedicating my life to helping my fellowman, and to sharing my talents and blessings with our fellowman throughout the world." He further learned the importance of man's physical existence: "I found that discipline grows naturally out of strong conviction. If we believe our bodies are temples of the holy spirit, we see to it that we discipline ourselves to take proper care of them. Believing this helped me overcome my problem with weight; in addition the allergies that bothered me for years are slowly disappearing."

Billy said, "When I am out using this God-given talent for golf, I find myself praying that I can give pleasure to the people who watch me and that I can be a good example of my faith to them." Casper's new life set a fine example for young people and golf fans everywhere.

In receiving the BYU Manhood Award, he said, "This is undoubtedly the most cherished thing I've ever been presented in my life. I hope and pray that I might live up to this award." It was presented for his service to the nation, his love of youth, his devotion to his family, his faith in his religion, and his professional accomplishments.

At a testimonial dinner in Los Angeles in 1971, Senator Barry Goldwater said, "We don't have enough Billy Caspers in America. He is an ambassador in America even more than he is a golfer. He is an example for all of us. Billy has proved that in America a person can be what he wants to be. Billy Casper has been a fine image for the young people of America."

President of the United States, Richard Nixon, said, "We admire you as a golfer, but we admire you more for the great American you are, for the good things you have done for so many people, for your generosity and high standards by which you live."

Casper's second U.S. Open victory was notable because he was the winner among the professional ranks, and Johnny Miller was the winner among the amateurs. What an honor for two Mormon golfers to participate together and win, each in his own right, one of the major tour victories. That was the year Billy Casper joined the Church, had notable tour victories, was the leading money-winner, and was named the PGA Player of the Year. It was also the year in which he proclaimed that he had found a better way of life than just playing golf. He said, "I received more blessings doing the work of the Church. I hope I can be a good example and light a spark in someone. I am proud to be a Mormon."

One of Bill's greatest victories was off the golf course. He once told Milton Gross in an interview for the *New York Post,*

"I used to be the fat man's dream and now I'm the thin man's hope." His weight loss of fifty-five pounds indicates the self-control and conviction of this great man. In his spiritual accomplishments, Casper has filled the void in his life, and perhaps filled a void in the life of his remarkable wife, Shirley. She also attributes much of her success to her baptism into the Church, at which time she more fully realized the purpose of life and the weight of responsibility given to a woman when she becomes a Mormon. As a mother of eleven children (six of whom have been adopted), she proves her courageous support of her husband. For her outstanding achievements in community and Church projects, she was selected the California Young Mother of the Year in 1971.

In 1966 Billy Casper visited Vietnam with Hack Miller. He was the first golfer to visit the troops. He made seventy-one stops in seventeen days, at aircraft carriers, hospitals, and two playing clinics.

Billy Casper has an amazing philosophy. He says, "When you come right down to it, there are only four interests in my life—religion, family, golf, and fishing, in that order.... Golf is the ultimate free agent's game. Each muscle must work in perfect harmony, under the control of a mind clear of self-doubt." He further says, "There is a close relationship between golf and the gospel. The challenge and enjoyment of golf, plus the high caliber of competition in recent years, builds patience and humility, both important principles. Golf has given me the opportunity to make a good living for my family, but more than that, it has enabled me to meet many people I otherwise would not have met....I have had the opportunity to touch the lives of many people who probably could never have been approached any other way. Golf was the common bond."

Billy Casper, superstar of golf, hallmarked by consistency, is indeed a brilliant Mormon athlete and an example of indefatigable self-mastery in athletic excellence.

KEY TO ABBREVIATIONS

AAU   Amateur Athletic Union
AAUW   American Association of University Women
ICAC   Intermountain Collegiate Athletic Conference
NABC   National Association of Basketball Coaches
NAIA   National Association of Intercollegiate Athletics
NCAA   National Collegiate Athlete Association
NEA   National Enterprises Association
NIT   National Invitational Tournament
NJCAA   National and Junior College Athletic Association
NL   National League
PGA   Professional Golfers Association
RBI   Run batted in
UHSAA   Utah High School Athletic Association
USBWA   U.S. Basketball Writers Association
USGF   U.S. Gymnastics Federation
WAC   Western Athletic Conference
WBA   World Boxing Association
WFL   World Football League

INDEX

Abraham Lincoln High School,
52-54
Abrams, Al, 95-96
Ah You, Junior, 5
Ainge, Danny, 9
Anderson, Harry, 29
Archer, Joey, 179
Arizona State University, 1-5
Armstrong, Ike, 218, 261-62
Arrhenius, Anders, 268-71
Atlanta Braves, 115-16, 119
Auto racing: Ab Jenkins, 80-84

Baker, Cecil, 203-10
Ballisteros, Steve, 57
Baseball: Harmon Killebrew, 74-79;
Vern Law, 90-98; Dale Murphy,
115-19; Mickey Oswald, 215-22
Basketball: Danny Vranes, 8-13;
Jeff Judkins, 9-10, 13, 59-63;
Devin Durrant, 27-32; Tina Gunn
(Robison), 33-39; Mel Hutchins,
135-37; Neil Roberts, 154-61;
Dick Motta, 195-202; Cecil
Baker, 203-10; Homer Warner,
211-14; Mickey Oswald, 215-22;
Eugene Roberts, 234-37; Marv
Hess, 263-64
Beattie, Bob, 65
Bell, Wade, 140-43
Ben Lomond High School, 140-41
Benson, Lee, 87, 191-92
Benson, Rose Ann, 34
Benvenuti, Nino, 179-80
Berry, Doug, 169
Berry, Rex, 168-71
Biederman, Lester J., 92-95
Bloomfield Hills High School,
125-27
Bluege, Ossie, 75
Bogs, Tom, 179-81
Boise State University, 145-46
Bonnell, Barry, 116-18

Boston Celtics, 13, 60-62
Bowerman, Bill, 141
Boxing: Danny Lopez, 85-89; Don
Fullmer, 178-83
Boyd, Bob, 161
Brigham Young Academy, 234,
236
Brigham Young University: Doug
Padilla, 19-22, 24, 26; Devin
Durrant, 27-29, 31-32; Tina
Gunn (Robison), 33-35, 37-38;
Curt Brinkman, 43; Johnny
Miller, 52, 54-55; Vern Law and
sons, 96-97; Linn Rockwood,
106-7; Kenneth Lundmark, 111-
12; Lelei Fonoimoana, 121-23;
Bob Richards, 125-32; Mel
Hutchins, 135-37; Mike Young,
144-46; Eldon Fortie, 148-53;
Neil Roberts, 155, 157-58, 160;
Rex Berry, 168; Richard George,
172-74, 176; Hansen brothers,
184-90, 192, 194; Clarence
Robison, 223-27; Eugene
Roberts, 234-37, 240-42; LaVell
Edwards, 243-50; Mike Reid,
251-52; Anders Arrhenius,
268-69
Brinkman, Curt, 40-44
Brown, Clay, 246
Buerkle, Dick, 22
Burgess, Smokey, 93
Burley High School, 155, 158
Burr, Glen, 86

Camp, Walter, 260
Carbon High School, 168
Carbon Junior College, 168
Casper, Billy, 56, 58, 272-78
Castanon, Roberto, 87-88
Cedar City High School, 154-57
Celion, Chris, 111
Chabot Junior College, 21

Chacon, Bobby, 86
Chicago Bears, 2
Chicago Bulls, 199-202
Collett, Don, 273
Coltrin, Bill, 156-57, 159
Cox, Bobby, 116
Crosby, Bing, 91
Curly, Angelo, 179

Dallas Cowboys, 2, 5-7
Dallas Mavericks, 200-202
Davis High School, 212, 263-64
Dempsey, Jack, 82, 87, 230, 236, 256-57
Deseret News Ski School, 103-4
Detroit Pistons, 62, 135, 137-38
Dixie College, 156, 158-59, 161
Duncan, Mark, 169
Dunn, Marion, 245-46
Durrant, Devin, 27-32

East High School, 215-22
Eaton, Lloyd, 150
Edmonton Eskimos, 151-52
Edwards, LaVell, 149, 151, 243-50
Ellis, Jimmy, 181
Engen, Alan, 105
Engen, Alf, 99-105
Engen, Corey, 100, 105
Engen, Sverre, 100-101, 105
Erickson, Bob, 189

Fernandez, Florentino, 87
Ferrin, Arnie, 60
Fletcher, Harvey L., 241
Fonoimoana, Debbie, 121
Fonoimoana, Lelei, 120-24
Football: Danny White, 1-7; Merlin Olsen, 45-51; Eldon Fortie, 148-53; Rex Berry, 168-71; Mickey Oswald, 215-22; LaVell Edwards, 243-50; Marv Hess, 263-64
Fort Wayne Pistons. See Detroit Pistons
Fortie, Eldon, 148-53
Foster, Bill, 10
Franks, Herman, 218-19
Fullmer, Don, 178-83
Fullmer, Gene, 87, 182

Gabriel, Roman, 49
Gates, Chuck, 31
Gavitt, Dave, 12
Geertsen, John, 53, 58, 254
George, Richard, 172-77
Georgino, Bennie, 86, 89
Goates, Les, 241, 256-62
Goitschel, Christine and Marielle, 65-66
Golf: Johnny Miller, 52-58; Mike Reid, 251-55; Billy Casper, 272-78
Gomez, Famaso, 86
Grace High School, 195-200
Granite High School, 149, 203-7, 244-45, 248
Grass, Ray, 266
Grier, Roosevelt, 48
Griffith, Calvin, 78
Griffith, Clark, 75
Griffith, Emile, 179
Gunn (Robison), Tina, 33-39
Gunther, Kurt, 246
Gymnastics: Kim Taylor, 14-18

Hall, Bob, 42
Hansen, Brad, 184-94
Hansen, David, 186-88, 190-94
Hansen, Laron, 186-88, 190-94
Hansen, Mark, 186-88, 190-94
Hansen, Mike, 185-88, 190-94
Hansen, Ronnie, 187-88, 190-94
Harvard Business School, 176-77
Havlicek, John, 62
Hess, Marv, 263-67
Highland High School, 59-60, 62-63
Hinckley, Gordon B., 204
Hislop, Chic, 141
Howard, Paul, 5
Hudspeth, Tommy, 244
Hunt, Paul, 15
Hutchins, Colleen, 139
Hutchins, Matt, 139
Hutchins, Mel, 135-37

Ice Capades, 69, 73
Idaho Falls High School, 144-45

Jackson, Reggie, 78
James, Paul, 29

James, Sherald, 22, 132
Jenkins, Ab, 80-84
Jenkins, Marvin, 80, 83
Johnson, Mike, 41-42
Johnson, Phil, 197
Jones, Deacon, 48
Jordan High School, 196
Judkins, Jay, 10
Judkins, Jeff, 9-10, 13, 59-63

Kansas City Royals, 74
Kemp, Harry Davidson
    (pseudonym). See Roberts,
    Eugene
Kendall, Andy, 181
Keyworth, John, 5-6
Killebrew, Cam, 79
Killebrew, Harmon, 74-79
Kimball, Edwin R., 236-37
Klein, Dick, 199
Knight, Bobby, 11
Knight, Ray, 116, 119
Kotey, Dave, 86-87
Krienbuehl, Franz, 163

Larson, Clint, 237
Law, Jessie, 97
Law, Vance, 97
Law, Vaughn, 97
Law, Veldon, 97
Law, Vern, 90-98, 118
Law, Veryl, 97
Lee, Harold B., 230-31
Lehi High School, 260
Leishman, Courtney, 35, 39
Lewis, Ed "Strangler," 230
Lier, Dolores, 162-67
Lincoln County High School, 205
Lindgren, Blaine, 264
Lingenfelter, Ben, 218
Logan High School, 46
Lopez, Danny, 85-89
Lopez, Ernie, 86
Los Angeles Rams, 45, 47-48
Lundmarks, Kenneth, 110-14
Lundy, Lamar, 48

Malvarez, Juan, 87
Marsh, Henry, 21, 174, 176
McKay, David O., 92
McMahon, Jim, 246-47

Melville, Alton C., 67-68
Meridan High School, 91
Millard High School, 172-73, 224
Miller, Hack, 248, 262, 276, 278
Miller, Johnny, 52-58, 277
Millett, Floyd, 136
Milwaukee Bucks, 135, 137
Minnesota Twins, 74, 78-79
Mitchell, Hal, 149-50, 244
Monrovia High School, 136
Montrella, Jim, 123
Mooney, John, 88
Moore, Kenny, 25
Motta, Dick, 195-202
Murdock Academy, 203-4
Murphy, Dale, 115-19
Murtaugh, Danny, 95

Nelson, George, 228-33
New York Knickerbockers, 135,
    137-38
Nicklaus, Jack, 52, 56-58, 274
Nicks, John, 70
Nielsen, Gifford, 249-50
Nilsen, Jorgen. See Nelson, George
Nixon, Richard, 277
Nyambui, Suleiman, 21-25

Ogden High School, 211-12
Olsen, Merlin, 45-51
Olsen, Orrin, 49-50
Olsen, Phil, 49-50
Oneida Academy, 230
Oregon State University, 67,
    140-41
Orem High School, 247
Oswald, Mickey, 215-22

Padilla, Doug, 19-26
Palmer, Arnold, 56, 58, 274
Patton, Joe, 34
Payette High School, 75
Payson High School, 155, 158
Petersen, Mark E., 83-84
Peterson, Vadal, 212
Pimm, Jerry, 12
Pittsburgh Pirates, 90-97
Player, Gary, 56-57
Pond, Michelle, 15
Provo High School, 27-28, 97, 271

Ralston, John, 50-51
Rand, Abby, 104
Reid, Bill, 254
Reid, Mike, 251-55
Rice, Grantland, 258
Richards, Alma, 237
Richards, Bob (Olympic pole vaulter), 224-25
Richards, Bob (steeplechase champion), 125-34
Richards, Danny and Golden, 5
Rigney, Bill, 79
Rimriders, 41
Roberts, Eugene, 234-42
Roberts, Neil, 154-62
Robinson, Doug, 13, 22, 25
Robison, Clarence: on Doug Padilla, 24; related to Tina Gunn, 39; on Bob Richards, 128-30, 132; on Richard George, 174, 176; about, 223-27
Robison, Tina. See Gunn (Robison), Tina
Rockwood, Linn, 106-9
Rodgers, Bill, 44
Romney, Dick, 214, 231
Rowe, Owen, 237
Runyan, Damon, 258
Ryun, Jim, 131, 141

Salazar, Alberto, 21, 24-25
San Francisco 49ers, 168-69, 171
Sanchez, Salvador, 89
Sanders, Tom, 60
Santell, Ad, 230
Saubert, Jean, 64-68
Schofield, Dale, 237
Scott, Steve, 21-22, 25
Seattle Supersonics, 9, 13
Seibu Lions, 96
Shelley, Ken, 69-73
Silvester, Jay, 268
Skating: Ken Shelley, 69-73; Dolores Lier, 162-67
Skiing: Jean Saubert, 64-68; Alf Engen, 99-105; Mickey Oswald, 218-20
Skyline High School, 8-10, 155, 158
South High School, 107

Spencer, Jim, 29
Sportswriting: Eugene Roberts, 237-41; Les Goates, 256-62
Starbuck, Jo Jo, 69-70, 72-73
Staubach, Roger, 5-6
Swimming: Lelei Fonoimoana, 120-24

Tanner, N. Eldon, 134
Taylor, Kim, 14-18
Tennis: Linn Rockwood, 106-9
Teton High School, 184-87, 192-93
Timpanogos hike and legend, 239
Torres, Jose, 87
Track and field: Doug Padilla, 19-26; Curt Brinkman, 40-44; Kenneth Lundmark, 110-14; Bob Richards, 125-34; Wade Bell, 140-43; Neil Roberts, 154-58; Richard George, 172-77; Cecil Baker, 203-5; Mickey Oswald, 215-22; Clarence Robison, 223-27; Eugene Roberts, 234-37, 240; Marv Hess, 263-65; Anders Arrhenius, 268-71
Tucker, Karl, 55, 58
Tuckett, Glen, 244

University of Michigan, 224
University of Southern California, 235, 240
University of Utah: Danny Vranes, 8, 10-13; Jeff Judkins, 59-60, 62-63; Jean Saubert, 67; Linn Rockwood, 107-9; Homer Warner, 211-12; Mickey Oswald, 215-18; Les Goates, 256, 260; Marv Hess, 263-67
Utah Academy of Gymnastics Nuggets, 15
Utah Jazz, 62
Utah State Agricultural College. See Utah State University
Utah State University: Merlin Olsen, 45-48; Dick Motta, 198; Cecil Baker, 203-5, 207-9; George Nelson, 228-33; LaVell Edwards, 243, 247-48

Vandeweghe, Ernest, 139

Vandeweghe, Kiki, 139
Vandeweghe, Tauna, 139
Vranes, Danny, 8-13, 158
Vranes, Lou, 10
Vranes, Shauna, 10

Walker, John, 21, 25
Warner, Homer, 211-14
Washington Bullets, 200-202
Washington Senators, 74-76
Watts, Stan, 158, 224
Weber Junior College, 195, 198
Weber State College, 195, 197-99
Welker, Herman, 75, 91
Westwood High School, 1, 3

Whelan, Danny, 93
White, Danny, 1-7
White, Wilford "Whizzer," 2
Whiting, Wendy, 16
Wilson, Mark, 245-46
Wilson High School, 115-16
Wood, Bob, 22
Wrestling: Mike Young, 144-47;
  Brad, Mike, Laron, Mark, David,
  and Ronnie Hansen, 184-94;
  George Nelson, 228-33; Marv
  Hess, 263-67

Young, Mike, 144-47